HARD GRASS

HARD GRASS

Life on the Crazy Woman Bison Ranch

Mary Zeiss Stange

University of New Mexico Press
Albuquerque

Library of Congress Cataloging-in-Publication Data

Stange, Mary Zeiss.
Hard grass : life on the Crazy Woman Bison Ranch / Mary Zeiss Stange.
    p. cm.
Includes bibliographical references.
ISBN 978-0-8263-4613-1 (cloth : alk. paper)
1. Women ranchers—Montana—Biography. 2. Ranchers—Montana—Biography.
3. Crazy Woman Bison Ranch (Mont.) 4. Bison farming—Montana. I. Title.
  SF194.S78A3 2010
  636'.01092—dc22
                          2010008316

Portions of the Introduction originally appeared, in different form, in "Coming Home to the Country" in *High Country News* (December 6, 1999).

A portion of Chapter 6 appeared, in different forms, in "Homestead Hunting," *Big Sky Journal* (Fall 2001), and "The Home Place," in Thomas McIntyre, Ed., *Wild and Fair: Tales of Hunting Big Game in North America* (Long Beach, CA: Safari Press, 2008).

A portion of Chapter 6 appeared, in different form, in "Living with the ghosts of the Indian Wars," *High Country News* (February 6, 2006).

Portions of Chapter 7 originally appeared in an essay that won a First Prize in Sierra Club's "Why I Hunt" essay competition in June 2006.

A portion of Chapter 12 was originally published in different form under the title "New West code for city folk: No whining," *USA Today* (March 31, 2004).

Cover Photo by Doug Stange.
Design and composition by Karen Mazur.

Dedication

For J and A, running with Artemis now
For Doug, always and in all ways
&
For all things gentle and tender, pure and natural

CONTENTS

Preface: Working "Off the Place"   ix

Acknowledgments   xiv

Introduction: Coming Home to the Country   1

Chapter 1
The Lay of the Land   11

Chapter 2
Being "Differnt"   39

Chapter 3
Intrepid Hippies, Homesteaders, and Other Survivors   61

Chapter 4
The Law of the Frontier   83

Chapter 5
Animal Affinities   99

Chapter 6
Hard Grass   125

Chapter 7
Hunting Nature, Hunting Culture   153

Chapter 8
The Business of Buffalo   173

Chapter 9
The First, and Last, Annual Buffalo Gals Hunt   201

Chapter 10
A Nice Place to Visit   227

Chapter 11
Next Year Country   255

Chapter 12
New West, True West?   275

Epilogue: Rockfall   295

Resources   297

PREFACE
Working "Off the Place"

🍂 Most farm and ranch wives have to work "off the place," to help make ends meet. This is one way to describe my situation. I simply work farther off the place than most.

It is a stark and simple fact of rural life that the majority of ranch operations do not generate sufficient regular, reliable income to sustain a family, let alone provide perks, like health insurance. So the women take jobs in town: as teachers or bank tellers or waitresses, working behind the counter in the grocery store, or pushing papers for the farm services agency. Such jobs produce a dependable supply of cash, to pay some bills and forestall having to make tough financial calls, like whether to put food on the table or a new sickle bar on the tractor mower, or whether to take one's daughter to the dentist or one's ailing Angus bull to the vet. Of course, for many of these women, as for their urban counterparts, work outside the home is as much a matter of choice as of necessity; they do it because they want to, and not merely because they have to. And most of them, again like their more citified sisters, can expect to work a "second shift" when they get back home. In the case of ranch wives, this means not only getting caught up on household chores like cooking supper and doing the dishes, but also anything from helping with the combining until well after sunset to staying up all night in a cold barn during lambing season. And then there are the myriad of practical decisions, large and small, that preoccupy a rancher's time and mental space.

So it is by no means unusual either that I have a day job "off" our ranch, or that a hefty proportion of my physical and emotional energy is channeled in the direction of day-to-day ranch matters. It's just that my town job, as a professor of women's studies and religion at a liberal arts college in upstate New York, is two thousand miles away from our remote southeastern Montana bison ranch. The long "commute" is possible, thanks to a flexible teaching schedule, generous vacation periods, mostly understanding colleagues, and the occasional extended respite of sabbatical time off for good behavior. These factors, plus a relationship in which my husband and I mutually pledged, twenty-seven years ago, that this marriage—the second for each or us, and we intended to get things right this time—would be based upon freeing each other to be and to do whatever it was that made us more authentically ourselves. For Doug, this eventually meant forsaking academe for the life of a full-time rancher. I held on to my day job, for a complex variety of reasons to be sure, but not least among them economic.

And so, I oscillate between two quite different worlds, my heart in one, my paycheck in the other, my head invariably in both. Friends and acquaintances in each setting seem to harbor private suspicions that I actually inhabit two different planets, and sometimes I think they may be right. This is perhaps especially true when those worlds collide: My office phone rings. Ranch business cannot always wait for evenings and weekends, let alone until my next trip home. It might be a relatively minor, yet nonetheless vexing, matter on which Doug needs a second opinion—things ranging from how best to fill out arcane government forms to which supplier we should contract with for custom bison feed. Then again, it could be a downright emergency, most of which have to do with large animals, heavy machinery, or some unfortunate combination thereof. There have been a few occasions on which I discovered, after the fact, how close I had come to becoming a widow. The call might, of course, also bring good news: of the births of healthy animals, of bad weather that didn't come or good weather that did, say, in the form of a desperately needed downpour. More recently, the less pressing matters—good and bad—have been relegated to e-mail, where they nestle among memos announcing campus-wide events and student requests for extensions on term papers. Meanwhile, considerations of how best to deal with a burgeoning prairie dog population in our west pasture cozy up to notes I am making on reproductive rights issues for tomorrow's Intro. to Women's Studies class.

Over the years I have had to become fairly adept, then, at occupying two different mental spaces more or less simultaneously, just as I do two time zones, Mountain and Eastern. Transiting from one conceptual terrain to the other is not infrequently a bumpy ride. But what might strike the casual observer as a jarring juxtaposition of radically different sets of information and their accompanying emotional states is, necessarily, just day-to-day living for me.

As to the physical commute: A mere few in-flight hours can separate my attending a faculty wine and cheese reception (this being Doug's favorite fantasy of how I spend my time at school) and struggling with a pipe wrench, sweat-drenched and up to my elbows in rusty muck, in the process of helping to pull a pump from a stock well—a two-person job that had awaited this particular trip home (and during which I mutter, "If the folks at Skidmore College could see me now . . ."). The gauzy Western-inspired Ralph Lauren skirt and Italian sandals I wore to that reception would not survive a single stroll across our hard-grass hayfield. Indeed, my "ranch wardrobe" doesn't even contain a skirt. I don't bother to paint my fingernails when I'm home, since the polish wouldn't outlast a day's work. I accessorize with the cuts, bruises, insect bites, and minor abrasions that invariably come with a day's work.

Yet in other ways these worlds I inhabit are not so distinct. Early on in our tenure on the ranch, the day before my departure to begin the school year, Doug and I met with Bureau of Land Management agents to work out a rotational grazing plan for our place. A week later and two-thirds of a continent away at Skidmore, I was sitting on the Committee on Educational Planning and Policy designing an improved all-college curriculum. Only the details differed; from a bureaucratic point of view, the two meetings were essentially a trade-off. More recently I have noted the structural likenesses between the pecking order of a buffalo herd and power arrangements on a college campus. As to the resemblance of year-end grading to mucking out paddocks . . . well, you get the idea.

My northeastern friends and colleagues for the most part seem to think I live on something like the Ponderosa, that Doug and I spend our time riding the range (for which we manage to find time all too rarely), line dancing to country music (which in fact neither of us can stand), and just generally whooping it up (although it's fair to say we are not, by temperament, much given to whooping). Their fantasies of High Plains ranch life are largely shaped by Hollywood, and outfitted by the Sundance Catalog. They find my "other life" at once intriguingly exotic and, as a "lifestyle," mystifying. Those who regard largely agricultural Saratoga County as sufficiently rural for anyone's tastes have asked, more than once, why doesn't Doug just move east to New York? Because, I tell them truthfully, it just isn't the same country. Even supposing we could find a piece of land there that we would want to buy, we would never be invested in it in the same ways and to the same degree as we are here.

My Montana friends and neighbors, meanwhile, generally view my life away from the ranch in light of whatever fantasy they nurture of the East Coast—fantasies sure to be informed equally by media images and shared local biases. One friend has put it to me this way: "Mary, every summer when you come home, you start out very city, but by the end of the summer, you're downright country again." She is probably right that, given my personal background (which is, in fact, East Coastal) and my commute, there are both "city" and "country" sides to me, although I experience these more as a tension—on good days, a creative one—than as an either/or proposition.

But for High Plains folks, my professional life occurs in a terrain radically different, in two very crucial ways, from anything customary here: it is big-city urban-focused, and it is intellectual. And, in these parts, both generate responses ranging from bemused skepticism to sardonic deprecation to downright distrust. The anti-intellectualism of the interior American West is oft-reported, and for the most part accurately. Underreported is the extent to which High Plains animosity toward anything that smacks of the "urban" is as much a product of media images and collective imagination as is the "coastal" dismissal of pretty much everything that happens in those big, square, traditionally red-voting "flyover" states.

The lesson of this continental cultural divide is learned and internalized very early on. I know of no other part of the country where "ethnic," meaning "not from around here," and roughly equivalent to "foreigner/city dweller," is a category in the supermarket aisles for interesting if somewhat spurious foods. One of my favorite local stories has to do with a physician who came to this area from New York, with a Bronx accent, an assertive personal style, and dark curly hair to match his cultural provenance. He settled down to a practice in Baker, Montana, some sixty or so miles north of here—which in eastern Montana terms made him downright local—and set about visiting his neighbors, with his wife and two young daughters, to get acquainted. At one place where they stopped, his daughter walked up to the little girl who lived there, and proudly announced: "Hi! We're Italian!" Perplexed, the little girl thought that through for a few moments, and ventured, "Well . . . we're Ranch!"

This book is, if you will, an extended inquiry into what it means to be "ranch" in a society that, like the weather here, runs to extremes and that, like the landscape, is simultaneously unforgiving, sometimes brutal, and yet capable of unalloyed charm and surprising, at times breathtaking, beauty. After more than twenty years, I remain to some extent an outsider here, in a place where "different" is the operative term for anything new or foreign or innovative or threatening. And yet, I sometimes think despite my better judgment, I have sunk roots here. And so I hope to use my sometimes-outsider's perspective to present an honest portrayal of what living in this powerful landscape can do, for better and for worse, to those of us who call it home.

Everything that follows is, to the best of my knowledge and of my powers of expression, true. Such altering of names, places, and other details as I have done, has been minimal, and it has been for the sake of protecting the privacy of some individuals or families.

ACKNOWLEDGMENTS

My thanks, first of all, to all those spirits of southeastern Montana, great and small, living and gone, who in myriad ways shaped this story and its telling. More particularly, I am grateful to the staff of the Carter County Museum for their assistance, and for the permission to reprint four archival photographs of downtown Ekalaka in this volume. Special appreciation also to Wayne Yost, Jackie Dalzell, and Rebecca Wolenetz of the USDA Natural Resources and Conservation Service, District Administrator Georgia Bruski of the Carter County Conservation District, and Bobby Baker of the Miles City office of the U.S. Bureau of Land Management, all of whom have been ever ready to answer my questions about regional flora and fauna and their "management."

I am grateful to Charlene Porsild for her astute suggestions early on in this project, and to Tovis Page, Hannah Stephenson, and Carol Oyster for reading and commenting on various parts of the work in progress.

Skidmore College provided welcome support for the writing in the form of a Major Project Completion Grant and a supplemental grant in support of the full-year sabbatical leave during which much of the text was produced.

After helping me put together the original proposal for this book and suggesting its title, Doug Stange, my life partner and soul mate in every sense, kept a sufficient distance from this project to allow me to develop it as my rendition of our shared story. Thanks, dearest: I think I got it pretty much right.

Every step along the way, Clark Whitehorn has been a dream of an editor for this book: perceptive and provocative, enthusiastic and ever-supportive, even when I knew I was trying his patience. And the entire staff at the University of New Mexico Press has been wonderful to work with. My thanks, particularly, to Managing Editor Elise McHugh for her sensitive, and sensible, handling of the manuscript. And to designers Karen Mazur and Melissa Tandysh, both for their willingness to take a risk or two, and for their commitment to producing a beautiful volume.

Finally, I am grateful beyond words to the pheasants who decided to make Spring Creek their home in the winter of 2010.

The "Mother Tree," 2009. Photo by Doug Stange.

INTRODUCTION
Coming Home to the Country

🖎 We called it the Mother Tree: a mature ponderosa pine on the crest of a small hill, with an acre or so of seedlings and saplings draping the hill's leeward side, a miniforest in the making that was the product of scores of pinecones shed by that lone adult. We drove past this tree and her progeny, which were on a nearby cattle rancher's place, whenever we took the gravel Chalk Buttes Road to and from town.

The Mother Tree was among the first landmarks Doug and I noticed, to our mutual delight, when we moved to Carter County, Montana, in 1988. She bore eloquent testimony to the character of the land we had determined we would call home. This isn't *Lonesome Dove* country. It isn't the part of the state that Hollywood rivers run though, or in which Hollywood stars buy property. It's a rougher, rather more austere terrain. But it is also surprisingly vigorous and diverse, fragile in some ways, yet able to withstand a good deal of abuse.

In the twenty-one years we've been here, we have come to appreciate that resilience. We have also come to understand that the forces of change at work in the contemporary West are more subtle and more complex when you're living through them than when you contemplate them from a comfortable, myth-infused distance. This is, perhaps, especially true when you have to count yourself among those forces.

It was 106 degrees the July day we moved in. No rain had fallen in two months. The Drought of 1988—which would attain legendary proportion in local memory—was in full swing. It would, by summer's end, spawn fires in Yellowstone Park and elsewhere across Big Sky Country, rendering the sun a bronze disc hovering high in a smoky-pale sky. We had just "taken possession" of our ranch. An odd phrase that: We were essentially clueless as to what we had gotten ourselves into. All we knew at that moment was that we were now the holders of a deed to roughly seven square miles of parched stubble, puckered-looking prickly-pear cactus, desiccated sage, and struggling ponderosa pines and junipers.

And dust. Lots and lots of dust. We began to figure we might be crazy. Before too long, we understood all our neighbors were pretty certain we were.

Neither Doug nor I come from rural backgrounds. He grew up in Kenosha, Wisconsin, a factory town (then home of American Motors) on Lake Michigan midway between Chicago and Milwaukee. His idea of "going natural" was to pick up his shotgun for an afternoon's bird hunting in some of the undeveloped fields on the outskirts of town or to spend a weekend camping in northern Wisconsin. I was raised in Rutherford, New Jersey, across the Hudson from New York City. I believed a good day's hunting was best accomplished on Fifth Avenue, and the closest I came to a gun in my youth was a pair of faux-pearl-handled Dale Evans cap-shooters. My idea of the great outdoors was a big backyard. That had changed, of course, after we met and married and he somehow brought out the hunter/forager in me.

Coming to cattle country, we harbored no illusions about becoming cattle ranchers. In fact, initially, we weren't interested in becoming serious ranchers at all. Our ambitions were modest, or so we believed. We wanted a place where we could work with, rather than against, nature. To cultivate wildlife habitat. To have some quality hunting for ourselves, and perhaps to operate a small hunting concession. To plant some trees. To raise a few pack llamas, maybe a couple of horses. To have a retreat where we could live a good, by no means ascetic but certainly simplified, life.

The previous owner of the place we had just purchased had been here for over forty years, meting out about as much punishment as the land could take. His cattle, before the Land Bank forced their sale so that he could make some delinquent interest payments, had overgrazed every pasture. He had dynamited beaver dams, had let most of his boundary fences fall into disrepair, and had dumped garbage in riparian areas. In forty-odd years, he had not, as far as we could tell, planted a single tree. This place, we felt certain, needed us.

At the time, we both still had full-time jobs in higher education. We didn't want to take on more than we could handle. We just wanted a place we could come home to. And where we could simply let nature be nature.

"But you *can't* just let it sit!" our cattle-ranching neighbors told us. "Fire'll take out the grass, if cows don't. That's nature's way. Best thing to do is to graze it down. Even if it don't burn or get grazed, it'll get so thatched over you won't *have* any grass in another year or two."

It didn't seem to us, what with it being so awfully dry, that we had much of any grass as it was.

"Look," our neighbor went on to explain over coffee at the Wagon Wheel Café, "you have to know when it becomes grazeable."

Another rancher at the next table over chimed in. "Guy over at the BLM told me to put the cows out on the grass when it's as high as a beer can."

"Now," our neighbor-friend replied with a sly wink, "would that be a beer can standing up, or a beer can lying on its side?"

Later on, driving home past cattle who appeared to be subsisting on barely inch-high stubble, Doug remarked, "I think that must have been a crushed beer can they were talking about." By that fall, with wells drying up and no hay for wintering-over livestock, our neighbors were all selling off their cows in record numbers. We remained happily, and smugly, committed to being cattle free. The deer and the antelope, both of which we had in good numbers, would have our sparse grassland to themselves.

Yet amazingly, the following spring was as gloriously lush as the previous one had been dire. A well-timed late-spring snowstorm followed by ample rains had brought the water table up and replenished reservoirs. The landscape was a profusion of wildflowers and almost unnaturally green and varied prairie grasses—the names for which we, of course, had no idea. Our neighbors rebuilt their herds, and renewed their friendly counsel about getting some cows on our place, but despite their well-intentioned urgings, we stuck to our let-nature-be-nature program. The closest we got to livestock were an obstreperous llama, the first of the small pack herd we hoped to build, a Maine coon house cat, and a couple of English springer spaniels. The deer and the antelope continued to play, at home on our range. It was a lovely summer.

But the next year, 1990, something appeared to be going wrong. We once again had sufficient spring moisture, but by early summer our pastures were all looking dry and thatchy and, with not even a dandelion in sight, decidedly the worse for wear. Watching nightly light shows crackle in a rainless southern sky, we began to comprehend why the phrase "dry lightning" could strike fear in the hearts of landowners. And we had to reconsider the conventional wisdom about fire being "nature's way" of managing for healthy grassland.

We reluctantly decided it might be a good idea, all things considered, for those deer and antelope to share their space with a few bovines after all. We placed an ad in the *Ekalaka Eagle* and immediately found a cattleman who was looking for grass and happy to bring over a hundred cow/calf pairs. The cows got right down to business, chewing their way through the summer. The next time we ran into our neighbor at the post office in town, we sheepishly admitted the error of our ways. "Well, there you go!" he exclaimed good-naturedly, with a slap to Doug's back.

It was about that time that we discovered we were known in town as "the people from Connecticut." That neither of us had ever had anything to do with the Constitution State was beside the point. We were outsiders. Also, about this time, we learned that when, occasionally, we would hear about somebody being from "out of the country," it didn't mean they were foreigners. It meant they grew up a few miles down the road, in western South Dakota, or maybe northern Wyoming.

We were *really* outsiders.

Of course, we knew we were. We also knew that, after a decade or so of farm foreclosures and the gradual swallowing-up of small family farms by corporate agribusiness, outsiders were not particularly welcome in these parts. We knew, as well, that despite the three doctoral degrees we have between us, our neighbors, who all seemed to be fifth-generation ranchers sharing a dozen or so surnames, knew a lot more about getting on in this part of the world than we did.

We were prepared to learn, and to listen. It shouldn't be that hard, at least in theory. Being academics, we were used to doing homework, and so we set about doing research. We learned the principles of rotational grazing, and resolved to work with the Bureau of Land Management (BLM) to bring our deeded and leased grassland back from the degraded condition in which we had found it—officially, of "no productive value"—to prime range condition.

We investigated the best trees, shrubs, grasses, and forbs to grow in this climate—some native, some introduced—and began a program of planting shelterbelts and wildlife habitat areas. We also studied up on the identification of the grasses and flora native to our place.

We learned what we needed to know about veterinary first aid, and about the care and feeding of cud-chewing quadrupeds, in order to get our llama operation going.

We learned about the construction and maintenance of barbed-wire fences and enclosures, and the pros and cons of various fencing systems, including electric fences.

In spite of ourselves, we began, however unsteadily, to evolve into ranchers.

One important thing we learned in those first years here was that you cannot run a ranch in absentia. A ranch is not a vacation home. In our second year on the place, Doug had taken a semester's leave of absence from teaching, to stay in Montana. He didn't much miss the classroom, and had grown increasingly impatient with academic posturing and politics. So he decided to quit his job at Cleveland State University, to close the door on academe and concentrate his time and energies on the ranch.

Another thing we learned, in those first three years: Ranches are money pits, especially when they need a lot of restoration as ours did, and more especially still when one is—as we were—starting from scratch, in terms of equipment. This had not been a "turn-key" property transfer. We didn't even have a tractor yet. Not only were we facing a steep learning curve, the challenge of making this ranch work without breaking the bank in the process looked steeper still.

I kept my day job, commuting to upstate New York during the academic year.

By this time our neighbors were no doubt betting on how long we would last in Carter County.

The early 1990s were our Llama Period. Our cattle-ranching friends had warned us against the critters. There had been a llama, once, in Carter County. "Never met a fence he couldn't get through, then he'd run for miles on end. Manage to get close enough to him, and he'd spit on you. That llama spit, it really stinks, too."

We were undaunted. The animals were intriguing, long-necked wooly wonders. They had multiple uses: not only for wool and as pack animals, but also as sheep guards. The llama industry was robust. They were a good investment. And every breeder we spoke with stressed how easy they were to handle. Not only that, we were assured, they were essentially indestructible. We fell for it, all of it, secured a line of credit from the bank, and assembled a small foundation herd: a couple of geldings (for pack purposes), six breeding females, and a gorgeous black herd sire with the fetching name "Silver Sage's Garth Brooks."

Between 1990 and 1997, when we sold off the last of our "indestructible" camelids, we lost two llamas (Garth being one of them) to rattlesnake bites, one to bloat, one to a congenital heart defect, one to an intestinal disorder to which llamas aren't even supposed to be susceptible, and one to stillbirth. In that same period, thanks largely to the USDA's lifting a ban (because of risk of foot-and-mouth disease) on the importation of South American animals, llama prices plummeted. Females that had commanded ten thousand dollars or more were selling for, at best, a tenth of that. Males you could give away, if you were lucky. Our llama venture yielded a net loss of about twenty thousand dollars, and we counted ourselves among the more fortunate llama folk. Spit happens, as they say in the llama trade.

Our neighbors, we were sure, mostly figured we were a little screwy to get involved with the long-necked woolies in the first place. The animals were just too different, and being "differnt" is not a particularly good thing in these parts. Nonetheless, they sincerely commiserated with us over our losses, particularly the two that succumbed to snakebite. "It's always the best animals you lose, the ones you love the most," they uniformly observed, with a look in their eyes both distant and guarded. One person was thinking about her quarter horse gelding that disastrously fractured his leg in a cattle grate and had to be put down; another about his prize Angus bull struck by lightning; yet another about a sheep-guarding Australian blue heeler herd dog that had been bushwhacked by a pack of coyotes.

If they could commiserate with us about how hard it is when livestock becomes dead stock, we could empathize with their economic distress, what with beef and lamb prices both falling through the floor at that point. Between the llamas (however "differnt" they were), and the grassland we annually leased (even though leasing to other operators is, by local measures, far inferior to running one's own cattle), we were beginning to gain a modicum of credibility. We were not exactly hobby farmers. We had suffered losses both emotional and financial. We had bought a tractor and some other implements. We had, with a neighbor's assistance, rehabilitated our alfalfa field, and had put massive amounts of time and effort into repairing our boundary fences. People stopped asking us what we did with all the time we had on our hands. They also stopped assuming we were "independently wealthy."

But if we and our neighbors were becoming closer in some ways, in others we were still very far apart.

Several times, during each academic year, I fly home for long weekends. On one such trip, in the mid-1990s, we were en route back from the Rapid City, South Dakota, airport. Dusk was falling. As we crested a hill on the gravel Chalk Buttes Road nearing home, Doug suddenly slowed the pickup and murmured, "Uh, Mare, you're not going to like this." At first perplexed, I was then stunned: he was talking about the Mother Tree. The familiar Mother Tree, still on her hillside but now achingly alone. The future pine forest, those scores, no, hundreds, of her seedling children, had been ripped up and plowed under. Mutilated branches littered the hillside. A handful of partially uprooted survivors leaned into the old tree's shade. All the rest were gone.

It was carnage. It was cold-blooded mass murder. A massacre.

Of course, from the cattleman's point of view, it was a good idea. Trees displace grass, and he was in the business of producing beef, not scenery. Besides, ponderosa pine needles can cause spontaneous abortions in cows that chance to nibble on them at the wrong time. Trees and cows don't mix, therefore. A month or so later, a second pass with the sickle bar took out the last few struggling survivors. The Mother Tree then stood in stoic isolation.

As if to balance our neighbor's karma, we were as busy planting trees on our place as he was eliminating them on his. And as our llama venture was heading south, we were also pondering what else to do with all that grassland of which we had become stewards.

From the start, we had regarded our cattle lease as at best a necessary, and temporary, evil. And the better we got to know beef cows, frankly, the less we liked them. Annie Dillard had it about right, we figured, when she described domestic cattle as "a human product like rayon," with "beef fat behind their eyes, beef stew." Yearlings jump fences, bulls walk right through them, and calves get tangled up, sometimes fatally, in wire or baling twine or whatever else is handy. Indiscriminate grazers, they are hard on pasture, and murder on riparian areas. They consume enormous quantities of water. It is of no small significance that when the great Crow chief Plenty Coups had his vision of the demise of the eastern Montana prairie, it took the form of these strangely misshapen spotted grazers displacing the buffalo from their homeland.

So that was it, then. We would bring the buffalo back. Actually, this had been Doug's desire from the outset. I had been skeptical, but something oddly having to do with the fate of the Mother Tree's progeny changed my mind.

Our neighbors warned against our getting involved with bison. So intense was their concern that a delegation came by to visit about it. Earnestly, they explained that they worried that, even if after five years we seemed to have gotten pretty good at the rudiments of managing a ranch, we were getting in over our heads with this buffalo idea. We had fences, but not good enough ones. We had no handling facilities at all. We lacked sufficient experience with large animals. Buffalo are big and wild and powerful, they reminded us. They're *different* from cattle. We could get hurt.

We allowed as how all this was certainly true. We were by now very used to the gut reaction against change in the way anything is done around here: "Dad didn't do it that way, and what was good enough for Dad is good enough." Of course, Dad is long gone. And it sometimes seemed to us that our cattlemen neighbors harbored some sort of a death wish themselves: the worse things got (and they were getting mighty bad by the mid-1990s), the more they dug in their heels and refused to do anything that might look, in a word, different. Two of our contiguous neighbors had gone belly-up since we moved in, another was close to it (and subsequently had to sell out). Everyone had cast us in the role of "outsider forces of change" anyway, so we decided we might as well embrace it.

In 1993 we bought our first twenty-five weanling bison heifer calves from a producer in Colorado. The following year we bought twenty-five more from a local producer, until then the only bison rancher in Carter County, a man who had a local reputation, not coincidentally, for being "a little differnt." In 1995 we bought three breeding bulls from him. Bison can be bred at two years old, so our first calves wouldn't be on the ground until 1996, with the full herd reproducing the following year.

Meanwhile, we fenced like crazy. No house guests of ours during that period left without a tutorial in the use of fence pliers and barbed-wire stretchers, and time out on the fence line, some major stretches of which bear their names today: The Rick and Bernardette fence, the Helene and David pasture, Ryan's hill, Maggie's gate, and so on. We invested in working facilities specifically designed for bison, since those designed for cattle did not have sturdy enough crowding tubs, squeeze chutes and crash gates (the terms alone were enough to give this Jersey girl the willies). We visited other bison operations, to learn how to work with the animals. We read every bison-related publication we could get our hands on. We joined the National Bison Association.

Our first calf was born on Mother's Day of 1996. We had been on our place for eight years, and in spite of ourselves, we had become ranchers. It's fair to say that that little one's arrival marked the end of our period of initiation into rural lifeways.

With initiations come new names. We were now the Crazy Woman Bison Ranch. And our adventure was only really just beginning.

Aerial view of Ekalaka, Montana, in the 1920s. Photo courtesy of the Carter County Museum.

CHAPTER 1
The Lay of the Land

EKALAKA, MONTANA:

A Short History

> "Ekalaka? Why, she was an Indian Princess. She married the first white settler in these parts, fellow named Russell. He was sort of a, you know, mountain man. Pretty little gal—there's a statue of her in the Museum in town."

The history of the American West is never an uncomplicated story to tell. In perhaps no other part of the nation do myth and legend intertwine so freely with more or less verifiable fact. And surely nowhere else are people, natives as well as outsiders, quite so prone to evaluating the truth of an historical account in light of its conformity to the accepted, larger-than-life saga of frontier times. The story of Ekalaka—county seat of Carter County, and one of the handful of off-reservation Montana municipalities with an Indian name—is an excellent case in point.

For the conventional version of the story of the town's founding (as for so much else these days), one need go no farther than the online encyclopedia *Wikipedia*:

The story of the early days of Ekalaka takes us back to the golden age of the west, to the brave, free life of the wilderness and plains—the most romantic chapter in American history. In the olden days, before there was any state or even territory of Montana, an Indian girl was born on the Powder River. Her parents were Sioux. She was of a restless disposition, something unusual among Indians, and on this account was called Ijkalaka, which in the Sioux tongue means restless—always on the move. When this restless, roving child of the plains was about sixteen years old she met David Harrison Russell, an intrepid scout, hunter and all-round frontiersman, who had been something of a rover himself.

In August, 1881, six years after their marriage, they settled in a beautiful valley at the edge of the forest, on the bank of a stream fed by numerous springs, where there was plenty of grass and where there were buffalo in droves and many kinds of wild game in abundance. Their location was many miles from any other settlement, in the domain of the old war chief Rain-in-the-Face, and was reputed to be infested by hostile Indians who at this particular time were in a dangerous and ugly mood. But the white man with an Indian wife was considered comparatively safe . . .

All that's missing in this once-upon-a-time account is the reference to Ijkalaka as an "Indian princess." Well, that and a cavalry charge under the command of John Wayne, routing out those Indians "infesting" the countryside.

There are, of course, some truths here, under the nostalgic overlay of "olden" times. Ijkalaka, also known as Mary Eagle Man, was born around 1858, somewhere along the Powder River in Wyoming Territory, into the Oglala band of the Lakota, or Sioux. Her father was Eagle Man; she was a niece of the great chief Red Cloud, and was also related to Sitting Bull. Mary's mother died when she was a young child. She went first to live with her mother's sister, who had married a white settler at Fort Laramie, and shortly thereafter to the home of her cousin Elizabeth Renshaw (Red Cloud's granddaughter), who had married rancher Hiram Kelly, in Chugwater, Wyoming. Thus, she appears to have been less a "roving child of the plains" than a displaced female child in a widely dispersed extended family. Settled in Chugwater, on one of the more prosperous ranches in the area, she took for herself the name Mary Ellen Kelly.

It was apparently through the Kellys that she met, and was courted by, David Harrison Russell, an Illinoisan fifteen years her senior. Ostensibly descended from Scottish aristocracy, Russell had indeed done a good share of roving by then. Orphaned at the age of eight, he enlisted at age thirteen to fight the Cayuse Indians in Oregon in the 1850s. He subsequently drove mules and oxen from Central America to the Canadian border, worked on cattle drives and as a bronco rider, and hunted buffalo. In the course of his travels he met and mingled with a virtual Who's Who of the American West: Brigham Young, Chief Joseph, Sitting Bull, Kit Carson, Theodore Roosevelt, Wild Bill Hickok, and Buffalo Bill Cody. It is said that the latter offered Russell and Ijkalaka roles in his Wild West Show, but they declined.

One may well imagine young Mary Kelly being swept off her feet by this dashing adventurer, a dreamer with big stories and bigger plans for the future. One may equally well imagine his being taken by this lithe Indian maid's easy rapport with people and by her beauty, the red satin ribbons she braided into her long dark tresses. And that is about as close to romance as we dare verge in this story. Russell paid Eagle Man a bride-price of eight horses and a hundred-pound sack of sugar, and the couple were wed near Laramie in 1874. Mary/Ijkalaka was sixteen.

The "particular time" in question was, of course, the period of the Indian Wars: George Armstrong Custer was defeated by Lakota and Cheyenne warriors at the Battle of the Little Bighorn two years after the Russells married, and the next sixteen years would see numerous conflicts between Anglos and Natives, along with the establishment of the reservation system. Rain-in-the-Face was among the most uncompromising of Oglala warriors. Hence the presence of those "hostile Indians . . . in a dangerous and ugly mood," in a region that the *Montana Travel, Tourism, and Recreation Guide* persists to this day in calling "Custer Country." Indians were at war with one another, as well as with the U.S. Cavalry. The traditional animosity that the Lakota and Cheyenne bore toward the Crow tribe over contested hunting grounds was exacerbated by the fact that Custer had used Crow scouts. No doubt Russell managed to live well in this country not only because of his marriage to a Lakota woman, but also owing to the prior good relationships he had nourished over time with Native leaders.

The area around the settlement that would eventually bear his wife's name was indeed lush hunting country at the time. It had, in fact, traditionally been a major hunting area for Lakota, Cheyenne, and Crow Indians. For the Lakota peoples, it also lay well within the "Hoop of the Nation," that broad swath of eastern Montana and Wyoming and the western Dakotas and Nebraska that constitutes a spiritual as well as a physical geography.

At the center of this map, both symbolically and economically, was the buffalo. The U.S. Army, well aware of this fact, recognized that the best way to break the soul and spirit of the Plains Indian peoples was to deprive them of that spiritual center. Indian fighter General Phil Sheridan—another of Russell's famous acquaintances, and the man who immortalized the phrase, "The only good Indians I ever saw were dead"—remarked that the buffalo was the "Indians' commissary." His solution to the Indian problem was summed up in the simple formula: Kill the buffalo, kill the Indian.

In 1880, the U.S. government issued an order to clear eastern Montana and the western Dakotas of their free-ranging bison herds. Private market hunters were free to keep or to sell the hides of any animals they killed. Settled in South Dakota, David Russell recalled a particularly bison-rich area he had hunted with Chief Joseph many years earlier, and sold off everything he had in order to move to southeastern Montana, to that "beautiful valley at the edge of the forest" (*Wikipedia's* phrasing here was originally Russell's). In 1881, Mary/Ijkalaka joined him here, with their four children. Hunting with a partner named Isaac Downing, between 1880 and 1882 Russell killed 2,650 bison, selling their hides. In 1883, he shipped another nineteen hundred bison hides to market. By then a few more homesteaders had drifted into the area, and Russell opened a trading post, to serve their needs.

That same year, an entrepreneur named Claude Carter was wending his way westward into Montana Territory, with a wagon loaded with whiskey and logs, and the intention of slaking the thirst of gold miners farther west. He had gotten as far as what by then was called Russell Creek Valley, when his wagon got mired in the muddy creek crossing and his horses balked. Carter declared, "Hell, anyplace in Montana is a good place for a saloon!" and set about building the sod-roofed, earthen-floored Old Stand Saloon, which he would operate profitably for the next fifty years.

Other small businesses followed, and by 1885 enough of a town had grown up here that it warranted a U.S. post office. Accounts vary as to how exactly it was decided upon, but "Ekalaka" (a phonetically accurate rendition of the Lakota "Ijkalaka") is the name that stuck. It was surely preferable to the contemporary alternative, Puptown, a reference to the numerous prairie dogs overrunning the neighborhood.

After moving to their Montana homestead in 1881, Ijkalaka bore David nine more children. Some of the Russell children went to the Indian boarding school in Pierre, South Dakota, and in 1893—perhaps owing to a succession of cruel winters, beginning in 1886—Russell sent Ijkalaka and all but one of their children to spend the winter on South Dakota's Pine Ridge Reservation. He and their son George followed them there, but Russell decided he liked Montana better, and the family returned to Ekalaka in 1894. Six years later, their eldest son Ben went to visit the Cheyenne River Reservation, in central South Dakota, where a smallpox epidemic had broken out. Ignoring the quarantine Ben returned home to Montana, where he subsequently developed the disease. Ijkalaka died of smallpox, along with Ben and another son Thomas, in the spring of 1901. She was forty-two years old.

David Russell went on to remarry a Canadian widow he had met through correspondence. He brought her to Ekalaka, where he enjoyed a reputation as "The Father of Ekalaka" and as the "Columbus and John Smith of Carter County." The latter title is particularly telling: Columbus-like, Russell was the white explorer who "discovered" this place, and like John Smith he chose a Native bride. Never mind that Native American tribes don't really have "princesses"; Ijkalaka *was* one, just like Pocahontas! And the conventional history of the displacement of her people from their own land, like that of the English conquest of the Algonkian in Virginia two centuries earlier, was ultimately written by the winning side, with enough of a mythic overlay to blunt later sensibilities to the harshness of its reality.

Of course, there are other actors in this historical drama, the ones who built the town and populated what became Carter County: the homesteaders, many of whose descendants still live here, and who have their own myths by which to live.

"GO WEST, YOUNG MAN"

In 1862, Abraham Lincoln signed the Homestead Act into law, opening up vast expanses of public land to private acquisition. The Act provided ownership of a quarter section (that is, 160 acres, or one-fourth of one square mile) of land to anyone who staked a claim on it, built a house and dug a well, and cultivated at least ten acres or planted ten acres of trees for timber, built some fence, and actually lived on the place for five years. At the end of that time the claim was "proved up," and title to the land passed from the government to the homesteader. The land had to have been previously unoccupied, or in the phrasing of the later Indian Appropriations Bill (1889) "unassigned," which means of course that tribal claims were rendered invalid. In a rather spectacular instance of bureaucratic sleight of hand, it seems to have been assumed that an ideal way to accomplish this was to allow title to pass from government into private hands—and with it, any chance that Indians could advance land claims in the future.

Homesteading came first to Nebraska and Kansas, and in the generation after the Civil War settlers fanned out, westward across the Great Plains. The 1889 Oklahoma Land Rush was perhaps the most extravagant homesteading event of that era, opening up two million acres of Indian land to white settlement, with millions of acres more platted and made available for homesteading in successive land runs in Oklahoma Territory between then and the turn of the last century. In all, between 1863, when the Homestead Act went into effect, and 1900, 1,400,000 people had applied for 160-acre family farms under its provisions.

Amazingly, the early years of the twentieth century saw the number of homesteaders per year double. As historian Walter Nugent relates it:

> Those first thirteen years of the twentieth century were the true heyday of homesteading. Compared with them, Kansas and Nebraska in the twenty years after the Civil War were a prelude, and Oklahoma for all its explosiveness was only an overture. The first dozen years of the century brought an extravaganza of settlement, from Texas north across the High Plains into the Canadian prairies.

This was the period during which Ekalaka and environs were settled. Indeed, eastern Montana was an epicenter of land development. Nugent continues:

> In 1890 two giant counties occupied all Montana between Wyoming and Canada for about 125 miles west of the Dakota line. Only 7,400 people rattled around in them. By 1920 they had calved off into sixteen counties with 117,700 people, settled on farms or ranches or in small towns sprinkled along the routes

of the Great Northern and Northern Pacific. None of these towns
came near having 10,000 people, or ever would.

David H. Russell and his Indian wife were, then, among the
first wave of homesteaders who would ultimately transform this
landscape's map. The transformation was abetted by two factors.
The first was the Enlarged Homestead Act of 1909, which doubled
the size of a claim from 160 to 320 acres. The opportunity to secure
more land was obviously appealing, especially to settlers who wanted
to run a few cows in addition to farming—a dream that was further
enhanced by the Stock-Raising Homestead Act of 1916, which opened
up 640-acre parcels specifically for cattle. In the second decade of the
century, homesteaders staked thirty million acres worth of claims in
eastern Montana. "Honyockers," these newest pioneers were derisively
nicknamed by their (if just barely) more established neighbors. As
many as half of these newcomers, propelled westward by the powerful
dream of self-sufficiency, had no agricultural experience whatsoever.

The second factor at work in this rapid expansion of homestead
activity was the transcontinental railroad system, which established
towns every twenty miles or so as quickly as the tracks were laid down,
moving steadily west. These towns could be expected to bring workers
and commercial interests into the region, but their primary function
was—and in those isolated outposts that survive today, remains—
evident in their uniformly most prominent architectural features.
Small towns in other parts of the country can boast of old ivy-covered
churches or venerable stone town halls dominating their civic spaces.
Here, by contrast, the most striking feature of any railroad town was
its hulking grain elevator, often visible on the horizon for miles of flat
landscape before the town itself came into view.

Not coincidentally, most of the homesteaders traveling west on
the Northern Pacific and other rail lines carried with them stacks of
literature, graciously provided by the rail companies themselves,
promoting the new agricultural technology of "dryland farming."
This revolutionary process promised to turn the semiarid mixed-grass
prairie of the northern High Plains, where annual moisture generally
amounts to between thirteen and sixteen measurable inches, into a
virtual paradise of wheat production. Pamphlets described near-barren
hardpan blossoming into amber waves of grain, thanks to a regime of

deep plowing, subsoil compaction, and mulching with fine topsoil. No need, would-be farmers were assured, to worry about lack of irrigation. Rain would "follow the plow," and besides, the relative lack of moisture was offset by the abundant sunshine. This method turned out, in fact, to be a recipe for rapid topsoil depletion, and little else. A few dryland farmers saw a couple of good years, thanks to back-to-back seasons of above-average rainfall. But then came six straight years of drought, from 1916 through 1921. "The golden twilight of homesteading" had, as Nugent puts it, "faded into dark." By 1922, three-quarters of those who had settled in eastern Montana had abandoned their claims.

The child of one such family, Percy Wollaston, years later chronicled their homesteading experience, near the now-defunct railroad town of Mildred. "One should be able to begin a story with the conventional 'Once upon a time' and have done with it," he wrote. "But what time? Any one of the factors influencing the advance of settlement would be a story in itself and each settler had some different reason for the move." Wollaston's memoir of life on the eastern Montana frontier was a major resource for English writer Jonathan Raban's travelogue of this region, *Bad Land: An American Romance*. Having retraced the eastern Montana homesteaders' failed odyssey, poking around their ruined cabins and interviewing their scattered descendents, Raban summed up his research this way:

> For two years, I had been living with a story so American that some Americans would not recognize it as a story. These people came over, went broke, quit their homes, and moved elsewhere? So? This is America, where everyone has the right to fail—it's in the Constitution.

Some Ekalakians of the period of homesteading's twilight surely exercised their "rights" in this regard. However, in many respects, the town was doing well. This may have had to do, in no small part, with the fact that it was not a railroad town. In fact, Ekalaka was once reputed to be the biggest inland town in the nation not served by a railroad: the nearest rail line (and the nearest commercial grain elevator) is in Baker, thirty-five miles to the north. While the area attracted a few farmers, Ekalaka from its beginning was, and would remain, essentially a cow town. Indeed, the eradication of the resident bison herd between 1881 and 1883 had served the interests not only of a U.S. government that wanted to rid the area of its Native American population, but also of large-scale cattle ranchers who had long seen central and eastern Montana Territory as prime range country.

Granville Stuart, at one time the most powerful "cattle baron" in Montana, who ranched in central Montana's Judith Basin, recorded the rapid transition from bison to cattle across the eastern half of the territory:

> It would be impossible to make persons not present on the Montana cattle ranges realize the rapid change that took place on those ranges in two years. In 1880, the country was practically uninhabited. One could travel for miles without seeing so much as a trapper's bivouac. Thousands of buffalo darkened the rolling plains. There were deer, antelope, elk, wolves and coyotes on every hill and in every ravine and thicket. In the whole territory of Montana, there were but 250,000 head of cattle including dairy cattle and oxen.
>
> In the fall of 1883 there was not one buffalo remaining on the range and the antelope, elk were scarce. In 1880, no one had ever heard tell of a cowboy in "this niche of the woods" and Charlie Russell had made no pictures of them; but in the fall of 1883, there were 600,000 head of cattle on the range.

By that same year, market buffalo hunters who arrived in Miles City, eastern Montana's commercial hub, found no bison left to shoot. But cattle were being trailed up to eastern Montana from Texas by the thousands, and soon overtook the landscape. It has been estimated that by 1890 there were more beef cattle on the High Plains than there had been bison a mere twenty years earlier. And Montana had become the forty-first state.

FROM ONE TWILIGHT TO ANOTHER

With cheap homesteaded land on the one hand, and good hard-grass prairie that needed to be grazed on the other, Ekalaka took root, along with other area communities—Ridgeway, Capitol, Mill Iron, Alzada, Albion, Boyes, Hammond. In 1917, Ekalaka was declared the seat of newly established Carter County (named, by the way, not for that enterprising barkeep, but for Thomas H. Carter, Montana's territorial delegate to the U.S. Senate), a land area somewhat larger than the state of Delaware. By this time the county had a public school system, with the high school in town and one-room grade schools strewn about the countryside. In 1920 the courthouse, still in use today, opened.

Most of the homestead deeds in the county were issued during Woodrow Wilson's administration. As happened throughout the plains, those boom years quickly turned to bust for many. The paint was barely dry on the new courthouse walls before the county began to seize land for nonpayment of back taxes, gobbling up quarter sections and half sections and then immediately selling them to more prosperous landowners at the bargain rates of two to three dollars an acre. Brokers cashed in on the bargain rates, consolidating land for sale at a quick profit. Meanwhile, the savvier (or luckier) area cattlemen could afford to secure larger tracts of land for their herds—and this was key to their eventual success as ranchers. On rangeland where the Natural Resources and Conservation Service today estimates that every cow/calf pair requires roughly 35 acres of forage, assuming there is the additional acreage available to produce hay for winter feed, those 160- or 320-acre cattle operations were obviously never viable in the first place. During the first two decades of the twentieth century, homesteaders' cabins had dotted the landscape within sight, or at least an easy walk, of one another. By the close of the 1920s, ranch houses were typically five or more miles apart.

Sepia photographs from the period, available from the Carter County Museum, eloquently attest to the town's growth and nascent

Ekalaka, Montana, in 1896. Photo courtesy of the Carter County Museum.

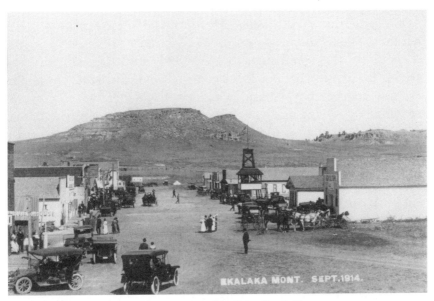

Ekalaka the boomtown, in 1914. Photo courtesy of the Carter County Museum.

prosperity at this time. A preboom picture taken in 1896 shows a scattering of buildings on what would become Main Street, the "street" itself being a muddy two-track. A man leads a horse in the distance, and a lone wagon is parked outside what appears to be the livery, where a trio of men are conversing. A later photo of the same view, looking up Main Street and dated September 1914, depicts a far more settled and obviously prosperous town. Businesses line both sides of the wide thoroughfare, which is filled with motor cars, horse-drawn carriages, and an assemblage of nattily dressed pedestrians, socializing and going about their business. A later aerial view, dating to sometime in the 1920s, shows (in addition to the courthouse) side streets and residential neighborhoods fanning out from the business center: a mini-metropolis in the shadow of the rugged Ekalaka Hills.

But pictures alone only begin to tell the story of what was going on in this frontier town. Narrative histories written by members of the founding families in the area survive, in a three-volume collection preserved in the museum. They tell stories of hardship and loss, of small joys and major accomplishments, dashed hopes and unanticipated good fortune, and a society populated by colorful, eccentric, and generally upstanding pioneers: hardworking ranchers, dedicated schoolteachers, enterprising businessmen, occasionally rowdy but good-hearted cowboys, and humble churchgoers. All the fairly predictable western themes are there, in other words.

A rather less sympathetic, but certainly revealing, account was written by Jennie Carlson, a Wisconsin native and graduate of the teachers college in Oshkosh, who moved progressively westward, teaching English and history in high schools in Wisconsin, Minnesota, and South Dakota, and finally landing in Ekalaka in 1921. Three years later, Carlson was elected superintendent of schools, and in that capacity traveled throughout the county, monitoring the progress of its one-room schoolhouses, and accumulating material for the novel—actually, by all accounts, a thinly disguised memoir—that she published in 1952, titled *Thru the Dust*. Its dedication, "to the beloved people of Carter County, Montana,—May your sins be forgotten," suggests that Carlson intends to take aim on a culture about which, it appears, she harbored rather mixed feelings.

In her telling, Ekalaka becomes the town of Cactus, county seat of Gumbo County. ("Gumbo" is Montana slang for the particularly noxious character of the mud around here: an impossibly slick and slippery ooze when wet, it dries to concrete hardness.) Carlson opens her story, set in the 1920s, with a detailed description of the county fair, with excited youngsters decked out in new clothes and shoes, ladies from town and country competing with their best pies and preserves and needlework, milking contests, and a midway complete with a fortune-teller and "a wild man from Africa," and the central event of the fair, its rodeo, with a robust cast of buckaroos and cowgirls. As dusk falls, people's thoughts turn to food and drink (especially the latter), and to dance. Here Carlson conveys a less romantic insight into prairie life:

> At such dances as this, the alley is far more interesting than the dance hall. Drunken men are lying among the boxes and garbage reveling in their drunkenness; small boys are creeping about to gather up the empty bottles and drinking anything that happens to be left; and young girls and women are heard cackling as if insane and calling for more moonshine; gambling men are cursing in vile language in the rickety poorly lighted old sheds used for this amusement. As you continue your visit in the alley, the blood in your veins begins to become sluggish; and you wonder if God can find His way to this loathsome den in order to guide your footsteps back to a place where you can think and act like a human being.

And then there is the county fair's aftermath:

> The next morning, the Main Street was a gruesome sight. There
> were bits of broken bottles strewn along the sidewalk, scraps of
> paper, darkened spots of tobacco juice, and patches of blood—
> indicating there had been several fights during the night. The
> dust and sand had accumulated in little mounds in front of the
> business places. The windows of the stores, banks, and other
> places were spattered up from the drizzling rain that had fallen
> during the day. The fruit, toys, and candies on display in the store
> windows were in a state of disorder; they looked as if the children
> of the village had played Hop Scotch over them. The people were
> sauntering up and down the Main Street in the morning looking
> bedraggled, sleepy, and disinterested in life . . .

As Carlson moves into her plot, it quickly becomes clear that Cactus,
Montana, is run by scoundrels and corrupt politicians, and while there
are a few generally upstanding country folk, the population of Gumbo
County primarily consists of charlatans, loose women, and sex-starved
ranch hands. Despite her prefatory "Note: The local coloring and
characters are truly western; yet, no character is a portrayal of any living
person," older residents of the town today—many of them descendents
of those characters from whom Carlson drew inspiration—dismiss
Thru the Dust as nothing more or less than mean-spirited gossip. They
call it "Through the Dirt." Undeniably an unflattering portrait of Carter
County's early history, from a literary point of view it is also, and this
may be its saving grace for Ekalakians today, virtually unreadable.

Carter County comes off rather better in one other fictional take on
homestead history, Russell Rowland's *In Open Spaces*. Rowland's 2002
novel is loosely based on the story of his homesteading grandparents,
amplified by interviews he conducted with descendants of their
neighbors in and around the now-defunct community of Albion, in the
southern part of Carter County. His tale is at once more fully imagined,
and more genuinely evocative of the region's history, than Carlson's
work. It begins in the same time period, but the bulk of its action occurs
during the "dirty thirties" years of national Depression and regional
drought, recalled by the narrator, a character named Blake Arbuckle:

> The interesting thing about our county was that by the time the
> Depression hit, we had already experienced a difficult decade. In

the twenties, half the banks in Montana had closed, rainfall had
been well below average, livestock and grain prices were down,
and many of the honyockers that inundated our little corner of the
state had gone against conventional wisdom and used farming
methods such as a machine that pounded the ground until the
topsoil blew away with the slightest wind. Much of the topsoil in
our county was gone before the Depression even started. Because
of this, the amateurs, the less dedicated, the disillusioned, were
mostly gone by 1929. Most of us who were left were survivors
already, so we knew what it took.

But if we had known in 1929 that the drought was going
to last another ten years, we could have set our fields on fire,
and shot three quarters of our stock. It would have had the same
effect.

The theme Rowland hits on here, of being a survivor—being tough
enough to make it on this unforgiving land, being illusion free when it
comes to what one can expect in return from this hard-grass prairie—is
both a leitmotif in his novel and an accurate assessment of the way
southeastern Montanans continue today to perceive themselves, and
to judge one another. Another of his characters says, "This place, this
land, it beats the hell out of people. Have you noticed that, Blake? Beats
the holy hell out of folks." I've heard the same thing myself, in the
Wagon Wheel Café.

This land, in Rowland's telling as in the homesteading reminiscences of its real-life residents, has plenty of hell to go around: children die of accidents and disease, farm work is always both tedious and
backbreaking and there is always too much of it for it all to get done,
machinery seems designed to malfunction, people drift into drunken-
ness and insanity, families struggle not only to make ends meet but to
remain more or less on speaking terms in a world of remote ranches
where they are, for the most part and often for interminable stretches
of time, the only human society they've got . . . and everyone, in his
or her own fashion, struggles to fend off "the loneliness," that crush-
ing sense of isolation in the face of such vast openness as few places
on earth offer in so raw a form as this easternmost fringe of Big Sky
Country. And yet, harsh as it can be, this same landscape catches hold
of one. Rowland writes:

In our country, there is a quietness, a silence that surrounds you
and fills you up, beating inside like blood until it becomes part

of you. The prairie is quiet even during the day, except for the sounds of work—the snort of horses, the clang of a plow's blade against rock, and the rhythm of hooves pounding the ground. But these sounds drift off into the air, finding nothing to contain them. No echoes.

. . . At night, the darkness seems to add to the silence, making it heavier, somehow more imposing. It is a silence that can be too much for some, especially people who aren't fond of their own company. And it seems that living in such silence makes you think twice before speaking, or laughing, or crying. Because when sounds are that scarce, they carry more weight.

A sensitive, and perceptive, description here, to be sure. But it may also be the sort of prairie poetry that perhaps only a skilled writer who also happens to be a native of western Montana, and who relocated to San Francisco, can venture more or less convincingly, and without a trace of irony. On the ground, as it were—and perhaps this is what Jen Carlson tried, and failed, to convey in her more amateurish narrative—the people who settled here, and those who lasted, took their cues from nature, for better and for worse. Their psyches could, and often did, become as calloused as their work-hardened hands, and their social interactions as chafed as their wind-chapped lips.

The population of Carter County peaked at 4,136 in 1930, and has been in decline ever since. A 2005 U.S. Census Bureau estimate put it at 1,320 persons spread out over the county's 3,340 square miles: this yields the statistical oddity of zero persons per square mile. The cattle population is, however, holding its own: there are 42 beef cows for every human being here. In the 2000 census, the town of Ekalaka's population had dropped to 410, from a high of 904 in 1950. People whose ranching dreams evaporated in the 1930s and 1940s often moved to town, apparently, before leaving the country entirely.

Another sepia photo from the Carter County Museum shows Main Street in the late 1930s. Horse-drawn wagons have given way to late-model cars. The street is paved and there are sidewalks. There are electric power lines, and a fire hydrant on one corner. Despite the autos, the photograph conveys the aura of a ghost town in the making. What I found startling, if not altogether surprising, when I first saw this photo is how similar Main Street looks today. It is not entirely as if time has stood still, of course. There are, in fact, fewer businesses in Ekalaka now than there were then.

For example, there used to be a hardware store, of sorts, on Main Street. It was locally owned, but participated in a national hardware franchise system. Around 1990, store owners from around the country were invited to bring their accounts ledgers to the national convention, where marketing experts would run their numbers and suggest ways they could improve or streamline their merchandising. When Bill, the Ekalaka store owner, had his information fed into the system, the computer spat out a printout declaring that according to its algorithm, his store had gone belly-up in 1927. That probably accounted for his disappointing receipts, of late. Bill finally threw in the towel, and closed the store in the mid-1990s. Gone as well, by then, some of them long gone, were the movie theater, the drugstore, the lumberyard, the farm implements dealer, the clothing/dry goods store, the barbershop, the liquor store, the steak house/supper club, one of two grocery stores, one of two propane dealerships, and two of four saloons.

In 1932, at the worst of the Great Depression, the median household income in America was $1,500. Adjusted for inflation, that would be around $22,573 today. According to the 2000 Census, the median household income in Carter County was $26,313, with a per capita income of $13,280. Roughly one in five residents of Carter County lives below the poverty line. In per capita terms, this is one of the poorest counties in one of the poorest states in the Union. This isn't to say that some people, especially some area ranchers, aren't doing well, and some of them very well, indeed, thanks to a judicious combination of hard work, government subsidies, and a cordial relationship with an understanding banker. But all the same it is difficult to shake the feeling that just as the early twentieth century saw the twilight of homesteading fade to black, scarcely one hundred years later we are observing the last gasps of the High Plains ranch economy, and of the culture that goes along with it.

A BEAUTIFUL VALLEY AT THE EDGE OF THE FOREST

A number of Carter County ranchers have sold their places in the last few years. Their motivations were various, and not invariably related to financial distress. But for every ranch sale resulting from retirement or relocation, three or four more have been matters of foreclosure—even the bureaucratic boondoggle otherwise known as the Federal Land Bank catches up with delinquent mortgagees eventually. In rarer cases,

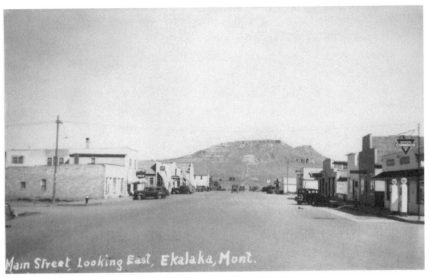

Ekalaka in the late 1930s. Photo courtesy of the Carter County Museum.

Ekalaka, summer of 2009. Photo by Mary Stange.

the country treasurer has seized property for nonpayment of back taxes, yet another echo of an earlier era.

This, of course, was where Doug and I came in, twenty-odd years ago. The cattleman we bought our place from had been on it since right after World War II. His name, like that of about a quarter of the adult males in southeastern Montana, was Bud. He and his wife Betty had had some good, even prosperous, years here, although their lifestyle was rather more hardscrabble than most. "He's the last of the old-time cowboys," one neighbor told us. "Lives on horseback. Never owned a tractor or a chain saw. Always fed his stock in the winter out of a wagon pulled by a team of mules, and cut his firewood by hand." And, we quickly surmised, depended on the kindness of neighbors to, say, plow him out after a snowstorm. Or else, more frequently—and the reason, no doubt, why Betty and the kids moved to town in winter—Bud just toughed things out, waiting for a break in the weather that was bound to come sooner or later. Like more than a few ranchers, he apparently managed his finances in pretty much the same way.

By the time we were in a position to be looking at ranch properties, in the late 1980s, Bud was in considerable financial trouble. Some of it was of his own making. Having owned the place free and clear, he took out a mortgage to come up with the money to lease a huge tract of land not far from here, so one of his sons could get set up in ranching on his own. In good economic times, this might have been a sensible, even lucrative, venture: between the income he and his son made off their respective herds, they'd be able to pay back the loan, possibly even cut some profit. But those were not good economic times. The 1980s was the decade that saw, essentially, the collapse of the farm and ranch economy. Land values were nose-diving, to the point where even if all the livestock and the machinery were factored into a farm loan as collateral, it still didn't cover the outstanding principle on the mortgage. A grim pattern emerged in the national headlines. A failed farmer, in some gritty little town in the Midwest or High Plains, driven to desperation akin to what the original homesteaders must have experienced, but even more impossibly leveraged, would walk into his bank manager's office, shoot the banker, and then turn the gun on himself. With luck, and a sympathetic claims adjustor, there might be some insurance money for his survivors.

Bud and Betty's situation was not quite so dire, although Bud must have suffered his share of anxious moments when he had to fess up to his wife about having mortgaged the ranch without consulting her. They didn't have any implements to speak of, for collateral, but they did have a nice herd of cows, and a pretty piece of land with a BLM grazing allotment. So the Land Bank was prepared to be patient. These folks were covering the interest on their loan, at any rate.

But then beef prices went into free fall. There were back-to-back very dry years: open, snow free winters followed by scant spring moisture. And the grasshoppers came, a virtual plague, clouds of them jumping around as if on a hot griddle and stripping prairie grasses to their stems. And so-called Mormon crickets, three-inch-long monsters that look like the kind of bugs that surely would survive a nuclear blast, moved overland in phalanxes, gnawing their way across entire pastures. The alfalfa developed some sort of blight, shriveling away, worthless as forage. None of this could have been planned for. Yet, life being what it is in this part of the country, it all could have been anticipated. The Land Bank began to lose patience. Bud reluctantly put the place up for sale.

The real estate agent in Miles City, a Wyoming native named Steve, dubbed it the Chalk Buttes Ranch, for advertising purposes. This was the very first ranch property we looked at, in the spring of 1987. It was not love at first sight, at least not for me. Beautiful it was, yes, with the stunning Chalk Buttes rising to the east, and the ranch spanning much of the southern end of a broad valley, its main entrance road swirling down a hillside through ponderosa pine woods. When one rounded a slight curve in the road and came out of the trees, the vista opened out toward sandstone buttes miles distant, and an expanse of rolling sage and grassland carved by seasonal creeks and deeply wooded draws. Three miles down the road, one came to a fairly new log home, a nicely sited, compactly built cabin. To the north and east of the house were groves of Rocky Mountain juniper trees and more mixed-grass prairie. A mile farther down the creek north of the homestead, there was a Quonset pole barn. East of that, more grassland, then a steep canyon that snaked its way toward massive mud buttes. It was undeniably ideal wildlife habitat, with those deep creek beds and draws for whitetails and rugged breaks for mule deer, those broad undulating plains for pronghorn antelope, the forest for turkeys, and hay land for upland birds—Hungarian partridge, sage grouse, sharp-tailed grouse, and maybe with luck, some pheasants.

But, while we had often hunted in this part of the state, it was not the Montana I had grown to love in the several years we had been calling the Helena Valley home. Montana is a state with a distinctly split personality. The western third of the state is Rocky Mountain high country. It features gorgeous scenery, clear mountain streams and deep blue lakes, lush national forests of towering lodgepole pine and Douglas fir, wilderness areas like the Scapegoat and Bob Marshall, Glacier National Park, and the Greater Yellowstone ecosystem. It is a recreational paradise, with prime hiking, camping, hunting, and fishing minutes, or at most an hour or so, away from just about anywhere. It boasts a few nifty smaller cities—the university towns of Missoula and Bozeman, the state capital of Helena, the historic mining center in Butte, resort communities Kalispell and Whitefish up near Flathead Lake—all with museums and theaters and arts festivals, and places where you could buy a *New York Times* on the same day it was published, and a cappuccino to sip while you were reading it, before there was a "Pony Espresso" stand in every backwater community. The west, in other words, has long offered something like recognizable culture, to go along with its Big Sky ambience.

Move east of the Rocky Mountain Front, however, and Montana is quite another story: an inland sea of grassland, sage, craggy breaks and rock-strewn badlands, with a horizon often stretching to infinity. Such forests as there are, are less immediately impressive than the west's, featuring the ponderosa pine and juniper trees that grow at somewhat lower altitudes, and offering less spectacular vistas. There is one major commercial center, Billings, in the south-central part of the state. East of that, there's Miles City—"the bucking-horse capital of the world"—and, frankly, not much else. The newspaper of record out here is the *Billings Gazette*, and the coffee in establishments "where the pot is always on" is generally overcooked and flavorless. Whereas the west tends to skew politically liberal/progressive, the east is rock-ribbed conservative. It is hotter here in the summer, colder in winter, and drier and windier all year round. The west has grizzly bears. The east, rattlesnakes.

Notwithstanding all these differences, this ranch was indeed a very pretty place. It was remote: twenty-five gravel miles southwest of Ekalaka, and once you got to town, there wasn't much there, nor was it near to much of anyplace else. But that didn't bother me so much as the mailbox did—or, more precisely, the fact that the mailbox was five miles from the house. Five miles up the dirt "road" (which was for long stretches nothing more than a two-track), three of those miles on this ranch and the last two out to the county road on an easement across a neighbor's land.

"Well," Doug said, when I raised this concern, "you run every day, anyway. You could just jog up to the get the mail the two days a week it gets delivered."

"Ten miles roundtrip, up and then back down something like a nine-hundred-foot rise, just to get some bills and the L. L. Bean catalog? No, dearest," I said, "I don't think so."

Doug was more taken with the place than I, but he agreed that this was, after all, just the beginning of our search. Over the next several weeks, we traveled around the state, and looked at as many more properties as we could find in our rather modest price range. But there was something about each one that led us back around to that place near Ekalaka. That something generally had to do with one or more factors: neighbors so close as to be in sight; the likelihood of neighboring land being subdivided and developed; a house on or within sight of a public highway; an old, dilapidated, or architecturally ugly house; proximity to a town offering even less than Ekalaka did in the way of conveniences, and farther still from the nearest shopping center or airport.

Doug was generally the one who drew the negative comparison between a place we'd just visited, and that first ranch we had looked at. I would counter that he just seemed to have his heart set on that Chalk Buttes place. But I also began to realize that I, too, was using that place as a standard against which to judge all the others. I finally admitted this to myself (it would take me a while to get around to admitting it to him) after we quite literally came to a crossroads in our search.

We had spent the day looking at what had promised, judging by the realtor's brochure, to be a real treasure. It was called the Buffington Ranch. It was in the Missouri Breaks, overlooking Fort Peck Lake and abutting the Charles M. Russell National Wildlife Refuge, or CMR as it's called. It had turned out to be a major disappointment. The house, supposedly designed to function as a hunting lodge, was not only devoid of anything like character, it was situated at the dead end of a paved county highway that afforded access to CMR hunting: in effect, the front yard would be a public parking area for hunters' pickups, and there would be a constant stream of traffic from September into January. The pastures were demarcated by cross fencing that bore no discernable correlation to the patchwork of deeded, BLM, and refuge land that comprised the acreage; this was especially troublesome because wherever CMR land was involved, it carried all sorts of use restrictions. The "lake access" promised in the brochure turned out to be a narrow, rocky, and near-vertical footpath; there was no way to get a boat down there, nor any place to moor one.

The ranch was in receivership, so any buyer had to act fast, the agent—a very nice guy who bore an uncanny resemblance to the television actor Jamie Farr, of *M.A.S.H.*—told us. The only reason the bankruptcy court hadn't sold the place already was that the owner had disappeared, and provided no forwarding address. He did this quite abruptly. One afternoon he was out haying, and at some point he pulled the tractor to a stop, got down from the driver's seat, and walked away. He didn't even turn off the ignition; the tractor just sat there idling in the middle of the partially mown hayfield, until it ran out of fuel. It was still there, door of the cab still hanging open. This felt like bad karma, to us.

After we bade adieu to Corporal Klinger, we decided to stop for a cool drink in the tiny town of Jordan. There we proceeded to have a reasonably vigorous row. We were both hot, we were tired, we were discouraged, and depressed, and hundreds of dry dusty eastern Montana miles from basically anywhere. To be fair, Doug started it. "You know," he said, opening a Montana state highway map out onto the hood of our·Toyota pickup, "we're only a couple of hundred miles from Ekalaka. We can drive down to Miles City, get a motel room, and call Steve about taking another look at that place tomorrow morning."

"Oh, right," I whined, "the place where the mailbox is five miles from the house."

"Do you think you could put that mailbox out of your mind for just once?"

"How do we know that place is even still on the market? It's been weeks since we looked at it." A reasonable question, I thought.

"Uh, I just know that it is," he hedged. For some reason, this made me furious.

"Look, I'm just sick of all this running around, looking at places that have all kinds of problems. We don't know what we're getting ourselves into, we don't know what we're doing, we probably should have our heads examined for even thinking about buying a ranch in the first place. We both have to be back at school in a couple of weeks and this is a hell of a way to spend the end of summer vacation." I was weeping by now, partly out of genuine frustration, but mostly for effect. "I want to go home."

"All right," Doug groaned, "let's get in the truck and get on the road, then."

We pulled out of Jordan, immediately coming to the junction of state highways 200 and 59. At the stop sign, Doug said, "All right, Mare, it's your call: 200 west to Helena, or 59 south to Miles City?"

He knew what my answer would be. "Miles City," I sighed. "But we probably should drive back into Jordan, to call ahead for a motel and see whether Steve is free tomorrow."

It turned out he was busy in the morning, closing on another land sale, but Steve suggested we meet up at the by now notorious mailbox around noon, for another tour of the ranch. It was somewhat disconcerting, when we three got down to the ranch house, to discover that not only were Bud and Betty at home this time, she had cooked up a hefty ranch "dinner" (the local term for lunch) for us all: roast beef with gravy, mashed potatoes, beans, tossed salad with assorted bottled dressings, Jell-O salad with marshmallows, Parker House rolls . . . standard eastern Montana fare for a ninety-degree mid-August midday working ranch meal. This one was punctuated by Betty's not always successful attempts to hold back tears, and Bud's stream-of-consciousness narrative about life on the place, how he had pretty much taken raw land and turned it into a cattle ranch. After dinner and a dessert of deep-dish apple pie à la mode, we went for a second tour of the ranch, this time with Bud driving and serving as our guide, a laconic Steve dozing (or pretending to) in the back of the truck's crew cab, his Stetson pulled down over his eyes.

That Bud loved this place was obvious. Equally apparent, though, was that—not unlike a lot of men in a region where horses have to be "broke" to be trained, and an alternative term for ranch hand is "cow puncher"—his regard for the land was of the "tough love" variety. Everything he had done to the place over the years had been for the benefit of his cattle. Bud had dynamited a beaver dam up in the woods, lest one of his cows fall into the beaver pond and drown. He hadn't flinched at putting out bait laced with poison—the highly lethal 1080, now banned in this country—to kill coyotes . . . as well as anything else that happened to come into contact with it. Such "improvements" as served the needs of his cattle—jerry-built boundary fences and a few rough-hewn corrals, and water resources like wells and stock tanks—

Bud maintained, after a fashion. Others, surviving from the earlier homesteaders who had tried and failed to make it on this place, had ages ago fallen into disrepair.

Water is always an issue of particular importance on a ranch. There were several wells here, two with electric pumps (one serving the ranch house, the other on an old homestead site), and the rest pulling water up with windmills. Bud seemed especially concerned that we understand how important the latter were, since they were the primary sources of stock water. "Those old Aermotor fans, they were made in Chicago and shipped out here back in homesteading days. They just keep on a-pumpin'. 'Course, a man wants to be sure to keep 'em maintained, oil 'em at least once a year, change the sucker rods and leathers when they need it. Those parts can be tough to find these days. But it's awful when a well goes out, and it always seems to happen when a man can least afford it." I could see Doug, squinting up at the fan spinning away atop its forty-foot tower, mentally taking notes. In weeks to come, he would become as fixated on those windmills as I had been on the blasted mailbox.

We drove the five hundred miles home to Helena that night, and by the time we pulled into our driveway, we knew we were going to make an offer on Bud's place. There were several reasons, but chief among them was the fact that at 4,400 acres—3,200 of them deeded, and another 1,200 BLM allotment—it was the biggest, and most scenic, ranch that we had seen, and that we could actually afford to buy. The bulk of the money was coming from the sale, after the deaths of both of my parents, of the suburban New Jersey house in which I had grown up. Tempting as it might have been to use that money as a sizable down payment on a pricey spread in western Montana, we mutually agreed that we were on safer ground—literally—purchasing a place outright, and forgoing a mortgage. That was why our search had led in the direction of eastern Montana, where land values were far more reasonable. It was, nonetheless, quite a proposition to wrap one's brain around. It amounted to trading an unpretentious ranch-style house on a 50' x 100' lot in Rutherford, New Jersey, for a ranch occupying nearly seven square miles, or roughly double the total land area of Rutherford, New Jersey.

It felt like an adventure. It felt a little crazy. It also felt like the right thing to do.

There was, however, one enormous hurdle—part mental, part emotional—Doug and I found we both had to clear. It was glaringly evident that Bud and Betty did not want to let go of the place. They were certainly old enough to call it retirement. Had they aggressively marketed the property sooner, they could have cut their losses, and made the appearance of a reasonably graceful exit. But by the time we saw their listing in the *Montana Land Magazine*, they had already been forced to lower their asking price, and were, in the realtor's euphemism, "motivated sellers." We understood from Steve that they had, nonetheless, already turned down one good offer. We gathered that he, like their creditors, was running out of patience with them. By their own admission, they were drowning in debt. Over dinner they had matter-of-factly explained that whatever they might have left over from the sale of the property that didn't go to the Land Bank would be sucked up by the IRS. As to back property taxes, well, those would fall to the buyer.

We consulted a friend who worked as a buyer's agent on ranch properties, and she assured us that the offer we intended to make was quite reasonable. It was below their asking price, and we were pretty certain less than the offer they had refused. But we were lucky, she said; this was a buyer's market.

Yet Bud and Betty were so dreadfully unlucky. Even taking into account that their current plight owed primarily to his bad business sense, they were at the same time victims of larger forces. Huge forces, in fact, that were totally beyond their control: the tanking ranch economy, the distant manipulation of the cattle futures market that caused local beef prices to fall through the floor, successive drought years and overall unfortunate weather patterns, insect plagues of seemingly Biblical proportion.

Now, in fact, that was all just a run-of-the-mill stretch of bad times for this part of the country. But we didn't know that, then.

All we knew was that it felt like we were cashing in on someone else's bad fortune. Here were two elderly souls, who had toughed it out over decades of hard times, and now faced homelessness. They had told us about the cruelly cold winters, when they were snowbound for weeks at a time, and the blindingly hot dry summers when they had to sell their calves at a loss. For many of those years, they had mostly lived apart, with Betty taking a job as a nurse in Miles City and schooling the kids there. The original ranch house had burned down, and for several years when she and the children came home to the ranch each summer, the entire family lived on top of one another in a cramped trailer. Then finally, not so long ago, they had been able to build their log house. Finally, after so many years Betty had a proper home of her own to take care of, a couple of meager flower beds, a tidy vegetable garden. I was going to take this away from her.

Meanwhile, ranching was the only life Bud knew. If he didn't have the range to ride, the myriad chores to attend to, he wouldn't know what to do with himself. His now-adult children had all moved away, but he was too proud to move in with any of them, and besides it would never work out. Doug, an equally proud man with a problematical relationship with his adult son and daughter-in-law, could relate. Perhaps, Bud ventured, he might stay on as sort of a ranch manager? Doug—those mysteriously complicated windmills haunting his apprehensions about how much he didn't know about ranching—thought about it. We talked about it. We lost sleep over it. We agreed it would not work.

It didn't occur to us that they were playing on our sympathies. It probably didn't occur to them, either, at least not consciously. Still, Betty somehow neglected to mention that they still owned the house she had lived in, in Miles City, so they did have a place to go. And, as Doug would eventually discover, while windmills can at times be devilishly temperamental, their general care and maintenance do not amount to rocket science.

Our friend Ann, the buyer's consultant who was also a Lutheran pastor's wife, reminded us that this was, after all, a business transaction, and a fair one. Her husband Tom, who had spent his adult life ministering to rural Montana folk, said he reckoned they'd be just fine in the long run. We were not our brother's keeper, or words to that effect. Nor were we the moral equivalent of the commercial interests that had swooped down on homesteads gone bad, a few generations ago, turning a calculated profit off the miseries of others. Betty and Bud were not victims, nor we villains.

We moved forward with the purchase, and after all the usual details were sorted through, with all the usual attendant delays, we closed on the sale in April 1988. We told Bud and Betty they could take as much time as they needed to leave, and they were gone by July Fourth. Later that month, we moved from Helena. We were just as clueless about the realities of rural life as those "honyockers" who first tried to set down roots here, and just as driven by the frontier myth of it all. Deep down, of course, we realized this. But never mind: like those first homesteaders in these parts, David and Ijkalaka Russell, we had our own "beautiful valley at the edge of the forest."

We also had a lot to learn: not only, as things turned out, about ranching, but also, in far more subtle and complicated ways, about the culture into which we were, both literally and metaphorically, buying.

Mama llama Jessica, babysitting. Photo by Doug Stange.

CHAPTER 2
Being "Differnt"

WHAT'S IN A NAME?

🐾 CWB—for "Crazy Woman Bison." We weren't quite in a position, yet, to begin marketing breeder stock, but when our now two-year-old and freshly bred bison cows would begin dropping their first calves in another year, we wanted to be ready with a bona fide herd identifier. That's the combination of letters, generally three and always unique to one producer, that precedes a registered animal's name or number. Because the bison industry was rapidly growing, with quite a few new herd identifiers getting listed in every issue of *Bison World* magazine, we wanted to get ours on the books before someone else grabbed that specific letter combination. So we filled out the requisite form and sent along the filing fee to the National Bison Association (NBA).

A week or so later, we got a call from a pleasant-sounding woman in the NBA office in Denver, her tone suggesting something between guarded amusement and outright concern. There was, it seemed, a problem with our application. Had CWB been taken, Doug, who took the call, asked? "Oh, no," she said soothingly. "But are you *sure* you want to use that name?" Well, yes, he replied, Crazy Woman Bison is our ranch's name, hence we want CWB for our herd identifier. "Uh huh . . . but, you know," she ventured brightly, after a moment's pause, "there are other names you could use, if CWB are the letters you want. Names that don't have 'Crazy Woman' in them. Clear Water Buffalo . . . or Covered Wagon . . . or . . ." But, he explained patiently, those were the letters we wanted because that *was* the name of our ranch. After a bit more back and forth, she relented. "I don't know, I *guess* it's all right, if you're sure that's the way you want it. But you do realize, we will have to publish your ranch name along with your 'CWB,' in the directory." Yes, we did realize that. That was the whole point of it, in fact. I'm sure that as the conversation concluded, she hung up the phone thinking we were, well, crazy.

This is a common enough assumption, after all, if one judges by the number of callers who, when I answer the phone, demand with a wry cackle, "Are *you* the crazy woman?!" The callers—always male, generally of the ol' boy persuasion, and each seeming to figure he's the originator of this bit of wit—are usually seeking information about the buffalo hunts we offer on the ranch. When I'm lucky, Doug's in the vicinity and I can hand the phone off to him. Otherwise, I finesse the question in a variety of ways, depending on my mood. The answer, in one way or another, is always no, and yes.

The actual inspiration for our ranch's name is literally written into the western landscape. Crazy Woman Creek threads its way south of here in Wyoming; one crosses it driving Interstate 90, outside of Buffalo. There are several stories of how the creek got its name. One account has it that the U.S. Cavalry ambushed a Lakota village, leaving all dead but for one surviving woman, whose mind failed as a result of the carnage she had witnessed. Yet another Lakota story tells of an old woman who had been "touched" by the Great Spirit, and who could be seen in the environs of the creek, phantomlike in shamanic trances, and later haunting it in death as she once had in life, which was thought to be good medicine for the people. A Crow variation on the tale has it that a Native woman married a white trader who opened a post where he served "fire water" to the Indians, systematically addicting them for his eventual profit. A warrior party avenged themselves on the man, whom they scalped, and his wife, whom they merely left for dead. She was, however, nursed back to life if not to sanity by other Crow women, and returned to live in solitude by the creek that was later named for her. In still other variations on the theme, the Crazy Woman was white, the lone survivor of an Indian massacre. One legend has it that the mountain man Jeremiah Johnson took pity on the miserable recluse, built her a ramshackle cabin, and periodically stopped by with provisions for her, until he at last discovered her dead from a combination of frostbite and starvation. A camp established at Crazy Woman Crossing, on the Bozeman Trail, was in the 1870s the site of several skirmishes between U.S. Cavalry, and Lakota and Cheyenne warriors. Crazy Woman Creek was also the site of one of the major pitched battles between cattle barons and homesteaders during the Johnson County Range War in 1882.

In Montana, the Crazy Mountains rise to precipitous heights (some peaks over eleven thousand feet), an "island range" that irrupts out of the rolling grasslands west of Billings. They are among the easternmost high mountain ranges in the northern Rockies. Beyond them, from their vertiginous summits, the vista is of vast prairies stretching out toward visual infinity. They were once, or so the story goes, called the Crazy Woman Mountains, and here as with the Wyoming creek, opinion is divided as to whether the Crazy Woman in question was an Indian maid who went mad for one reason or another, or a white pioneer who was driven to lunacy by some facet of the "westering" experience. Either way, the stories have the woman wandering off into those remote and forbidding mountain fastnesses, her spirit forever haunting them, her insane lament still keening in the wind. There are those who argue, reasonably I think, that in their separate ways these stories attempt to downplay the role that the Crazies, as they are more popularly called today, played in Plains Indian religion. Crazy Peak was where warriors and holy men went on vision quests, where becoming "crazy" (as in "Crazy Horse") meant gaining nonrational, spiritual insight.

The author of the *Wikipedia* entry on the Crazies therefore objects that "The 'Crazy Woman' legend is one more denial of Indian culture." Perhaps. Then again, for my part, I'm uneasy about the erasure of the Crazy Woman—whoever she may have been, whatever the nature of her madness—from that ruggedly austere landscape. The documented history of the westward expansion abounds with the stories of women who gave up or lost everything—friends and relatives back home, security and creature comforts, their health, their children, and too often ultimately their sanity—as a form of collateral damage in their menfolk's enterprise of "winning" the West. Back in the early 1990s, Natalie Merchant recorded a moving song about these women, entitled "Gold Rush Brides." In it, she reconstructed the westward expansion from the point of view of these women who were, essentially, bystanders to the men's adventure. They were also the ones who paid the highest price for that adventure. "The land was free," Merchant sang, "yet it cost their lives."

In my first book, *Woman the Hunter*, I had at one point, and at roughly the same time as Merchant, been thinking along very similar lines. After recounting the story of a failed elk hunt on the CMR, along a nasty gash in the landscape that drains into Fort Peck Lake and is ominously named "Kill Woman Creek" on one map I was consulting and "Killed Woman Creek" on the other, I concluded with a series of questions that led me back to those women whose spirits haunt this part of the country:

> Had it been the country that had gotten the better of me? Or was it what the country had become as the result of human manipulation? Was there, at this point, any difference? Those other women—the crazy ones, the kill women/killed women, whose follies and tragedies are encoded in this harsh landscape— what portents would they have read in a prize hunt that had felt like all bad luck?
>
> Better to have stayed at home, they might have said. Better to have owned your limitations and let the wild things be. But then again, they might have reflected, nothing ventured, nothing gained. You never know what's around the next bend in the trail or what change in the weather tomorrow will bring. That's what keeps a body going—that yearning anticipation; that belief in luck, or providence, or one's own misguided wits.
>
> They might have said all that and more. And it might all have been the truth.

It was Doug who suggested that we name our place Crazy Woman. It immediately felt right—even romantic—to me. It is our way of acknowledging our foremothers and sisters, of remembering them, paying tribute to their sacrifice as well as their strength.

There are visual reminders of those women here, Native and Anglo; we live with them every day. The northernmost prominence along the ridge of the Chalk Buttes to our east is called Starvation Butte—a steep-sided escarpment of rock, freestanding and accessible only via one narrow upward trail. There is a local legend to account for its name. A Crow war party attacked a Cheyenne encampment in this area—for all we know, it might have been at one of the locations where we have discovered teepee rings on our place. A lone Cheyenne woman escaped, along with her infant daughter, and fled up into the Chalk Buttes, picking her treacherous way up that narrow trail, Crow attackers on her heels. The men blocked her escape route, to trap her into submission. Refusing to surrender to them, she remained in hiding atop the butte, where she and her baby eventually succumbed to hunger and thirst.

It used to be that, when the light was right as the late-day shadows snaked their way across the Buttes, you could just make out what appeared to be the silhouette of a slender figure up there, poised at the precipitous edge of Starvation Butte. Perhaps that's what gave rise to the story. These past few years, that figure has been joined by others. More ghosts are with her now. In literal fact they are a tribe of ponderosa pines, spreading along the edge of the rock. A trick of the eye these phantoms are—but not, surely, of the mind. One must tread carefully in this awesome country. There are powerful spirits dwelling here.

Down in our valley, the ruins of several homesteads bear witness to other women who once walked this land. Collapsed dugouts that once were root cellars yield feral gourds, and rhubarb springs seemingly eternal on plots of earth that were kitchen gardens. Transplanted wild roses still trellis their way along the log remains of caved-in cabins, the interiors of which contain hints of the ways homestead women attempted to domesticate their rough space: a sliver of broken mirror on one wall, a fragment of picture frame on another, whatever image it once contained long ago surrendered to the elements . . . rotted scraps of hooked rug, perhaps once calico but faded now to lifeless gray . . . a shard of a china teacup, embossed with faded sweetheart roses . . . an ornately scrolled bit of decoration from a long gone iron cookstove . . . a child's doll, its filthy dress in tatters and hair disheveled, one arm missing, one glass eye squeezed permanently shut, the other open, staring dully. The women who lived in these homesteads moved on, and died elsewhere. But they are still a presence here, nonetheless.

Ever since we moved here over twenty years ago, I've had an odd recurring experience. It happens when I am by myself, in some wilder part of our place. I am hunting, perhaps, or out walking a fence line to check for needed repairs, or doing some other solitary chore or exercise. Distantly, I will hear the chime of a Westminster clock, faint but distinct, striking the hour. We ourselves have such a clock, but this always occurs miles from our house, well beyond earshot. I like to think that it must be some echo of former lives hereabouts, a ghostly reverberation perennially drifting along in the wind, a fragment of the soundscape of the past. Perhaps it is my foresisters' way of keeping me company here.

MIRAGE COUNTRY

I should probably point out at this juncture that I am not unduly susceptible to visual or auditory hallucinations. It is simply a fact of life here, in a terrain the original inhabitants of which understood to be spirit-infused, that one becomes accustomed to—and reasonably comfortable with—the experience of perceiving things that are not actually, or factually, there. Paraphrasing a line from one of Wallace Stevens's poems, one becomes acclimated to seeing nothing that isn't there, as well as the nothing that is. The boundary between the physical and the immaterial is relatively permeable in a landscape like ours.

To explain this more prosaically: mirages are relatively common in these parts. So common, in fact, that it is not unusual to hear a casual exchange like the following, between two people who discover they had been driving the same stretch of highway at roughly the same time:

"Did you see that mirage off to the north of the interstate yesterday morning, then?"

"Yeah, that was a really good one! Lasted a long time, too."

Or this one, which occurred between myself and a neighbor a few years ago:

I: "It's been a long time since I've seen a good mirage around here."

She: "Why, now that you mention it, you're right. It's been ages since I've seen a good one."

I: "I miss them after a while, when I don't see them."

She: "Me, too."

Before I moved to this part of the world, I naïvely assumed that mirages were confined to the desert, and invariably involved camels and palm trees and, most likely, thirst-crazed wanderers whose eyes were playing tricks on them. I'd have thought anyone engaging in such dialogues as those above would therefore have to be on the "crazed" side, themselves.

But what did I know? It turns out that mirages are a universal phenomenon; they have to do with the way light refracts through air masses of different temperatures. The most common ones—we all see them, all the time—are those stretches of roadway ahead which are dry, but nevertheless look wet or slick. It is actually the sky we are seeing, reflected on the asphalt surface. These, and like phenomena—including those desert oases the word "mirage" typically conjures up—are technically referred to as inferior mirages, because what we are seeing is below its actual location: the blue of the sky transposed to earth as a pool of water, say.

But there is a far more interesting, and somewhat rarer form of mirage: the superior mirage, in which the image seen has been transposed from a focal point elsewhere, someplace below or beyond the horizon. There are several types of superior mirages, but the one of interest here is called—after the fairy sorceress of Arthurian legend—the Fata Morgana. In what is essentially a weather phenomenon, objects that are far distant are transposed to the visual horizon, often gaining in size and scale, sometimes reduplicating. Fata Morgana mirages are most commonly observed at sea, where clifflike seashores seem to loom or ghostships to float above the horizon; and in Arctic climes, where strange towers and turretlike snow sculptures rise over distant ice floes.

Such mirages are also very common throughout eastern Montana—although it's likely most tourists passing through the area are unaware that they have seen, perhaps even photographed, one. You wouldn't be aware that those flat-topped buttes and weird rock outcroppings that form the distant scenery off I-94 outside of Terry aren't actually there, for example, unless you travel the road often enough to know what's really there and what isn't, on a day-to-day basis. But if you do, then you become aware that the vista before you is always capable of shape-shifting, rearranging itself, challenging you to take its rock-solid predictability for granted, and occasionally throwing up fantastic surprises for your delectation. You stop, you take it all in. These fairy buttes, that momentary mountain range, they are not "optical illusions." They are real buttes, real mountains. They happen to really *be* someplace else. But they are, just as really, there—you *can* photograph them if you like—and then, gradually or sometimes quite suddenly, they're gone.

There is obviously something about meteorological conditions in Carter County that is conducive to mirage formation. And, equally obviously, there is something about the topography here that is, in itself, miragelike. The typical Fata Morgana—whether it appears at sea, in the Arctic, in the desert, or elsewhere—looks like bluffs or buttes or rimrock or, basically that is, like most of the major features of our topography. And on a typical late-summer late afternoon, when the Chalk Buttes are shimmering in the hazy heat, their spectral whiteness evaporating, stone merging with the translucent clouds coalescing in a milky blue sky, they could easily be mistaken for a mirage that has returned home, after a day's work gracing other horizons.

Much about this country has a now-you-see-it, now-you-don't quality. The wildlife, for example, tends to specialize in evanescence. Pronghorn antelope, native to here and a species unique to itself (being in no way related to African antelopes, that's a misnomer), often in winter snows seem to materialize before one's eyes: you are looking at them long moments before you are seeing them. The same is true of mule deer in late fall or early spring, when what had appeared to be a rock nestled on a dull gray-brown hillside suddenly stotts away, startled by your presence. Observe closely the dusty ground in summer, and if you are lucky a horned lizard will come into focus, looking like a miniature dinosaur, and so perfectly camouflaged as to appear nearly transparent against the sandy soil. This country teaches you to trust your senses, but only up to a point.

Is that blue-gray cloud drifting over the far horizon an incoming rain shower, or smoke from a wildfire sparked by last night's dry lightning? That quick sound just now, something between a buzz and a snap: was it a grasshopper taking flight in the dry grass, or a chickadee branch hopping in the chokecherry bush, or a well camouflaged rattlesnake coiling to strike? Or, for that matter, that snake right before your eyes, now menacingly coiled: is it a rattler, or an innocuous bull snake taking advantage of its uncanny resemblance to a diamondback (a triumph, that, of evolutionary protective coloration), and mimicking the more lethal reptile's buzz? Sights and sounds can be deceiving, a moment's dread can become delight, and vice versa.

If it becomes more or less routine to second-guess one's perceptions, at what point does that bleed over into pondering one's sanity? This must have been a question increasingly near to the surface for those venturesome souls who first homesteaded here, as nature turned on them, and times got hard, then harder still. It lingers, I think, on the periphery of their descendants' consciousness.

And it accounts, at least in part, for the widespread aversion to anything "different" (or, pronounced more accurately, "differnt"). The term is used in two major ways. On the one hand, it is an indicator of anything that falls outside of some tacitly agreed upon social or cultural norm, as in, "Well, *that's* differnt!" This can cover a variety of situations, ranging from a person's deciding to vote Democratic or buy Japanese rather than American-made farm implements, to ordering white wine rather than a beer or a shot of Canadian whiskey in the Old Stand Bar, or questioning whether it's really appropriate to refer to cherry-flavored Jell-O with miniature marshmallows as a meal's "salad" course. More broadly, this is the operative judgment about anything that challenges conventional wisdom about the way something is, or should be, or always has been done: backing off on pesticide use, for example, or forgoing "summer fallowing" of one's fields, or planting alternative crops to those that are federally subsidized, or deciding not to hot brand one's calves.

The second main use of the term has to do with judging a person's mental or moral capacity: "That Clyde, you know, well, he's just . . . differnt." (There is always a moment's pause there, for effect.) That is, by implication, Clyde is a bit on the nutty side. He grows canola instead of alfalfa. He's owned up to having voted for Ralph Nader, maybe more than once. He's been observed using chopsticks, rather than a fork, at the Chinese buffet in Miles City. If the person in question is seriously divergent from the accepted norm, then (often with a wink) "he's . . . a . . . *little* . . . differnt—*if* you know what I mean." What is meant by "a little" in this context is, of course, a lot. The listener must fill in the blanks: Is Clyde deranged? Abusive? Stupid? Gay? A horse thief? An opera lover? All of the above? Probably.

There is, additionally, a third sense of difference, pertaining to "foreign" or "not from around here." In this case, the fact of being "differnt" is acknowledged, but unspoken, because it is self-evident. An example: Early in the summer of our fifth year in Carter County, two recently graduated Skidmore students of mine were stopping at our place for a few days' visit, en route to graduate school in California. Because this young couple was driving a small sedan and were unaccustomed to our kind of gravel roads, we had agreed they would call us when they got to Ekalaka, and we'd drive to town to escort them back to the ranch. This they did, and we suggested they wait for us at the Wagon Wheel Café. When we got to town, between a quick stop at the post office to pick up our accumulated mail and the two-block walk to the Wagon Wheel, no fewer than a half dozen townsfolk good-naturedly informed us that our friends were waiting for us there. Now, not a single one of these people had actually spoken to Helene and David. They hadn't needed to. Two pretty obviously Jewish kids, East Coast types sporting Birkenstocks and Ray-Bans, driving a Toyota Corolla with New York plates? Had to be friends of the Stanges, nobody else around here would know anybody like that.

Interestingly, a kind of backhanded civility seems to be at work in all of this. Southeastern Montanans—perhaps because they themselves have for so long been on the losing end of unflattering antirural stereotypes—take a dim view of outright name-calling. "Differnt" thus becomes convenient code for the strange, the unusual, the dangerous, the unfamiliar, the foreign—basically anything that would, upon closer linguistic scrutiny, cry out for some sharper definition. And to define another, or oneself, in any terms that depart from the familiar parameters of cowboy culture would be to limit that other person's, and thereby one's own, freedom and autonomy. In a place characterized by so much bigness, so much openness and room to move, it is nonetheless important to give every person their own share of space.

This leads to a good deal of indirect communication. For example, one person will never tell another what he or she should do. "A fella might want to get his feed at the Co-op up in Baker" means "You'd better buy your grain up there: we support local businesses around here." A seemingly random comment by a neighbor that "A man, he wants to keep his fences in good shape" means you'd best ride that fence line we share first thing tomorrow, and find out where that stretch of boundary fence that is your responsibility needs work, and fix it, pronto.

A variation on this theme is criticism in the third person. Sometime early on in our time in Carter County, Doug was in town running errands, and dropped into the Wagon Wheel. He was wearing a T-shirt, cutoff jeans, and Docksiders ("differnt" apparel, to be sure, from the local norm). A crusty old cowhand snorted, ostensibly to his table mates but loud enough for the entire room to hear, "I don't mind if a grown man wears shorts in public. But he sure oughtta wear socks when he does!" It is far from unusual, actually, to hear southeastern Montanans debating some aspect of "this guy here"—with a gesture of the thumb indicating the person in question—as if this guy weren't actually *here*, to account for himself. Becoming the subject of a conversation from which you are quite unselfconsciously excluded is not necessarily the same as being pegged as "differnt," but it generally does imply that there is something about you that warrants attending to.

Or, as it would more likely be put around here, something about you that "needs fixed." There is a linguistic tic shared by virtually all southeastern Montana natives. They readily lose track of the verb "to be." They literally misplace it, as in such common locutions as "The truck's tires need rotated," or "That colt of yours, he's got one ornery temper: he needs broke," or "With fire season coming on, that tall grass near the house needs cut," or "That Jake—he's so differnt, he needs kept a close eye on."

You could chalk this verbal habit up to mental laziness, I suppose, or to some shortcoming in the primary and secondary English education rural schools provide. But neither of these explanations is convincing. You might, as well, attribute it to eastern Montanans' inbred tendency toward the laconic: if your listener is going to *get* the point anyway, you might as well save time and a couple of words getting *to* it. It's a kind of verbal shorthand. This is probably somewhat closer to the truth.

But I wonder whether this seeming aversion to this essential grammatical building block isn't unconsciously symptomatic of a broader insecurity, having to do with the power of that innocuous-seeming little phrase, "to be." Perhaps it is a by-product of growing up in a landscape that is so wont to shape-shift, to play tricks on both the eyes and the mind, calling into radical question whether things *are* exactly as they seem. Unquestionably, the uneasiness with difference is rooted in that same hard, rocky soil. Sameness, the reliability of things to remain relatively and consistently what they are, equates with sanity.

Difference, on the other hand, often equates with change. And the lesson of living in this environment is that change is seldom for the better. Indeed, it is often disastrous. Enough of it might just drive you crazy.

A SUMMER OF NO DISASTERS

At the close of the summer of 2007, a day or so before I would be hitting the road for my annual drive east at the start of the school year, I remarked to Doug: "Well, an entire summer has gone by without any disasters." He nodded in agreement, but I think we both probably felt a sudden urge to knock wood, just in case. Disasters, or emergencies, or, as the locals are more likely to call them, "wrecks," are common enough occurrences as to be a shopworn part of the fabric of ranch life. Most of ours seem to happen in the summer. Over the years, and not in any particular order, they have included the time we lost two llamas, on consecutive days, to rattlesnake bites; the time Doug's favorite horse was attacked by a cougar; the year we spent an entire summer coping with one well failure after another; the year grasshoppers wiped out our entire hay crop; the year a neighbor shot and killed one of our dogs; the year my favorite horse nearly died of a freak infection; the time Doug's favorite dog developed tick paralysis; the drought year when the grass was so poor that Doug resorted to shooting almost all of our bison calves, to preserve their mothers; the two different summers we pitched in to battle forest fires on our neighbors' places, fearing our own ponderosa pine woods could be next.

What all these events—call them what you will—have in common is that, with rare exceptions, they happen suddenly. Nowhere else, in our shared experience, does the world turn upside down or inside out more quickly, and utterly, than on a ranch.

For example . . .

One moment it's a lazy July morning and we're taking our time, easing into the day's worth of chores, the next Doug checks a pasture to discover a llama, flailing his neck back and forth, his head swollen to watermelon-size, blood dripping from both eyes, blindly trying to stagger his way clear of the pain of the rattlesnake bite he sustained some time in the early morning hours. This is our beautiful black herd sire Garth Brooks, who has become something of a local personality for his habit of running up to greet any vehicle that comes down our road and race it back toward the house. This is the llama I so had my heart set on having that I tried to bid against myself for him at the llama auction in Oregon. This is the llama that lets me walk right up to him and put his halter on in the middle of an open field, my big wooly pet.

I put in a frantic call to Greg, our vet—thank heaven, he's in!—and he says to try to keep the animal as quiet as possible and apply a cold pack to counteract the swelling. Greg, a pilot, will fly out to our place; that cuts the travel time from town in half. Haltering Garth is out of the question, but Doug manages to get a rope loosely around his neck. Hearing my voice, Garth calms somewhat, and leans into the bag of ice I'm holding up to his now horribly disfigured face. His breathing

Silver Sage's Garth Brooks. Our house is in the background. Photo by Doug Stange.

is labored, and he is obviously in agony. Greg does what he can when he arrives, gives him antibiotics and cortisone and painkillers, but it isn't enough to save Garth. Later that afternoon, I find him dead in the corral, in the cool shade of a cottonwood tree. Doug says he wishes he had put him out of his misery that morning; he was obviously too far gone by the time we discovered him in such distress. I can only, tearfully, nod agreement.

The next morning, we check the same pasture, and find another llama has been bitten, very possibly, Greg will later speculate, by the same snake. This time the victim is a female, Portia, and she has a baby we have named Pistol. Her condition, at least, doesn't seem quite so dire as Garth's had been. Greg figures she has a fighting chance. Over the next three days, we grow guardedly optimistic: her facial swelling begins to recede, she is drinking water and appears to be eating some, she is nursing the little guy. We have to drive over to Miles City on ranch business. When we return in the late afternoon, I stroll over to the corral to check on Portia and her cria. She is dead, lying in exactly the same cool shady spot where I found Garth. Her baby is snuggled up next to her. It happens to be my birthday. We postpone the cake and champagne.

Greg comes out the next day and performs a necropsy on Portia, whose major organs, he says, were all destroyed by the toxin. What kept her alive for three days was apparently sheer maternal instinct, and those final few nursing sessions no doubt sapped the last of her ebbing strength. As the vet leaves, we notice little Pistol is still keeping a vigil by his mom's now disarticulated corpse. Doug has to use the tractor loader to scoop up her remains, to dispose of them. He had buried Garth, for me, but says he can't make a habit of digging graves for large animals; besides, as I well understand, scavengers will put her body to good use. It will be several days, as things turn out, before the baby llama stops staring down the road, in the tractor's wake, keeping a vigil for his mother's return.

Doug took photographs of both llamas, to share with a herpetologist friend who had chided us for killing rattlesnakes. I have never been able to look at them.

We bought calf milk replacer for Pistol, but he would have none of it, either via a bottle or in a bucket. It did turn out that, at the age of roughly eight weeks, he was just old enough to make it on his own, on grass. We had another female llama, Jessica, who had her own baby, Juliet. (If you are sensing a pattern here, aside from Garth Brooks, all our other llamas, bred on our place, had Shakespearean names.) Jessica wasn't willing to nurse Pistol, but she did keep an eye on him. He had a lot of pluck, all things considered, and went on to a career as a sheep guard on our friends Gib and Verna's ranch.

I recall watching a film once, about life in rural India—another, though vastly different, landscape of climatological and other extremes. A farmer was quoted as saying, "We are disaster-proof men." I admire such tenacity. Perhaps it's easier to sustain it in the context of a world view like Hinduism's, in which whatever else one knows from the brute testimony of one's senses and emotions, one recognizes it to be at the same time all, ultimately, an illusion. Real and not real. A trick of the mind. Fata Morgana.

But the heartache precipitated by such sudden irrational turnabouts, such disasters large and small as characterize ranch life, doesn't work like a mirage. It doesn't dissolve and go away. One learns, at best, to navigate around the memory of it. And to celebrate, with guarded optimism, the happy stability and sameness of reasonably uneventful days, to hope for a season of no disasters.

One also learns that it probably takes a little bit of craziness, just to get up in the morning in these parts.

CHRISTMAS IN THE COUNTRY

Looking back, it was only natural that, when it came to making friends in Carter County, we gravitated toward another couple who were generally deemed to be on the "differnt" side: Gib (short for Gilbert) and Verna, whose ranch being roughly fifteen miles away made them near neighbors. While we had met them in the fall of 1988, at a "welcome to the neighborhood" open house given for us by another near-neighbor couple, we were at best passing acquaintances until Christmas of the following year.

That Christmas marked the beginning of the closest friendship we have had in Carter County. These were two people with whom we had virtually nothing in common, in background or education, or even interests. But, as we increasingly learned over the years to follow, we nonetheless shared a certain degree of being "differnt." This was largely a matter of temperament: Gib, a Carter County native, shared with Doug a wry skepticism about the workings of the world of men, as well as an inclination toward a more or less reclusive lifestyle. Verna, originally from Baker just north of here, is far more independent-minded and self-assertive than any southeastern Montana woman is supposed to allow herself to be, outspoken to a fault, and—in the broadest sense of the word—a smart woman. I felt an immediate affinity there.

By late December 1989, Doug and I were still learning how much we didn't know about quotidian ranch existence. Since Thanksgiving time we had been essentially snowbound, with several inches already on the ground after a protracted cold snap, the primary road into our place drifted in, and another Alberta clipper in the long-range New Year's forecast. We decided a snowmobile was in order, and ordered a Yamaha "Bravo" model, arranging for it to be shipped to the RV dealership in Miles City. It would arrive on Christmas Eve. So that morning we bundled up and, as the first gray streaks of dawn lightened it up enough outside to see, we cross-country skied the five miles up the divide, our springer spaniel Jorinda trotting gamely along with us, to our truck parked on the county road. By the time we got there, the weather had warmed considerably, and we paused to shed our sweat-drenched long underwear. We made it to Miles City before noon and, what with some businesses closing early for the Christmas holiday, hastened to the RV dealer. He gave Doug, who had never been on a snowmobile before, a quick lesson in operating and handling the thing; we signed the loan papers, and loaded it into the back of our little pickup. The sun was shining and the afternoon was awash in glistening icicles and sparkling, settling snow. It was by now unseasonably warm, but it was nonetheless beginning to look a lot like Christmas.

We celebrated with a decent lunch, and then made the rounds of the stores: groceries, some "potent potables," Christmas cards to the post office (at least they'd have a pre-Christmas postmark), a few last-minute gifts. At dusk, our pickup laden and our spirits high if a bit frazzled, we were ready to head for home. Then something started slapping against the windshield. We were by now so acclimated to deep cold and snow that it took us a few disoriented moments to recognize it: freezing rain was starting to fall. We would later learn that the temperature that day had risen a record seventy degrees in the space of about twelve hours.

There are two ways from our ranch to Miles City and back. One, a route called the Powderville Road, is mostly on dirt and gravel. At eighty miles each way, it is the short, and therefore preferred, route. But in wet weather, an ungraveled stretch we had learned (the hard way) to refer to as "the longest thirteen miles on Earth" becomes impassable. The longer route, via Baker, nearly doubles the miles each way, but has the advantage of being mostly on pavement: a brief stretch of Interstate 94, then U.S. Highway 12 to Baker, and State Highway 7 down to Ekalaka, with the final twenty miles on the Chalk Buttes Road being the only gravel to contend with. Since we were driving what would turn out to be the last two-wheel drive vehicle we would ever own, prudence dictated the longer route. We figured that as the temperature dropped back below freezing after sundown, the rain would at worst shift back over to snow, and the now-slushy gravel road would harden up again. With so much melting having occurred, we might even be able to drive down into our place.

The eighty-mile drive from Miles City to Baker took us upward of two hours. As road conditions progressively worsened, the rain continued and a wind came up, glazing the pavement with an inch or more of "black ice." Around Baker the rain turned to sleet, and the thirty-five miles of highway down to Ekalaka was—as we could see by the headlights of the very occasional oncoming vehicle—mirror slick.

Counting off the mile markers one by one to trace our nerve-rackingly slow progress, we inched along the highway, passing widely spaced ranch homes—their Christmas lights twinkling, and their inhabitants no doubt sipping hot cocoa and humming Christmas carols as they arranged presents under the tree, safely warm and sanely out of this atrocious weather.

When we finally got to Ekalaka, and onto the Chalk Buttes Road, snow was falling. We took this as a good omen. The gravel road was a crunchy icy mess, but we made it to our mailbox. Driving down to the house was still out of the question. But, hey, we had a snowmobile now! We had to half unpack the truck to get our little red Bravo out. As we were going about this, a truck came down the road, and slid to a stop at the mailbox. It was our neighbors Verna and Gib, heading toward their own place. "Some weather we're having, huh?"

"Yah, a person would have to be crazy to be out on a night like this!" we and they laughingly agreed. Then, slightly more seriously, they asked, "You folks gonna make it home OK?" Oh yes, we assured them, pointing with pride toward our brand-new mode of overland transport. These last five miles would be a piece of cake, compared to the trip from Miles City. They were obviously anxious to get on home themselves. We waved them on their way, wishing them a Merry Christmas.

Then, we quickly foraged through our parcels for whatever absolute essentials couldn't wait until morning, and packed whatever we could into a large backpack, which Doug helped me shoulder. He got the snowmobile started, and its little two-stroke engine chugged gamely. Doug mounted the seat, I climbed on in tandem, somewhat unsteadily under the weight of the pack and twining my arms around his waist. Doug signaled Jorinda to jump onto his lap which, after a few moments' skeptical hesitation, she did. "*Hang on tight,*" he shouted back at me, revving the engine. And we were off, snow surfing over drifts, into the snowy darkness, toward home.

After close to two miles, and several stalls and spills, we were hopelessly lodged in a snowbank. Smoke was spewing from under the Bravo's hood. Doug managed to start the engine, but its desultory putt-putting was to no avail; after several tries, the machine was basically nonresponsive. It was by now past midnight. The snow had finally stopped. We were both wet and cold, and beyond exhausted. "Well," Doug sighed, "the truck is a couple of miles that way," pointing vaguely in the direction of the road, "and the house is three miles that way," gesturing into the blue-black darkness. "I guess the best thing to do is to go back to the truck until morning."

"Speak for yourself, dearest," I replied, with the sort of bravado only severe overtiredness can muster. "It is mostly downhill to the house, and I'm sleeping in my own bed tonight." There was just enough moonlight through the high thinning clouds to make it possible to discern the road. I trudged off, and Doug caught up with me, to relieve me of the backpack. I could see he was smiling, in a that's-my-girl sort of way. We hiked home, cracked open a bottle of champagne when we got there to celebrate the fact that we had actually survived the day, and tumbled into bed in the wee hours.

I awoke early Christmas morning to a sound somewhere between a groan and a heavy sigh. Doug was staring at the ceiling. "We killed it, Mare," he moaned. "We haven't even made the first payment on it yet, and we killed the bloody thing." I asked him if he was sure. "Well," he winced, "I've worked on a lot of engines in my life, and I've never seen one where smoke billowing out from every orifice is a good sign." Add to this the fact that most of our Christmas presents were up in the truck, along with a couple hundred dollars worth of food, much of which would probably go to waste: fresh fruits and vegetables probably hadn't survived overnight freezing and certainly wouldn't survive a second night, whereas perishables like shrimp were doomed to spoil as sunshine warmed the closed truck cab where they were stashed. The day was off to a pretty depressing start.

I got up to make us some tea. The phone rang and Doug picked it up. It was Gib; he and Verna just wanted to make sure we had made it home all right last night. Doug told him what had happened with the Bravo, and Gib said he'd try to make it over to our place after they finished feeding their cows, to see if he could help with the snowmobile. Doug protested that while we appreciated this, we didn't want to take time away from his Christmas. Well, Gib said, we'll see.

We couldn't just do nothing, and the prospect of a Christmas dinner of peanut butter and jelly didn't appeal, so we began gearing up for a day's worth of hiking the ten-mile trek up to the road and back. If we both carried empty backpacks, and pulled a sled behind us, we could with luck salvage a good deal of food and drink. The gifts, and the snowmobile, would have to wait until tomorrow . . . the latter, for all we knew, until the spring thaw. We were just about to set off from the house, when we heard the buzz of snowmobiles racing down our road: first Gib came into view, towing a second machine behind him, followed by his teenage son Dale, riding our Bravo. They had ridden over, quickly found the Bravo, and just as quickly discerned that the problem was not with the engine, but with the fact that the drive track had become so impacted with wet heavy snow that it simply couldn't turn. The smoke was apparently generated by the friction of a belt slipping. This, as we would subsequently learn, is your basic Snowmobile 101—although Gib was too polite to observe (as he no doubt was thinking) that any fool could have figured that much out for himself.

"Now," Gib continued—basking in our palpable relief, and probably fearing that at any moment either or both of us might spontaneously kiss him out of sheer gratitude—"Verna and I want you to come for Christmas dinner. Turkey's already in the oven. She says to plan on getting to our place by one o'clock. Don't worry about bringin' nothing, just yerselves." Then he and Dale hopped on their snowmobiles and headed for home. Never mind that the now-retreating figure who had bailed us out was wearing cow-shit stained Carhartt coveralls. It felt like the closest either of us had come in our adult lives to a visit from Saint Nick.

Doug took the Bravo for a trial spin. We changed our clothes and rode our little dream machine up to the truck, with packs and sled in tow for the later return trip. With some delight, we discovered that most of the food would survive after all. And so we set off to spend Christmas day with a family we barely knew at that point, beyond exchanging pleasantries when we ran into them in town.

There was nothing particularly special about the way the rest of that day unfolded. Verna showed me around her house, while Gib took Doug on a tour of his shop. The men retired to the living room, to talk about tools and machinery, while their adolescent daughter Karen and I helped Verna get dinner on the table. It was a no-frills traditional holiday meal, turkey with the appropriate "trimmings," pumpkin pie, and ice cream. Afterward, the men adjourned to the living room once more, to make small talk and watch the sun sink in the afternoon sky, while Verna—an indefatigable craftsperson—showed me how to make little Rudolph the Red-nosed Reindeer statuettes out of wooden cooking spoons and pipe cleaners, with bits of ribbon and felt. I've always been on the crafts-averse side myself, and my wonderment at the cleverness of a hot glue gun must have given her as much of a chuckle as Doug's snowmobile naïveté earlier had her husband.

It was the very ordinariness of that Christmas Day that made it remarkable, as if a cosmos thrown somewhat off-kilter had been righted by an offer of plain good food and homespun hospitality. As the sun began to set, we thanked them and made our farewells. An hour later, we were snowmobiling home over sparkling snow, provisions and Christmas presents in tow, singing "Here Comes Santa Claus" under a moonlit starry sky.

The road down into our place. Photo by Mary Stange.

CHAPTER 3
Intrepid Hippies, Homesteaders, and Other Survivors

🐾"Geez, only a couple of intrepid hippies like yourselves could choose to live in a place like this!" So Doug and I were informed, jocularly if not altogether kindly, by a western Montana native—I'll call him Bart—who had come to our ranch on a business matter. He harbored the western bias against the high plains portion of Big Sky Country, the same sort of dismissive smugness that led one former governor of the state to refer to its eastern two-thirds as "nothing but miles and miles of sage and gumbo," or words to that effect. It is a bias shared by all those, on both coasts, who regard southeastern Montana as the epicenter of "flyover country." Or, as the *Los Angeles Times* book review of Jonathan Raban's *Bad Land* phrased it, "the ugly half of a beautiful state they may never visit."

The question implicit in Bart's statement, of course, had to do not simply with why just anybody would want to live here, but why *we*—midwestern and eastern by upbringing, "professor-types" from nonagricultural backgrounds—would opt to settle down in a place so far off the beaten track, a place where we were so obviously "differnt." It's a fair enough question.

"Hippies" we certainly are not, and never were. Doug is old enough to have been rather too mature for the summer of love; the 1960s led him in the direction of radical politics, not flower power. And while my psyche bears some residual scarring from the fact that my parents wouldn't let me go to Woodstock, my hippie experience was largely confined to an undergraduate preference for peasant blouses and gypsy skirts, and some casual experimentation with mind-altering substances.

"Intrepid," however . . . well, that did fit, up to a point. As I mentioned earlier, this ranch was anything but a turn-key operation, in terms of heavy equipment. In snowy periods during our first couple of winters here, whenever our road threatened to become drifted in, we parked a truck up at the mailbox on the county road, and hiked or cross-country skied the five miles out to it, and back. We thought of this as an adventure. When that idea gradually lost its appeal, we bought that Yamaha snowmobile, which we rode in tandem out and back, sometimes pulling a makeshift trailer (I had sacrificed my skis for the runners) filled with groceries, mail, and other provisions. Eventually, when we bought our first tractor and a blade for plowing, life got a bit easier. We also discovered, in our third or fourth year on the place, that a seldom-used back route out, across sage-covered terrain over which the snow tended to blow free of the two-track, tended to stay open much of the time. We had, in our early years here, been not simply intrepid, but somewhat stupid.

Such steep learning curves aside, a yen for adventure has, ultimately, more the makings of a vacation than of a lifestyle. We learned, over the first few years, that while some risks we took—being out on iffy roads in deteriorating weather conditions, for example—more or less came with the territory of living here, these "adventures" at the same time could become seriously life-threatening. Everyone around here knows stories of hunters who got lost and suffered from exposure, and ranchers who became disoriented in blinding snow on the way from the house to the barn, and travelers, stranded when their trucks slid off of icy roads, who unwisely wandered away from their vehicles.

The stories generally have unpleasant outcomes. They serve as cautionary tales. The lore comes to mind periodically, as it did for us several years ago at Thanksgiving time. We were making our way home from the Rapid City airport where Doug had picked me up. Our three springer spaniels were along for the ride, and the extended cab of our Toyota Tundra was stuffed with groceries, holiday fare, and household necessities. Perched precariously atop everything else was a garden-gnome-like Jolly St. Nick statue we had bought for our curio collecting friend Verna. A few miles from our mailbox we found ourselves engulfed by whiteout blizzard conditions. The Chalk Buttes Road was rippled with knee-deep drifts ahead, the night sky invisible above, and saucer-sized snowflakes swirled dizzyingly in the headlights. The temperature was dropping precipitously. Doug was bone-tired and, while he had brought along a winter parka for me, I was nonetheless underdressed, having flown in directly from a conference in San Francisco. We readily, if reluctantly, reached the conclusion that the only sane thing to do was to pull off the road wherever we safely could, cuddle up with the springers—it would be a bona fide three-dog night—and wait it out until dawn, starting the engine and running the heater intermittently, dozing as best we could as the truck shuddered in the howling wind.

Things calmed down by daybreak, and the snow had backed off to mere flurries by the time of first, somewhat uncertain, light. But Carter County rarely sends its snowplows out on country roads, and never on a Sunday morning, as this was. We covered the eight or so miles to the gate into our place slowly, taking turns with one of us driving and the other walking ahead armed with a shovel, carving ruts in the deeper drifts for the chained-up tires. When we got to our turnoff from the county road, fingers crossed, we bumped and busted our way through snowdrifts the last five miles down to home, several times high-centering the truck and having to stop to shovel it free. We finally arrived hours later, relieved—and exhausted—at the house, Jolly St. Nick being by this time decidedly the worse for wear.

Why would we want to go through all this? Why would anybody?

Well, by now the sun was shining brilliantly. We had good German beer in the fridge, and were just in time for the coin toss in the Packers game on TV. A fire was quickly crackling in the wood stove, warming up the house. The snow cover would make for superb deer hunting in the coming days. We had a Thanksgiving holiday week ahead of us, and no other place we needed to, or would rather, be. We had everything to be thankful for. These were reasons enough, surely. At any rate, they were reasons enough that sunny Sunday afternoon in November 2000.

LIVING IN GIANT SHADOWS

To be sure, one of the gifts this landscape can bestow is a deep sense of gratitude for the fact of one's mere survival. And I suppose one way of accounting for what brought us here, and what has kept us here, is the sheer challenge of making it in a climate of extremes. But, especially as middle age sets in, in earnest, intrepidity clearly has its limits. There have to be other, deeper and more various, factors at work, elements of biography and temperament and chance that created the particular chemistry that brought us first to Montana, then eventually here.

Doug's story, in this regard, is perhaps more straightforward. He and his first wife had, in the 1970s, decided they wanted to live someplace west of the Mississippi. They scouted out a few areas in the Rocky Mountain region, and felt especially attracted to Helena, Montana—an attraction that deepened into a commitment when he got a job as head librarian in the Montana Historical Society, and she began working for the state. A lifelong hunter and all-round outdoorsman, he rapidly fell in love with just about everything under the Big Sky. A political and social progressive, he found the spirit of prairie populism congenial as well. When the job at the Historical Society didn't pan out, he returned to college teaching, in Wisconsin and later in Michigan, but maintained Helena, where his wife and son remained, as his permanent home.

My way into Montana, and the West's way into my heart, was a bit more roundabout. While I grew up as a more or less typical Jersey Girl, I did spend three childhood summers, when I was six, seven, and nine years old, on a family friend's ranch—an orange grove, to be more precise—in Ventura County, California. My memories of those years, like most childhood recollections, are in some ways quite vivid, but more or less scattershot overall, often more moods or feelings than events. Disneyland, of course, Pacific Ocean Park, Marineland, Olivera Street in Los Angeles, the Santa Barbara Mission, oil derricks, the Coast Highway, crossing country first in a TWA Constellation and then on the Santa Fe Super Chief . . . I have a sizable inventory of picture postcard vignettes on which to draw.

But beyond those snapshots, and much realer and more substantial, there were the mountains, looming in purple profile at dawn, and shape-shifting throughout the day in an interplay of shadow and light, until each sunset brought the show to a close in a wash of ruby brilliance. I was fascinated by them, and marked each summer day according to their rhythm. This nexus of memory also involves the scents of sage and orange, and the grittiness of sand between my toes. But the mountains are the lodestone around which all the pleasures of my western summers coalesce in memory. I can at best speculate about whatever they represented to my evolving consciousness of the world about me: their bigness, their solidity, their consummate *there*-ness. But I knew, from the first, that one could do much worse than to live in such giant shadows.

And so when, nearly a quarter century later, I first laid eyes on Montana, it was with an inborn sense of homecoming. That was on our honeymoon. Doug and I had met and fallen in love when we were on the same religion faculty at Central Michigan University, both of us in temporary appointments, and both in marriages that were imploding. When we eventually came together, acknowledging that what had evolved between us over the course of two years was much deeper than the "good friendship" we professed it to be, it was with a profound sense of a new beginning, a second chance . . . and, I suppose, yes, intrepid hippielike adventure. It was the spring of 1983, we had both been pink-slipped by the university, we loaded up everything of ours that had any meaning to us and would fit into a Toyota 4WD pickup and a small trailer, and headed west. He had a teenaged son from his first marriage he wanted to be close to. I understood, and—madly in love with him and feeling no particular ties to any other part of the country at that point—found it easy to pledge "Whither thou goest, I go." Or something like that, anyway.

Moving west, finding a place we could afford and settling down in the Helena Valley, I readily gave myself to my surroundings. I found it relatively easy to fall in love with this place that already claimed my husband's heart.

PROVING UP

Of course, that is a very romantic way of telling this story. There was certainly a more ironic edge to it. For example, when we married I had taken his name, a matter over which my feminist friends raised an eyebrow or two. And I had committed what some "Second Wave" feminists of the period considered the cardinal sin of "following my man." I had, in other words, acted in distinctly divergent fashion for a fledgling professor of women's studies.

And yet, viewed against the backdrop of the history of western settlement, I had merely done what so many women in generations before me had—and many of them with a kindred sense of adventure and romance. Indeed, the West would never have been "won," had it not been for the enterprise of women working alongside the men. As sociologist H. Elaine Lindgren phrases it in *Land in Her Own Name,* her ethnography of high plains women homesteaders in North Dakota, the "marriage, madness, and marginality syndrome" has been greatly exaggerated in the mythology surrounding female pioneers. There were surely those women who succumbed to "the loneliness," or who were beaten down figuratively by the landscape or literally by the dominant men in their lives. But, as feminist historians and literary critics have amply borne out via combing the treasure trove of frontier women's letters and diaries, the vast majority of these women experienced themselves as actors in a historical drama that they well knew couldn't take place without them. You might say they were the "intrepid hippies" of their era.

Historian Elizabeth Jameson quotes an interview with one such woman, native Coloradan May Wing: "I lived the history that I can tell. And of course the history today in books that's written a lot is not really the true thing, as it was lived." The eighty-nine-year-old Wing was speaking in 1979. This was about the time when historians were beginning to seriously question the "history . . . that's written a lot" in books—the same history that Jameson summed up with reference to Dee Brown's 1958 book, *The Gentle Tamers,* which "portrayed an image of western woman as the reluctant pioneer who, while her man tamed the physical wilderness, gently and passively tamed the man and brought civilized culture to the frontier." Think Grace Kelly and (Helena, Montana, native) Gary Cooper, in *High Noon.*

As Jameson explains, a specific cultural mythology has shaped conventional histories of the American West. She writes:

> I do not think May Wing would recognize herself in much of the scholarship on western women, which has been influenced by the assumptions of both traditional western history and the Victorian Cult of True Womanhood. Assuming that men's and women's worlds were separate, that men's lives were public and women's were private, that men were active and women were passive, historians have created a number of polarized images of western women. Common stereotypes divide them into good and bad women, either genteel civilizers and sunbonneted helpmates, or hell raisers and bad women.

The idea of women as "reluctant pioneers," tender flowers too fragile for the savage landscape into which their husbands nonetheless persisted in dragging them, goes back to the early twentieth century. Lindgren cites a 1930 novel, *An Army Without Banners*, by one John Beames. He wrote:

> It is not in women that the pioneer spirit stirs; the horizon does not beckon them; hills and rivers are to them a barrier, not an invitation to explore. It was the men only who pressed on across the great plains; the women had little more to say than the horses who drew the wagons in which they sat. Where women had the deciding word no move was made.

This is so much hogwash. The average western woman's experience was far more active and complex than the stereotype, and she was neither the "Prairie Madonna" popularized in pioneer art nor the Calamity Jane of dime novels. Lindgren's fascinating study of High Plains women who homesteaded on their own—many of whom subsequently married, a fair proportion of whom did not—presents a gallery of women who experienced themselves as, if not necessarily men's equals in the work of taming the land, then most definitely men's partners. Women, more often than not, primarily did the "womanly" work of homemaking: cooking, cleaning, doing laundry, churning butter and putting up preserves, gardening and suchlike, and of course child rearing. Some took in sewing or taught school. Men, meanwhile, worked the cattle, tilled the earth, and ran businesses in town. But, for the women at least, the social model was collaboration, not domination: "Whatever the actual division of labor was," Lindgren writes, "many women who chose to take homesteads seemed to support the idea that cooperation of the genders represented a partnership instead of a dominant male with helpmate."

According to western historian John Mack Faragher, somewhere between thirty and forty thousand women homesteaded in their own right. And they "proved up" alongside the men, in a society where, as Faragher has observed, "Proving up meant more than meeting legal requirements. It meant proving oneself."

Lindgren concludes her volume with the story of Pauline Shoemaker, a middle-class Pennsylvania native who graduated in 1897 with a bachelor's degree in education (or "the Elements," as it was then called) from the State Normal School in East Stroudsburg, and earned her teacher certification three years later. A striking brunette with delicate features and large, liquid eyes, she was proficient in both Greek and

Latin. And she had a yen for adventure that only the West could satisfy: She would pore over maps of the interior West, where there was in her words "sort of a blank in the middle," and she wondered what might be there. In 1902, she set out on her own to find out.

Not unlike Jennie Carlson, the author of the Ekalaka "exposé" *Thru the Dust*, she drifted from one teaching post to another, in North Dakota, then out to California, then—after a summer sojourn sheepherding in the Sierra Nevada Mountains and an extended tour of Yellowstone Park—back to North Dakota, where she filed a claim, supported herself by running a rural school out of her homestead shack, and eventually married a neighboring rancher. Adept with a rifle and an expert horsewoman, she was also a voracious reader, with a keen eye for current affairs and an interest in state politics. She went on to become the first woman appointed to the State Board of Higher Education. After her death at the age of ninety-one in 1970, her daughter Sheila summed up Pauline's life in one sentence: "After Mother came West, she never rode side-saddle, she always rode astride."

Coming from the same part of the country as she, and with a similarly middle-class background and education, I wonder whether, had I come of age at the time she did, I'd have been as audacious as Pauline Shoemaker. I suspect I wouldn't have been. But I nevertheless see in her story—as in the scores of other pioneer women's accounts I've read—a deeply kindred spirit. Or, perhaps more accurately, a kindred spiritedness. I was a slower study than Pauline, taking up hunting and shooting in my early thirties, and serious horseback riding only when I turned fifty. But it seems that, whenever this particular spirit moves, it heads in a westerly direction.

Now, as then, of course, that spirit is bound to bump up against obstacles for which "sexism" is perhaps too genteel a term. While pioneer women may have conceived of their relationships with men as partnerships, the men themselves easily assumed their own superiority. They were, after all, the ones who did the heavy lifting. In *Women of the Northern Plains: Gender and Settlement on the Homestead Frontier 1870–1930*, historian Barbara Handy-Marchello notes how the language employed by homesteaders belied the women's assumption of partnership: "Women spoke of 'helping out' in the fields; men frequently used the first-person singular when describing farm work." The division of labor was largely defined by who got to use which tools: "Use of even the simplest tools was governed by a hierarchy based on gender.

Mary checking on the bison herd. Photo by Doug Stange.

Men usually operated the more advanced tools while women worked with primitive tools or none at all." Men worked with machinery and animals. Women did "stoop labor," like removing rocks from fields in advance of the men's plowing.

> Primitive or not, a tool in a man's hands signified power over those with no tools. If the tool had to be sharpened or repaired, if the oxen needed rest or water, the work halted. Those toiling with their hands had no such external and compelling means of pacing the work of everyone in the field. This hierarchy should not be understood to mean that the women were "just helping out" but rather that the authority over field work and field labor remained a masculine privilege. . . . Though women occasionally worked with horse-drawn equipment—usually while alone in the fields—the exchange of labor was uneven, for men did not perform stoop labor while women operated equipment.

The prairie "hierarchy" established in the homesteading period remains essentially unchanged today. The machinery has gotten bigger and more sophisticated, and while women sometimes take the wheel, it is invariably in a subordinate capacity. A woman might operate a mower or a swather, to cut or windrow hay, or drive the grain truck accompanying a combine. But in all the time I have lived here, I have neither seen nor heard of a woman either baling the hay, or running the combine itself.

When any of these machines break down, however, halting the field work, it's up to the ranch wife to drop whatever else she may have been doing, and head out to the farm implements dealer—an errand which may well be upward of a hundred miles each way, depending upon what is needed and who in the area has it in stock—to fetch the part her husband has called ahead for. Meanwhile, since he can't work in the field until she gets back, he'll putter around the place attending to light chores . . . or maybe drive into town for a cup of coffee or a beer, and an afternoon of palavering about cattle markets, grain futures and the weather, with other men on a break from haying or harvesting.

Here, too, contemporary ranchers are playing out patterns laid down by their homesteading forebears. As Handy-Marchello recounts of those earlier days, "In addition to field work, women performed tasks that both supported and decreased the time necessary to complete the work of plowing and harvesting." One woman "drove the oxen one-half mile to the river for water while her husband ate his noon meal and rested." While another man was on his midday break, his wife "walked four miles to have the scythe sharpened by a neighbor who owned the area's only grindstone."

On several occasions, when she and her husband Gib were still ranching down the road from us, I accompanied our friend Verna on these parts-fetching excursions. She liked to have the company, on those numbingly long stretches of gravel roads, country highways, Interstate. Generally, it was long past sundown by the time we got back, from Miles City or Glendive, Montana, or Bowman or Dickinson, North Dakota, or some combination of those far-flung towns. Sometimes, either through miscommunication or misunderstanding at one end or the other, she turned out to have gotten the wrong thing, and would have to set out again, the next day, to exchange it. Why, I would ask her, didn't Gib just run the errand himself? "Because he has other things to do," she would respond. I supposed this was true enough; I don't think Gib ever voluntarily took time off from work. But, then, couldn't he call and have them ship him the part overnight, via UPS? "No," she would explain patiently, "UPS doesn't deliver out here until late afternoon, and that tractor needs fixed right away." Besides, I understood without her saying it, this is what a wife is supposed to do. It was part of her uneven half of their partnership.

Over the years, I too have run my fair share of ranch errands: hauling fence posts and wire and PVC pipe and the like, picking up sacks of feed cake and salt-and-mineral supplement. I've done it because Doug needed the help, of course. But I'll be frank: it is also because, as I came to realize fairly early on here, every solo interaction I had with the folks at the farm and ranch store or the grain elevator bought me a lot more local credibility than the books and articles I was publishing, or my status as a college professor. Conforming to the gender stereotype made me a little less "differnt." Or so I hoped.

Meanwhile, the historical division of rural labor has yielded an interesting contemporary side effect—and one noteworthy to me, as a feminist. Anyone passing through Ekalaka today might readily jump to the conclusion that the place is run largely by women. The county clerk and recorder, the county treasurer, the school superintendent, the postmaster, the justice of the peace, the director of the federal Farm

Doug oiling one of our windmills. Photo by Mary Stange.

Services Agency, the head of the county conservation district, the manager of the Carter County Federal Credit Union, and two of three managers of the First National Bank are all women. Women also own and operate the two restaurants in town, one of two motels, and the grocery store. In whatever "spare time" all these women have, they too are probably running around in search of replacement parts for heavy machinery. But even as some things stay more or less the same in terms of gender roles, others are clearly, and decidedly, changing.

PRAIRIE VIOLENCE

There is another, darker side to this story. You might say that, as a women's studies scholar, it's part of my job to be alert to the shadier side of any story that has to do with gender roles. In the case of southeastern Montana, one needn't look very hard, or very far.

Almost immediately after Doug and I moved into our place, we mutually remarked how precarious the distinction was between feeling safe from harm on the one hand, and vulnerable to danger on the other. On a day to day basis, as we settled into the rhythms of country living, we were utterly secure, miles from our nearest neighbors, in something like our own private wilderness area. But let an unexpected, or—as we got to know what all our neighbors' trucks looked like—unfamiliar vehicle come bumping down the road toward our house, and it was impossible to suppress an involuntary quiver of anxiety. It remains so today. Geographical isolation is, by turns, splendid and unsettling. Especially when one is at home alone. Rattlesnakes are not the only reason we keep a shotgun propped by the front door, with ammunition within easy reach.

Neither of us has had to reach for it yet, to fend off a human intruder. Our unanticipated visitors generally have been along the lines of out-of-state hunters who have become separated from their hunting buddies, linemen working for the electrical or telephone cooperatives trying to trace a problem, back-to-nature vacationing campers who have become hopelessly lost trying to decipher BLM and National Forest Service maps, and—on three separate occasions thus far—parties of Jehovah's Witnesses, undaunted missionaries from New York, California, and Illinois respectively, who were more skilled than the campers at map reading and actually intended to find themselves in our front yard. These last did inspire in my Lutheran spouse a jovial urge to fetch that shotgun, drawling *Deliverance*-style "In these parts, we shoot Jehovah Witnesses," but he restrained himself.

Here again, our present experience is rooted in the history of this place. The literature of westward expansion is, of course, filled with stories of potentially dangerous, unwanted visitors—who most commonly seem to drop by, either by chance or intent, when the woman of the house is there by herself, or alone with her children. Marauding Indians, drunken Cavalry deserters, and outlaws seeking a place to lay low: they are the stock in trade of the Hollywood version of how the West was won, drawing ample inspiration from both fictional and nonfictional homesteading-period accounts. To be sure, such wide open spaces might well be attractive to criminals seeking to get away with murder. A woman's brutalized corpse was discovered, by antelope hunters, in a culvert outside Alzada in southern Carter County several years ago. Also several years ago, law enforcement traced a convicted murderer, escaped from the state penitentiary in Deer Lodge and believed to be armed and dangerous, to southeastern Montana. When the man was finally apprehended in northern Colorado, it turned out our county sheriff had actually stopped to help him fix the flat tire on his stolen getaway car, before waving him on his way. The sheriff was just being neighborly, and in his defense, the All Points Bulletin hadn't reached him yet.

As to those encounters with Indians: Revenge killings, like the purported one on Wyoming's Crazy Woman Creek, undoubtedly occurred. But it seems that many Native/Anglo interactions were more benign than the Hollywood version that features befeathered braves swooping down on helpless farmwives. Gerard Baker, a Mandan-Hidatsa and (in a delightful piece of historical irony) the park superintendent of Mount Rushmore, tells a story, passed down among his people, that nicely brings home this point. Picture, if you will, a North Dakota homestead, a hundred or so years ago. The husband has gone off with other neighboring men, to drive cattle to market. It has been a lean year, and the wife is left to fend for herself and their several children. Within a few days, their meager cupboard is all but empty. There is a loud knock on the door and she opens it to discover a party of young Indian men. They are days from their village, and ravenously hungry. Lacking English, they try to communicate with her by crude sign language: pointing to their mouths, their stomachs, gesturing their hunger. The woman basically dissolves in a pool of terror—we might imagine her crowding her children to her, shaking violently, weeping uncontrollably. Meanwhile, the Indians, having given up on trying to make sense to this hysterical white woman, start poking around, looking through the cupboards, the larder, the root cellar. Finding essentially nothing worth eating, they leave the frantic woman and her cowering children to their shared misery. Several days later, her husband still away and her own and her children's stomachs now gnawingly empty, the woman hears some scuffling outside, then yet another knock on the door. Peering apprehensively through the window curtains, she recognizes that same band of Indians, although they are already mounting their horses to leave. On her porch, they have deposited a freshly killed deer, a sack of cornmeal, some molasses, and dried berries. It is a poignant story and, I think, has a ring of historical truth about it.

What we don't know about this nameless woman, whose story survived through Native memory, is how it might have happened that her husband left her in such dire circumstances in the first place. Perhaps they had, like many homesteaders, suffered disastrous bad luck, and he had taken their last starving cow to market. But maybe he had just given up, and deserted his family—this too was known to happen, and not infrequently. He might even have been habitually, systematically, neglectful, depriving them of all but the slimmest means of sustenance. And if he did eventually come back home, he might well have beaten her to within an inch of her life, for "consorting" with those Indians: What exactly had she done, to buy the favor of their feeding her?

It is with these possibilities that we engage the darker side of the pioneer story. There is a violent undertone to life on the hard-grass prairie, and the biggest dangers don't necessarily reside outside the homestead. Handy-Marchello reports that during the homestead period, violence against children "appears to have been widespread and not generally considered excessive unless the child suffered permanent damage." In some cases, especially among some immigrant groups, men—and while there were female child abusers, most were male— offered a biblical rationale against sparing the rod and spoiling the child. It was a matter of teaching respect for authority and upright behavior: as North Dakota historian and descendant of homesteaders Pauline Neher Diede puts it (quoted by Handy-Marchello), it was better "to have a dead son than a disobedient one." Given the patriarchal structure of society at the time, most men probably didn't even feel they needed to resort to Scripture to justify their violent outbursts. Frontier life was hard, and if a man needed from time to time to vent the aggression that built up inside him in the face of the quotidian pressure to survive, then his family was the perhaps inevitable outlet. A boy just needed to "cowboy up" and learn to take it.

And a girl—well, she needed to learn her place in the scheme of things. This was especially true if she was a displaced orphan like the somewhat more fortunate Ijkalaka, or illegitimate, or one of a family with simply too many mouths to feed. Handy-Marchello recounts the awful story of one such hapless child:

> At age seven, Margaret Kottke had been sent to work as a servant in the home of Mr. and Mrs. Walter Zimmerman near Granville [North Dakota]. On a cold, snowy October day in 1919 she was beaten and then sent to bring in the cows. The Zimmermans later reported her missing and asked neighbors to help search for her. The next day her bruised, dirty body, clad in light summer clothing, was found next to a haystack in the farmyard. Her stomach contained only a few grains of wheat.

While the Zimmermans were awaiting trial (for manslaughter), little Margaret's stepfather Arthur Kottke, who had sent her to the Zimmermans, was charged with neglect of his own children. The case attracted some brief public notice but, as Handy-Marchello notes, "did not spark any discussion among community members about the treatment of children in their own homes or in service positions."

Around the same time, an adolescent girl I'll call Marie was sent by her family in Carter County, Montana, down to a ranch in Wyoming, to spend the summer working as a housekeeper and helping with the children. A mere child herself at fourteen, she returned home for school in the fall, and was quickly discovered to be pregnant. Her father and brothers immediately drove down to Wyoming to have a talk with the rancher who had impregnated her. He, of course, protested his innocence. But his wife—appalled by what she realized her husband had indeed done, and sensing that the men from Carter County meant business of the "frontier justice" variety—stepped forward. "When Marie has the baby, we'll adopt it and raise it as our own," she offered. One can well imagine the conversation that must have ensued between the rancher and his wife, after their visitors had turned back toward

Montana. But, not only did they follow through with the adoption, the girl to whom Marie gave birth later reported having grown up in a warm and loving household.

This story was told to us by our friend Keith, one of whose brothers was working on a family genealogy and had pieced it together. The discovery rocked the family. Well into his sixties, Keith learned that he had an older half sister living in Nevada. The "Marie" of this story had, in fact, been his own mother. She, now deceased, had never breathed a word of the story to anyone, perhaps not even the man she eventually married, Keith's dad. Closing the circle of a lifetime of silence, Keith contacted his half-sister. It must have been as tough for her as it was for him. She knew she had been adopted; she did not know the circumstances of her conception. After decades, indeed generations, of concealment, with all the main actors in this drama dead and buried, there was little point to bitterness now. She and Keith savored their mutually extended family. They visited back and forth, and on one visit he brought her out to our place, to introduce us and take her on a tour of our bison herd. When she died a few years ago, he remarked how genuinely happy he was that he had the chance to know her.

Of course, abuse of the sort reflected in the stories of Margaret Kottke and of Keith's mother was hardly historically unique to the High Plains, but it does seem endemic to the frontier experience. Phoebe Ann Mosey, the little girl who would grow up to take the stage name Annie Oakley, suffered abuse very similar to that endured by Margaret Kottke, at the vicious hands of employers she later referred to as "the wolves." She escaped Kottke's fate only by literally escaping from their farm. This was in Ohio, at a time (the early 1870s) when it was pioneer territory.

Stories like these are embedded in a history we, as a culture, have worked hard either to forget or to ignore, largely because they fly in the face of our more cherished frontier mythologies. In an early feminist article on violence against women and girls in the pioneer West, literary scholar Melody Graulich observed: "Few Americans have been willing to believe that the frontiersman or pioneer was a woman abuser; that the real Davy Crocketts, Natty Bumppos, Virginians, and Ben Cartwrights took for granted a patriarchal authority that sanctioned woman abuse; that the frontier's cherished freedom and individualism, which helped shape American history and culture, might encourage the violent domination of women." Graulich's remarks occur in a fascinating study of female frontier writers who took up the theme of violence against women and girls, and who—largely against the writing conventions of their day—portrayed that violence as a "widespread and inevitable" consequence of male domination.

The most compelling story is that of Mari Sandoz, whose memoir of her father *Old Jules*, published in 1935, portrays his marriages to four women, including Mari's mother, as a marathon of battering and humiliation:

> When his first wife disobeyed an order, "Jules closed her mouth with the flat of his long muscular hand"; when his second wife asked why he did nothing, "his hand shot out, and the woman slumped against the bench. . . . [Later] he pretended not to notice [her] swollen lip, the dark bruises on her temple, and the tear-wearied eyes." When Sandoz's mother, Mary, asked Jules to help do the farm work, he responded: "'You want me, an educated man, to work like a hired tramp!' he roared, and threw her against the wall."

One would think that a family history like that would produce a writer at the very least skeptical of the myth of the rugged frontiersman. But Sandoz instead went on to focus in her later works on classic Western themes, what she called "the romantic days." Graulich suggests this may have been because she was either unwilling or unable to identify with "her mother's West." But it may also have had to do with a fact noted by any number of writers, before and since, about this theme: that Western men who routinely engage in violence against women and children are not conventionally perceived as being particularly at fault for it. It is simply a fact of life on the prairie.

Physical isolation, of course, exacerbates the problem for women and children at risk. Driving by night the long stretches of gravel road that crisscross southeastern Montana, one is stuck by the distance between ranch lights, flickering in the darkness. There is no neighbor to run to for assistance, or to see the struggling silhouettes behind the window shades. By day, that same distance can take the form of a vast, empty stillness. Were someone to shout, to plead for help, to scream, there would be no one to hear, aside from hawks and prairie dogs, preoccupied by their own prairie dramas. Telephone service only came to some of these areas as recently as the 1960s. Most are still out of cell phone range. One sheriff, and one deputy, serve the entire three-thousand-plus square miles of Carter County. The Domestic Violence and Sexual Assault Program, based in Miles City, serves five southeast Montana counties: Carter, Custer, Fallon, Garfield, and Powder River. That is a whopping land area of just under seventeen thousand square miles. Help, even if it is on the way, might take an eternity to get to where it needs to be.

But then, in this part of the world, one isn't really supposed admit one needs help, let alone ask for it. The social codes of silence surrounding the routineness of rapes and beatings has, historically, been as rigid as the gender codes in which men are in charge and women—if they know what's good for them—keep their mouths shut. Federally funded domestic violence services, such as they are, only came to southeastern Montana in 1996. That is late in the development of these agencies across the country, most of which were established a good ten to twenty years earlier. I suspect this owes in part to the fact that folks around here were reluctant to look for, let alone at, the problem of domestic abuse. Or, perhaps better said, to see abuse as a problem. It doesn't square with the stories they like to tell, and believe, about themselves. Women grow up in these parts with a thick skin. Indeed, they're capable of throwing the odd punch themselves, and are uniformly proud of that fact.

There is an inescapable casualness about interpersonal violence here, especially violence against or between children. In *Breaking Clean*, her bestselling memoir of growing up in rural northeastern Montana, Judy Blunt writes about her own ranch upbringing, in which "whippings" figured so prominently that "It got to be a joke in later years when a parent eating dinner might suddenly raise a hand to bat a fly, then stare in amazement at the answering wave along the table, the four of us ducking sideways with jet precision, the whole of it so automatic we never stopped chewing."

Among our Carter County friends and acquaintances, off-the-cuff recollections about the times fathers and mothers have "had to" beat their children pepper ostensibly fond reminiscences, sometimes even as the punch line to a story, and with no discernable sense that these stories might raise any moral or ethical qualms in the hearer. Boys, particularly, are encouraged to settle disputes by resorting to a good tussle. And a favorite sort of "practical joke," perpetrated by both adult and adolescent males, involves putting a greenhorn rider on a horse known to be dangerous, even deranged, and then standing back and watching the fun.

Short of beating, other sorts of physical abuse crop up as a part of the ordinary scheme of things. One friend of ours tells the tale of how he used to like to take his youngest son out when he was checking and repairing his cattle fences, when the child was little more than a toddler. The boy came in handy, the man chuckled, when he needed to test an electric fence line. A touch of the son's hand to the wire, a quick yelp on the three-year-old's part, and the father knew the wire was hot. Some ranchers employ their dogs' noses the same way.

I have to emphasize that many of the people who do these things are friends of ours, people with whom we have over the years developed deep and abiding relationships. They are good people. They are also, as was Mari Sandoz, products of and believers in a Western "romance" in which violence is necessarily a central, virtually inevitable, motif.

"DADDY'S HANDS"

Perhaps nothing sums up the complexity of this rough story better than Holly Dunn's country ballad "Daddy's Hands." It has become something of a standard at cowboy funerals. Doug and I first heard it at Gib's burial. He and Verna, our best friends in Carter County, were among those who, over the years, matter-of-factly described their son's and daughter's upbringing as involving a good licking on a regular basis. "Daddy's Hands" recalls a daughter's relationship with her now dead father, through homespun images of his saying bedtime prayers with her, hugging her to dispel a nightmare, patting her on the back for some childhood accomplishment, and fondly embracing her mother. Dunn also sings about his hands being cracked and calloused, "working 'til they bled," to put food on the table, and presumably some money in the bank. But it's the chorus of the song that carries its message home. In it, "Daddy's Hands" are alternatively described as gentle and harsh, meting out reward and punishment in equal proportions, and with equal alacrity. But whether softly compassionate or cruel, Dunn concludes that "There was always love in Daddy's hands."

Standing at Gib's graveside, in the chill of a January sunset, as the funeral director cued this song on his CD player, I glanced over at Gib's daughter Karen. Now in her thirties, she has from early childhood suffered from a degenerative disease that had been undiagnosed when her parents adopted her. Given actuarial tables, she probably never expected to outlive her father. Holly Dunn may or may not have had a disabled daughter in mind when she wrote this song. And Gib and

Verna surely thought the best thing to do for Karen was to treat her like any other child, which meant using "those hands of steel" from time to time.

It was, now in the fading light, impossible to read Karen's face. I believe it was the funeral director who chose "Daddy's Hands" for this moment in the memorial, probably on the basis of its being a regional favorite. I had the sense that, not for the first time, he had chosen right.

It is possible, of course, to exaggerate the level of everyday violence that seems so endemic to prairie life. And it doesn't take an outsider like myself to do it. Indeed, Judy Blunt succumbed to the temptation in her aforementioned memoir. And there is an important lesson to be learned from her story. One of the most shocking vignettes in *Breaking Clean* occurred early on in the narrative, and provided the sort of image that resonated in the reader's mind throughout the entire book. In it, Blunt's father-in-law seized her typewriter, took it outside, and "killed it with a sledgehammer." He didn't care that his daughter-in-law was a fledgling creative writer; all that mattered to him was that she hadn't gotten lunch on the table in a timely manner, when the men broke from their morning ranch work. The scene was viscerally emblematic of the indictment Blunt was building in her narrative—against her hard growing up in rural eastern Montana, against the unhappy marriage her own father had brokered for her with a neighboring rancher, against the confining strictures of being a ranch wife.

The only problem is, the sledgehammering of the typewriter had never happened. By the time the book was published, to glowing reviews most of which referenced this powerful scene (and one of which I myself wrote, for the *Women's Review of Books*), Blunt was long-divorced from her husband, and had relocated to Missoula, in western Montana. It was when she ventured back to the eastern part of the state on her book tour, with a *New York Times* reporter in tow, that the story broke: Her ex–father-in-law had written a letter to the *Phillips County News*, their hometown paper, declaring "No such event ever occurred. This is her story as she chooses to tell it." Other friends and family members had rallied around him, proclaiming his innocence and his fundamentally upright character. Blunt at first tried to finesse the situation, with a reporter from the *Great Falls Tribune* who surprised her after a reading at the public library in Malta. She said the incident, as she described it, was "symbolic" of what it was like on her husband's ranch, and admitted that the lived event was "less dramatic." She later owned up to the *Times* reporter that, in actual fact, "The old man pulled the plug on the typewriter and shouted and screamed, but the typewriter survived."

Knopf, her publisher, withdrew the scene from subsequent printings of the book. The incident precipitated a brief, but lively, debate in the publishing world, about the issue of truth telling in memoirs. And that was, supposedly, that.

As a reader, and reviewer, I felt cheated. And as a transplant to what Raban's reviewer had called this "ugly half of a beautiful state," I felt insulted. In Blunt's telling, her former father-in-law achieves the status of a monster, something approaching Simon Legree. To say nothing of his wife, whom she portrays as the original Mother-in-Law From Hell. Was it just possible, I could not help but wonder, that these were simply ordinary folks, just like our Carter County friends and neighbors? Like Gib, who once when Doug complained about how hard it is to maintain quality guns and good tools in our harsh climate, responded with a mixture of bemusement and annoyance, "What makes you think you deserve nice things?" Like Verna, who gave Karen the occasional thrashing even as the girl was the Montana poster child for cystic fibrosis: to make her tough, Doug and I assumed (albeit somewhat uneasily), to teach her daughter the survival skills she needed in this life.

For all the seemingly inevitable scars these people bear as a result of their eastern Montana upbringing—and, in her telling, in the early years of their marriage Verna certainly suffered in-laws no less cruel than Blunt's ostensibly had been—Verna and Gib, as we had learned early on in our Carter County "adventure," were capable of genuine graciousness, simple no-frills generosity, real friendship.

Of course, it is one thing to come to some comprehension of other people's woundedness, how they cope, or persevere, or overcome, or whatever it is they do to make sense out of day-to-day living. It is quite another thing, to learn to lick one's own wounds, to reconcile oneself to the fact that no one survives in this part of the world unscathed, or unchanged.

It took but one small disaster, one brush with "the law of the frontier," to teach us that.

Ayla as a puppy. Photo by Doug Stange.

CHAPTER 4
The Law of the Frontier

"I HAD TO SHOOT YOUR DOG"

The phone had rung just as we got home from a shopping trip up in Baker. Doug was standing, the phone still in his hand, his lips parted, shoulders stooped, looking as if he had just been punched in the stomach. As I walked through the door, kicking my dusty shoes off and stumbling toward the kitchen table with a couple of bags of groceries, he slowly turned his face toward me, shaking his head and blinking, as if trying not to see the implications of what he had just heard.

The voice on the phone, slurred and sullen, was that of a rancher in our general neighborhood—I'll call him Judd. Doug said he must have been calling from one of the bars in town, judging by the cowboy jukebox and boozy laughter in the background. Maybe, Doug said, he had to get a few drinks in him, to make the call at all. "I had to shoot your dog," he had said. "It was killing my chickens. Couldn't let that happen. Didn't know whose it was until after I shot it, and cut the collar off, saw your name tag on it. Thought you might want to know."

"I'd . . . where is she? I'd like to come over and get her . . ." Doug's voice faltered.

"In the hayfield, southwest of the barn. Happened hours ago. Nobody's home right now, but you're welcome, I guess, to go get the body, if you want to."

It had been a blistering hot June day. Too hot for working outside much, and we had needed supplies anyway, so we decided to head up to Baker. Ordinarily, we would have piled the dogs into the pickup. But it was hot, and we had company, in the form of two young brothers— Matt and Ryan, aged about eleven and thirteen, friends' sons visiting from their farm in Minnesota. The boys could be a handful at times, and trundling them around and keeping track of them was challenge enough, without two or three springer spaniels thrown into the mix. So we left the younger dogs—the ones who ordinarily rode with us— at home.

The day had gotten off to a difficult start: I had come upon a rattlesnake close to the house, had to run back to get a pistol and load it with shot cartridges, and returned to find our scrappy little Ayla, hackles up and barking, just about ready to take on the snake herself. Shouting at her and warning her away with one hand, I'd shot with the other and, in the heat of the moment, had needed two shots to hit the snake. I then had to submit for the next several minutes to being ribbed by two adolescent boys over the fact that I couldn't shoot straight enough to kill it with one. Meanwhile, Ayla had run up the road, thinking I was angry with her, and refused to come back when I called. Doug was impatient to get on the road. Our other springers were doing what bird dogs generally do when they hear gunfire, that is, running around in a generally celebratory frame of mind and clamoring for more action. But we humans were all more or less out of sorts at this point—a rattlesnake in the immediate vicinity can have that effect. Ordinarily, we would have gotten the dogs calmed down and sorted out. Ordinarily, we would have made sure Ayla was back at the house before we left.

But this turned out to be one of those days that give the lie to the seemingly innocuous word, "ordinarily."

"I had to shoot your dog," Judd had said. It was painfully easy to imagine what had happened. He came upon Ayla at his hen house. Some chickens had been killed. He went and fetched his .22 rifle, approached her, and Ayla—a bright, somewhat headstrong little dog who thought life was a superbly interesting game—probably briefly stood her ground, probably wagging her tail. And then she ran, zigzagging into the field behind the barn, where true to form she would have spun around to look back in Judd's direction. A totally trusting little girl, she may have had no idea she was in danger. She may even have seen the gun and assumed, employing springer logic, that they were going to hunt that hayfield. Instead, he shot her.

Then again, knowing Judd's temperament, he was probably shouting at her, cursing his head off. She may have run to escape his wrath. She may well have been very frightened. But we knew she did stop, and turned around to look at him. We knew that much because, as we discovered when we found her, he had shot her in the face.

We also discovered, when we found her, that his shot did not kill Ayla. Judd had to have known this, because after he shot her, he walked up to her, bent down and grabbed her collar and cut it off. She might well have been unconscious at that point. Perhaps he gave her body a kick. But he should have seen she was still breathing. A rancher and a hunter who has dealt with killing all his life, he had to have seen that. He had left her, severely wounded, lying in the searing hot afternoon sun, to die.

But Ayla hadn't died. Hours later, she was still clinging to life, in that sunbaked hayfield.

We and the boys had rushed over to Judd's place immediately. Judd is not exactly a near neighbor; indeed, Ayla had covered a surprising number of miles to get there. We drove the dusty roads in stunned silence, our mood as flat and as darkening as the late-afternoon shadows stretching out ahead of the pickup. We drove down the two-track to behind Judd's barn, and parked the truck. Ryan and Matt were already pretty seasoned upland bird hunters by then, and knew the drill as well as we did. We four would quarter back and forth in systematic fashion, to cover the entire hayfield, just as if we were searching for a downed pheasant. The problem, in this case, was that none of us really wanted to be the one to find the object of this grim field exercise. That awful phone call barely an hour old, I don't think any of us wanted to believe what was happening, what had happened. We soon were wandering randomly, backtracking, walking in circles. Maybe, I thought, if we couldn't find the little corpse we unwillingly sought, maybe it hadn't really happened after all. Maybe she would be waiting on the porch for us when we drove back home.

Then, in a far corner of the field, Ayla raised her head. Lying there dazed, dehydrated, suffering, she had heard us calling back and forth to one another. This roused her, weak as she was. We all saw her small, dark silhouette more or less simultaneously, but it took a moment to comprehend what we were seeing. Doug ran to her, stumbling through the grass at breakneck speed, and by the time he had dropped to his knees to gingerly gather her limp little frame in his arms, he was sobbing. Ayla was alive! She was also horribly, hideously hurt, her face grotesquely swollen on one side, its eye bulging nearly out of the socket.

"Call the vet!" Doug shouted to me. This was before the advent of cell phones, at least in our part of the world. I ran to the ranch house, was grateful to find the door unlocked, found a phone and rang up the vet in town. He said he'd be waiting for us at the clinic.

Doug carefully ferried Ayla to the truck, and slid into the passenger seat cradling her in his arms. She was dazed and disoriented, breathing but not without difficulty, whimpering. I drove, and covered the fifty or so gravel miles into town from Judd's in at most forty minutes. All the while, we were chanting as if the phrases formed a mantra, "It's OK, Ayla . . . Hang in there, Ayla . . . We love you, Ayla . . . You're a *good* dog, Ayla . . ."

It took Greg, our vet, some doing to even find the bullet's point of entry, a tiny spot on her swollen muzzle. He did what he could—started her on an intravenous drip of glucose, administered painkillers and antibiotics, tried to make her reasonably comfortable and to stabilize her. As he was working, we told him about what we knew to have happened. "A few chickens?" he said softly, matter-of-factly. "Well, that Judd has a temper. I guess it just got the better of him. It's a shame, she's a real nice little dog." The prognosis was not good, obviously.

But Ayla was still alive the next morning. His Ekalaka practice being limited mostly to large animals, Greg lacked the specialized equipment needed for testing and treating her. He recommended we take her to a vet with a more specialized small-animal practice in Miles City, and arranged a referral. We had Ayla there by noon, and this vet, after examining her and running a few tests, was guardedly optimistic: Ayla was in awful shape, but her vital signs were reasonably good, her little heart strong, and the swelling beginning to subside somewhat. An X-ray showed the bullet to be lodged in her skull in a spot where it could remain without further harm. She would lose the sight in that one eye, but likely not the eye itself. Her reflexes were good. As to brain damage and the extent of disability, well, we would have to wait and see.

We headed home, to await an update later in the day. When the call came, it was fantastic news: Ayla was drinking water on her own, was responsive when called by name, and even managed a few wags of her tail. She was resting comfortably in the cool air-conditioned clinic, and seemed to have turned a corner. The little kid had a lot of fight in her. A few more days of hospitalization, and we should be able to bring her home to continue her recovery. Massively relieved, we celebrated with popcorn and a movie on TV with the boys. Then, also massively exhausted, and having barely slept the night before, we turned in relatively early, ignoring the phone's ringing as we were turning out the lights.

When I checked our voicemail in the morning, it was the Miles City vet. She was very sorry, she said. She had returned to the clinic later in the evening, to look in on our little girl. Ayla had by then died— "peacefully," she was quite certain. The cause was probably swelling of her brain stem—"Usually, if this is going to happen, it happens sooner, so I thought she was in the clear, but it's the likeliest explanation"— and, realistically speaking, nothing could have been done about it.

So, finally, after two awful days, Ayla had breathed her last all alone, in the dark, in a strange place. We had left with her a blanket from home, and the shirt Doug had been wearing when we drove her to Miles City. We had to hope that had helped, that she knew we loved her and hadn't abandoned her. We had to trust she had indeed been comfortable, and that the end came to her in a dreamless sleep, softly and suddenly.

We also had to figure out how we could survive any longer in Carter County.

"I had to shoot your dog."

We bore our share of responsibility for what had happened. Ayla had liked to pal around with another of our springers, named Helene—a year or so younger than Ayla, but about the same size and so like her that from any distance they looked like twins. That past spring, the two little dogs had developed a habit taking a daily walkabout on their own. Like clockwork, when midmorning rolled around, we would see them head off down one of our roads, mutually absorbed in a mixture of play and serious hunting. They'd be gone for an hour or maybe two, and then come scampering home. Neither Doug nor I particularly liked this bit of limit testing on their part. But it had seemed fairly innocent, given the size of our place, and the bigness of this country. How far could two little springer spaniels range, anyway? They probably never lost sight of the house. We were, quite frankly, far more concerned that the dogs could fall prey to predators like coyotes, or could otherwise hurt themselves by, say, tangling with a badger, than that they could do any serious damage to anything bigger than a ground squirrel.

We were naïve, of course. We weren't thinking. Dogs are born hunters, and even a petite springer spaniel knows that deep down she is a wolf. We should have known better than to let them out of our sight.

This truth bore heavily, now, on us both. But did Ayla deserve to die for our foolishness?

The consensus in town, where apparently Judd told whoever was within earshot that he had to shoot Stanges' dog that afternoon, was that the answer was yes. In the ensuing weeks, in casual conversations in town, as well as from people we regarded as friends, even confidents, we heard the same recurring themes:

"Chicken killers, why, they're ruined as dogs. Once a dog gets the taste of blood, the only thing is to put 'em down."

"Judd was within his rights, you know. A man can kill to defend his stock, even if it is a bunch of chickens. That's the law of the frontier."

"Them chickens was his kids' 4-H project, I heard. You got to think about how disappointed they must've been."

"It's too bad about your dog, I know you were real fond of her. But you know, it's always the animals you love the most that get killed."

And, running like a leitmotif through every conversation, as if in itself it were sufficient rationale for what had happened: "That Judd, well, he's got quite a temper."

Of course, Judd did not have to shoot our dog. He could have tied her up, called us to come and get her, and read us the riot act about Ayla's ruining his boys' 4-H project. We would have deserved that.

Judd did not have to shoot our dog. Nor did he have to cut her collar off, as it had a very serviceable brass buckle. But perhaps getting close enough and taking the time to undo a buckle would have forged too intimate a connection with the thing he had just shot in the face, the still-living thing he was about to leave to die in the hammering afternoon heat. He didn't have to do that, either. Seeing she was still breathing, he could have put a second, more humane bullet into her to finish her off. But he didn't.

Of course, he also didn't have to call us. He could have left Ayla to the coyotes, and we would have been none the wiser as to the cause of her disappearance from our lives. But he did call, just as he did roughly cut her collar off, just as he did shoot her in the face and leave her to finish dying by herself. Was his call an act of belated civility, or a further act of aggression?

Or was it simply another requirement of the "law of the frontier?" If we couldn't find answers to these questions, how were we supposed to find a way to sustain our living in Carter County?

WHAT MAKES A MAN A MAN

In her provocative study of the western genre, *West of Everything: The Inner Life of Westerns*, literary critic Jane Tompkins posits—as I have—an immediate connection between the way westerns construct their characters and their society on the one hand, and the landscape around them on the other:

> Nature makes it obvious, even to the most benighted, who her chosen are; the sage-dotted plains, the buttes, the infinite sky tell more plainly than any words what is necessary in a man. The landscape established by contrast an image of the corrupt, effete life that that [western] genre never tired of criticizing—the fancy words and pretty actions of the drawing room, elegant clothes, foreign accents, dusky complexions, subservient manners, of women, Easterners and non-white males. We know that the people who get off the stage wearing suits and carrying valises, sporting parasols or mustaches, are doomed, not because of anything anyone says about them but because of the mountains in the background and the desert underfoot which is continuous with the main street of town.

Call it all a mythology, if you wish, but as a professor of religion, I know mythologies powerfully shape lived reality. And the scenario Tompkins describes is as evident in Carter County as in the novels of Louis L'Amour and the films of John Ford. It bears, I think, somewhat closer scrutiny.

Every western, Tompkins suggests, begins in emptiness: the panoramic vastness, the absence of shade from the sun or shelter from the gritty wind. And every western ends in death, which may or may not be redemptive, but in any event comes, literally, with the territory. The topography of the western is spiritual as well as physical, and inspires a "code of asceticism":

> [T]he negations of the physical setting—no shelter, no water, no rest, no comfort—are also its siren song. Be brave, be strong enough to endure this, it says, and you will become like this— hard, austere, sublime. . . . The landscape challenges the body to endure hardship—that is its fundamental message at the physical level. It says, This is a hard place to be; you will have to do without here. Its spiritual message is the same: come, and suffer.

The lesson this land teaches, then, is ultimately about one's own vulnerability, indeed about the fragility of life and of breath itself. It is not a landscape for the fainthearted.

Yet it is, at the same time, not without rewards, both physical and spiritual. Southwestern writer Sharman Apt Russell enumerates some of them, in her provocative environmental study *Kill the Cowboy: A Battle of Mythology in the New West*. She notes that while, strictly speaking, the term "cowboy" refers to those ranch hands who spend their days riding fence lines, herding sheep or cattle, and doing myriad sorts of grunt work—all for Spartan room and board and a subsistence wage of a few hundred dollars a month—the term, in popular imagination, extends to the entire ranching community and its support systems, and carries a much broader symbolic significance:

> Cowboys are the icon of the rural West. They have much to do with how all Americans think about the West. They have much to do with our cultural dreams of freedom and solitude, of riding a horse across golden fields as thunderclouds roil across the sky, of sleeping peacefully under the arc of the Milky Way, of waking alone to the bitter light of dawn. In these dreams, we test ourselves on the anvil of self-sufficiency. In these dreams, we know the grandeur of an untrammeled continent. We are intimate with animals. We are intimate with earth.

Russell remarks—quite astutely, I think—that while ranchers inhabit this world of intimate intercourse with nature, they do not typically spend any time analyzing their relationship either to the land or to their own "animal body." Simply put, they don't have time to spend interrogating the Western dream. They are too busy working in it.

> In the course of this job, they see sunrises, mud puddles, hoarfrost, willows, aspens, junipers, pines, rimrock, slickrock, ponds, stream banks, meadows, gullies, sunsets, and stars. They touch horsehair, cowhide, horns, bones, wounds, rope, and fence posts. Centaurlike, they can run twenty miles an hour, cover thirty miles a day, and have a great view all the while. They are physically alert and competent because they must be. They learn to endure. They live with their own company. The feel at home in the dark.

"Buckaroos" (the term is a corruption of the Spanish *vaquero*, "cowboy") will be the first to tell you theirs is not a lifestyle for everyone, nor is every man up to it. In *The Cowboy Kind*, a coffee-table compendium of western lore edited by Darrell Arnold, New Mexico rancher Stuart Major sums up the specific commitment it takes: "We ride every day—every day we're on a horse. If you've got ambition enough to get out there, there is always plenty of work to do. This life ain't for just anybody. If you don't understand it and like it, you can't do it. It's the longest hours, lowest pay, and hardest work you can find. If it ain't in ya, you wouldn't be satisfied." Texas ranch manager Buster McLaury states the case even more simply. You don't do it for money, that's for sure. "You do it because it is really what you want to do. If you truly want it bad enough, then you'll do it. All you have is knowing you're the man who can do the job. And that's enough." Another New Mexico rancher, Jeff Lane, spins it this way: "Life is pretty special, and the people around you are special. Anyone who starts to think he is unique or better than anyone else is foolish. For all that you might do, there will always be others who will accomplish much more and be much greater." And you may or may not make it. So-called day cowboy and western singer R. W. Hampton explains, "You can work as a cowboy and you can draw a cowboy's wages for a long time before they will say you are a cowboy. I've heard a man say, 'Did ol' so-and-so ever make a cowboy?' and the other guy will say, 'Nah, he never made it,' or 'Yeah, by golly, he made a good one.'" He made it, the message is clear, by hard work and harder living.

Come, and suffer. In the cowboy world view, the capacity to suffer, to sacrifice, to do without, to tough things out—to "cowboy up" in other words—is the measure of a man. "What," Gib had asked Doug, "makes you think you deserve nice things?" We would subsequently come to understand that this question bore a then unspoken, probably unspeakable, force for him. A man who was a rancher to his very core, whose body and soul were adapted to the daily rhythms of doing whatever needed to be done, who never took time off and wouldn't have known what to do with himself if he did . . . this man was beginning to experience his own body's turning against him. Odd, anomalous sensations of numbness in his extremities, muscle weakness and weird spasms, the occasional fainting episode, all were early symptoms of what would eventually develop into the degenerative illness that would take his life: ALS ("Lou Gehrig's disease"), or something very like it, his doctors were never quite sure.

What makes you think you deserve nice things? It was, for him, a natural enough question. What came just as naturally was the ready assumption that if one essential part of ranch life is to absorb physical abuse, another equally inevitable part is to inflict it. After all, one cannot *be* a cowboy—"punching" cows, "breaking" colts—without understanding from the get-go that life hurts. And that you are bound to be the cause of a lot of that hurt. It doesn't bear too much thinking about, not if you want to keep your wits about you, anyway.

On one occasion, during the years we were leasing pasture land to cattlemen, Doug went out with our then-lessee, whom I'll call Roy, to ride the range in search of a calf Roy had spotted, that needed some doctoring. With no small difficulty, they eventually managed to isolate the right cow and her wounded calf from the herd. Roy expertly lassoed the little critter, and Doug helped hold the terrified calf steady, while Roy applied some salve to its wounded leg and gave it a shot of antibiotics. The calf's mother, meanwhile, looked on from a few yards away, mooing her disapproval. All the while Roy was talking to the calf, softly, soothingly, almost tenderly. When he was done, he released the rope, and gave the calf a swift, hard kick in the butt, hallooing at it to get the hell back where it belonged. "What'd you do that for?" Doug asked.

"Do what?" Roy responded.

"Kick the little guy like that. He was going to run right back to his mama anyway."

Roy whistled under his breath. "It's just a calf. And we spent this whole entire morning chasin' after the danged little son of a bitch."

Roy's a longtime friend of ours. He is the same person who sometimes used his three-year-old son as an electric fence tester. It's not only the casual infliction of pain that warrants particular note here, it's the uneasy coupling of affection and emotional distancing at work in the cowboy's relationship to his world. Jane Tompkins takes up this theme in her study of the western ethos:

> In the course of providing a set of master images that tell men how to behave in society, Westerns teach men that they must take pain and give it, without flinching. The education of the hero and of the hero's audience moves in the direction of induration, hardening. We are taught not to cry out or show that we care. For to show that your heart is not hard, to cry when you feel pain, your own or someone else's, is sentimental . . . soft, womanish, emotional, the very qualities the Western hero must get rid of to be a man.

Sharman Apt Russell strikes a similar theme in *Kill the Cowboy*. Even as he inhabits our dreams of freedom and suchlike, she suggests, the cowboy also reminds us that such seductive dreams inevitably have a dark side. The cowboy's affinity with the land, his intimate connection to his surroundings, is offset by his need to control and subdue that same nature from which he derives his livelihood, indeed his life. Grass is there for the grazing. Livestock are destined for feedlot and slaughterhouse. Wild predators that interfere with that destiny— wolves, cougars, coyotes—deserve to be shot. The same goes for elk or deer that "compete" with cows for grass.

And it also goes, an outsider who ventures into this territory comes uneasily to suspect, for anybody who's just too damned "differnt." In a chapter entitled "Neighbors," *The Cowboy Kind* quotes one Little Walt Greeman, co-owner of a Colorado spread:

> The hippies cause us some troubles, but this place is no different than anywhere else. You've always got somebody who will give you hell. It doesn't make any difference where you are. Like when we sprayed the alfalfa for worms, they gave us hell about the pesticide. We have a little trouble with their dogs. They give them their freedom and those dogs like to run our cattle. Every once in a while, some of those dogs disappear.

That's prairie justice for you. The law of the frontier. The cowboy way. "I had to shoot your dog."

A social psychologist would, I suppose, say Judd was simply a product of his environment. My feminist colleagues would remark the role violence plays in the "construction of masculinity" in these parts. And, in theory, I would certainly concur. The problem is, you can't live in this country, you can't survive it, "in theory."

AFTER AYLA

Of course, we had to apologize and to make restitution for the chickens. The day after Ayla's shooting, when we got back from taking her to the Miles City vet, one or the other of us—I cannot remember which—managed to "cowboy up" enough to call Judd's number. Their answering machine picked up and a message was left. Later in the day, the phone rang and, with some trepidation, I lifted the receiver. It was Judd's wife—I'll call her Chris—returning our call. She began by saying she was sorry about the dog. That made it marginally easier for me to string a few words together. I apologized about the chickens. I asked how much we needed to give them, to make good on the chickens. Sixty-five dollars? We'd drop a check in the mail next time we got into town, first of the week.

Then I told Chris that Ayla was in fact still alive, and the vet in Miles City was guardedly optimistic about her chances. "Oh, that's great news," she replied, sounding authentically relieved. "No dog's first mistake should ever have to be its last. I'm glad to hear that, I really am." I thanked her for that, and we said good-bye.

For all I know, to this day she probably believes our little Ayla survived.

And for all I know, Judd has likely long since forgotten he even shot her.

It is not, after all, as if we were able to sustain anything like a cordial relationship with these people. Mind you: A couple of years before Ayla's shooting, Doug and I had been among a cohort of Chalk Buttes area ranchers who helped fight a forest fire on their place. Judd had, I'm pretty sure, been among the ranchers who, during a vicious fire season shortly thereafter, came over to help put out a grass fire on our BLM allotment. We had had the usual sorts of interactions with Judd and Chris in our first several years here. Judd had sold Doug some used machinery he needed. I had gone to a Mary Kay cosmetics party over at their place once. We would sometimes run into one or the other of them, when visiting mutual friends.

After Ayla . . . Well, immediately afterward, we seriously contemplated leaving, putting the place on the market, getting the hell out of Dodge. It was hard not to take Ayla's death personally, as a slap in the face for being outsiders. We were both pretty raw, pretty emotionally exposed over it, for very a long time. For me, the predominating emotion was anger. For Doug, it was something more complex—something I don't pretend to be able to fully understand, other than comprehending that there was something insidiously man-to-man about it. Judd had to shoot Doug's dog, because that's the cowboy way, the law of the frontier. A lot more was a stake than a few chickens. Or a lot less, depending upon one's perspective on codes of masculinity.

Judd killed Ayla thirteen years ago. Time does not heal all wounds. Some remain disturbingly fresh, festering, like scabs itching to be picked at. But, like Roy with that calf, perhaps there's a certain wisdom to just slapping some salve on the itch, and kicking that suppurating memory back into its place. And remembering to ride a wide berth around it in the future, whenever possible.

It has been some years now since I've crossed the street in town to avoid having to say "Howdy" to Judd or Chris. We have had occasion, as far-flung neighbors in this part of the world must, to talk on the phone—spreading the word about incoming weather or power outages, trying to track down the owners of random cattle that turned up on our place or an out-of-place buffalo on theirs, the usual sorts of things. Four years ago, we mourned together, if on opposite sides of the room, at Gib's funeral. More recently, we made small talk at a housewarming.

Forgiveness doesn't come easily. But, haltingly, it nonetheless comes. I have to believe that.

AN EPILOGUE

In August of the summer of Ayla's death, a vicious storm roiled its way through Carter County. It was the season for thunderstorms, but the one that blew up that late summer afternoon was unlike anything we had ever seen, nor have we seen another storm quite like it since. One moment, the sky was deep blue and the air dead calm. The next, a strong wind had come up out of the south, bringing with it storm clouds that churned the sky, gray-green, mile-high monsters, behemoths tumbling over and falling into one another. It was like watching time-lapse film of storm clouds, except that this was happening in real time.

And very, very quickly. Shopworn clichés and insurance disclaimers notwithstanding, it was like watching an act of God.

Our mama llama Jessica nosed her baby toward the shelter of a three-sided shed. Doug came tearing back in the pickup, from some chore he'd been doing back behind the house. I, meanwhile, was running around the yard, gathering up gardening tools, dog bowls, anything that wasn't fastened to the ground. Then the storm exploded on us with ferocious intensity. Rain came down in shock waves, wind gusts punctuated by jagged flashes of lightning, the thunder rumbling, growling, crashing. But the worst of those ever-darkening time-lapse clouds, blessedly, steered clear of our valley. The worst of the storm rode the top of the divide, along the Chalk Buttes. While we were getting rain by the barrelful, sheets of hail were falling up there.

The storm subsided as quickly as it had come. After a while, power was restored. After a while longer, it got to be possible to get around the country again. A few days later, when we ventured up our road to see how our alfalfa field had fared, the landscape told its own story. Numerous trees, ponderosa pines most of them, had been broken like toothpicks. But our hayfield had survived. As had one of our neighbor Floyd's fields, the one abutting ours. But his field adjacent to that one showed significant damage: some of the wheat mangled here, some cut off at the stem there, yet other parts of the field seemingly untouched. And his next field over, which had a few days previous been thick with summer wheat, looked as if it hadn't been planted at all. It had, as it were, been storm fallowed.

Word gradually got around, about the nature and extent of local damage. The Chalk Buttes area had been the epicenter of this weather event, which the National Weather Service had classified as "tornadic." Given the intensity of the storm, Carter County had made out OK, all things taken into account. Considerable crop damage had been reported, but property damage was sporadic. Some folks reported hail damage to their vehicles. Most folks lost a few shingles from their roofs. There was one ranch, however, that suffered a more direct hit: a windmill blown over, satellite dish upended, the main house's roof half gone, and most of the windows shattered.

That ranch was Judd's place.

I didn't feel good about that. I didn't feel bad about it, either.

Bison cow in winter. Photo by Doug Stange.

CHAPTER 5
Animal Affinities

🐾 I have never been to a branding. In Carter County, this fact marks me as being not simply "differnt," but downright antisocial. Brandings are, after all, a crucial element of each spring's social schedule. Friends, neighbors, and relatives are expected to pitch in, making the rounds from one ranch to another throughout the month of May. The work is long and hard, the socializing afterward a welcome respite for folks, before returning home to get back to their own ranch chores. Most of the labor is voluntary; the reward is a big meal—beef being the main event, naturally—washed down by a few beers. And it is reciprocal. Brandings therefore constitute an important cost-saving dimension of the cattleman's economy. And as social occasions, veritable rites of spring, they rank right up there with family reunions, anniversary celebrations, and high school graduations.

In popular mythology, brandings are akin to barn raisings. Distinctly American rural rituals, they are emblematic of the ways a community can pull together to get a big job done, neighbor helping neighbor. But at barn-raisings—in which I have participated, although in upstate New

York, not here—the pain and suffering involved are generally along the lines of, say, a sore thumb from a misplaced hammer stroke, or a strained back from exercising muscles too seldom used, or a wicked sunburn. In the movie version of this rural custom, the credits could easily read: "No animals were harmed in the making of this film."

Not so, for any branding. Even the Hollywood version allows as how it isn't an entirely pleasant experience for the calves involved, although in the cinematic cliché, each calf is expertly roped, quickly immobilized by agile cowhands, subjected to the momentary sting of a single branding iron, and within minutes is scampering about once more, reunited with its mom and playmates and looking none the worse for wear.

Real life is rather more complicated. And it is not for the fainthearted. An editor's note in the July 2008 issue of *Rural Montana* magazine (published by the state's electrical cooperative association) took umbrage with readers who complained that a photo they had published, of a calf being branded, had "glamorized" cruelty to animals. The photo in question—picturing a calf stretched its full length on the ground, with its legs rope bound, an iron yoke around its neck to hold it down, smoke pouring from the branding iron being applied to its flank, its tongue lolling and its eyes rolled back in their sockets—is reasonably grisly, by my lights. But, the editors chided: "It's branding, folks. Two red-hot irons, multiple inoculations, occasional ear clips, tags, and castration are all part of the drill."

So there.

And while we're at it, the "drill" may also entail dehorning, ear marking (cutting a slit or a notch in one ear, as an additional identifying mark), wattling (cutting the calf's neck to create a distinctively disfiguring scar for marking), and/or the application of an insecticide drench, some of which have a tendency to be flammable and therefore dicey to use around burning coals and red-hot branding irons. An ad for one such product used to run on the Miles City radio station, KATL. (Sound out the call letters. Their motto is "Rockin' 'til the cows come home.") It boasted the product's particular advantage at branding time: "No more fireworks!"

For our first several years in Carter County, I managed to wiggle my way out of invitations to join the seasonal fun. More often than not I had the bona fide excuse of not having arrived home yet, at the end of the school year. Or failing that, pretending not to have. It is reasonably easy to keep a low profile in this country when one wants to.

Doug wasn't so lucky. He generally was responsible for the ear tag-ging aspect of the "drill," one of the several tasks that occur more or less simultaneously, once a calf has been immobilized. Things can get pretty chaotic, and on one occasion he found himself on the receiving end of a sci-fi sounding Ralogun, wielded by a fellow buckaroo. The Ralogun delivers subcutaneous implants of Ralgro, a hormonal growth enhancer widely used in the beef industry. Exposure to this class of hormones has been suspected of increasing breast cancer risk for girls and women (and, for that matter, lactating cows: its use is contraindicated for heifer calves intended for reproduction). Fortunately Doug didn't exactly take a hit of the stuff himself. He was just pricked by the needle that implants the drug, and subsequently suffered no discernable ill effects.

Doug invariably came home from a branding filthy, exhausted, and depressed. He wasn't above trying to make me feel guilty for not having gone with him . . . but he never pressed me to rise to the occasion, either. I did toy with the idea. I knew that sooner or later, one way or another I'd be writing about branding, and probably ought to know what I was talking about from first hand experience. But I knew, equally well, that participating in an event that I regarded as animal cruelty pure and simple, and rationalizing my participation as "research," would place me in a light at least as morally ambiguous as those wranglers who rhapsodize about the lofty cultural traditions surrounding branding day. Besides, I didn't need to have been there to imagine the acrid smell of burning hair, the sizzle of living flesh under the irons, the squeals of pain, the choking clouds of manure-laden dust, the shouts, the cursing, the sweat, the blood, or the laughter.

After the Ralgro incident, Doug decided he didn't need to be there either, and began finding reasons—they may not have been excuses, exactly, but they were plausible enough—for having to decline invitations to brandings. After a while, the invitations stopped coming. We were both relieved.

From our neighbors' vantage point, we knew, we were essentially thumbing our noses at a tradition so venerable that, along with a few others—the cattle drive, the rodeo, and more recently and perversely, the demolition derby—it epitomizes the spirit of the cowboy West. An article published in 1997 in the Lubbock [Texas] Avalanche-Journal and titled "Annual ritual of branding cattle still alive on many ranches," stated the case succinctly: "The battle between man and beast and a harsh environment all remain part of a tradition." Colorado rancher and writer Peter Decker describes branding as "a perfectly choreographed cowboy ballet in which everyone moves carefully within a specifically defined space to perform a very specialized job." Promotional materials for Arizona's Grand Canyon West guest ranch proclaim that "Cattle brands have been used as a mark of identification at some time in all countries and civilizations. Cattle branding scenes can be seen on Egyptian Tomb walls dating back as far as 2000 B.C." The grandiosity of such claims set aside, it's clear that when it comes to branding, we are solidly in the territory of The Way Things Have Always Been Done. Cowboy literature about branding is fairly dripping with tradition. But, more prosaically, what it comes down to is that if it was good enough for Dad, then it's good enough.

And besides, cattle ranchers will quickly and invariably add, it's required by law.

Well, sort of. It is incumbent upon livestock producers to make their animals identifiable. Hot iron branding, a holdover from the days of free-ranging cattle herds on the open prairie, has conventionally been assumed to be the best form of identification ever since then, in cattle country. But it is far from the only way of doing it these days. There are actually several far more humane alternatives for marking animals. Freeze branding, for example, uses liquid nitrogen to permanently leave an indelible mark on an animal's hair, and is relatively pain free. There are ID chip implants that can be read electronically, and RFIDs, radio frequency ID ear tags. Bar-coded ear clips have also been tried and, with somewhat more success, ear tattoos. The noted animal behavior specialist Temple Grandin, of Colorado State University, advocates abandoning hot-iron branding in favor of DNA testing which, she believes, would "fingerprint" cattle for ready identification.

As bison ranchers, Doug and I haven't had to wrestle with these alternatives. Buffalo calves do not tolerate hot-iron branding well—it can throw them into shock—and so, aside from a few ranchers who have experimented with freeze-branding, as a rule bison producers stick to using ear tags for identification. So I suppose our neighbors could accuse us of being hypocritical, where their traditions are concerned. Still, we have the 75,000-member American Veterinary Medical Association on our side: the AVMA strongly urges finding alternatives to hot-iron branding, and played a key role in leading the USDA, in 1995, to ban the particularly brutal practice of face-branding cattle being imported from Mexico.

Cattlemen routinely characterize critics of traditional branding as a bunch of bleeding heart animal-rights crazies. But you certainly don't have to be a vegan to question whether a calf's first initiatory step on the way to becoming meat should be the experience of being grilled while still alive. With large franchise chains like Burger King and Applebee's taking the step of asking their vendors not to supply iron-branded meat, you would think cattlemen would think twice. Yet a 2002 story in the *Dallas Morning News*, titled "Cattle branding is chapping more than just PETA's hide," shows how slippery the argument about branding "tradition" actually is. Countering PETA's reasonable charge that branding is "more of a tradition than a necessity," a Texas cattleman explains: "We do, of course, embrace our lifestyle and appreciate those good points about it, [but] there is not much romance left. We're trying to produce a product."

A product. Hence the growth enhancers and suchlike, and the resorting to a method that—whatever its questionable status as ritual or tradition—is, to be sure, cost-effective. Long before they are shipped off to feedlots, to be "finished" on grain supplements (laced with more growth-enhancing hormones and a hefty cocktail of antibiotics), beef calves are effectively commodified to the extent that not only is their pain inconsequential, it is also possible to overlook the aftereffects of the third-degree burns administered by those hot irons. Some calves manage to heal up fairly quickly, yet in any given pasture you'll also see animals sporting inflamed, suppurating wounds weeks, occasionally even months, after branding. And, of course, a few calves never make it from the branding back to the pasture at all.

FANTASIES OF DOMESTICATION

My cattle raising neighbors would protest, of course, that in pointing out such unpleasant facts I am starting to sound like an animal rights "anti" myself. And they would further protest that what I, and PETA, do not understand is that they really do care about their stock, and they really do know what's best for them. And this is where things get sticky, indeed. Because, in balance, they would be correct. After all, I'm the one who assiduously avoids getting up close and personal with beef cattle. I don't even eat them, if I can avoid it. I didn't grow up in these parts; I don't know the culture of cows and cowpunchers.

Barney Nelson, however, is someone who does, and so I look to her for guidance. A Texas cattle rancher and a professor of English at

Sul Ross State University in Alpine, she says her "rural family heritage stretches back for fifteen agricultural generations on North American soil." (She is a direct descendent of the Mayflower's William Bradford.) In her fascinating book *The Wild and the Domestic: Animal Representation, Ecocriticism, and Western American Literature,* Nelson takes dead aim on the fantasies urban Americans harbor about the quotidian facts of ranch life: "Western movies always leave out the cowshit and horseshit; ever notice that?" she observes. "Shit just doesn't fit into the western myth. Buffalo chips might be useful as fuel, but not cow chips—well, maybe in India, but not in the American West." She goes on to say:

> Cowshit creates memories. When it appears between your sandaled toes, under hat brims, inside a torn shirt pocket, up a pant leg, gets into boots or eyes or hair, is imbedded between your teeth, or smeared all over your rope—usually you have just finished learning a cheap lesson. The cowshit sort of says, "And don't ever try that again."

Of course, in constructing this paean to bovine excreta, Nelson herself is mining another vein of western mythology, the one having to do with cowboy endurance. Maybe it takes one myth to deconstruct another, but in any case her instinct here—both as a rancher and as a writer—seems sound. In order to achieve a realistic view of cattle, one must quite literally work from the ground up. Nelson writes:

> I think it's time someone stuck up for cows. They have been getting a lot of bad press lately. Cows supposedly produce methane gas, eat like locusts, cave in creek banks, compete with wildlife, drop disgusting "pies" around campgrounds, and just, in general, look stupid.
>
> I've worked enough cows that sometimes even I have a hard time coming up with something nice to say about them. I've been stepped on, dragged, butted, pushed, kicked, smashed, knocked down, run over by, humiliated by, and hurt by the beasts, especially my feelings. I've also questioned their intelligence on many occasions. Baby calves are cute, true, but only for a couple of weeks.

Why make the effort, then, to defend the critters? Maybe it's because we are what we read as well as what we eat, and Nelson finds more god's honest truth in a pile of cowshit than in the spate of literature that's come out in recent years, generated by environmentalists and animal rights activists, attacking the cattle industry. And she has a point. No, make that several, with all of which our Carter County neighbors would, I think, readily concur.

First of all, Nelson notes the fairly widespread prejudice that sees farmers and ranchers as undereducated hicks who don't appreciate the ecological complexity of the lands upon which they have for generations lived and, in good times, prospered. Whether it's coming from government agents or professional environmentalists, this prejudice yields the same result—and one which she cannily implies would be recognized as ethnocentric bigotry were it applied, say, to Eskimos or other natives, with regard to their knowledge of their land:

> Observations by modern rural people whose families have lived on the land for four or five generations are . . . usually considered useless anecdotes. College-educated people who have managed farms and ranches for forty years are frequently required to submit to the judgments and ideas of young, newly graduated federal employees whose field experience can be totaled in hours, and who may never have seen the particular range they were sent to manage.

At least in theory, "science" trumps mere "anecdote" every time—even if that science turns out to be pure junk, like the dryland farming craze that drove the westward expansion during the homesteading era, and left millions of acres of formerly healthy grassland depleted of its fragile layer of topsoil.

Working from her own shit-imbued experience of cattle ranching, Nelson takes especially accurate aim at the anthropomorphic fantasies harbored by urban-based environmentalists—especially those influenced by animal protectionism. She cites Jeremy Rifkin's "comical tirade" against the beef industry, *Beyond Beef: The Rise and Fall of the Cattle Culture*, as a particularly egregious example of an unfortunately all too common way of thinking about animals in American popular culture. Here is Rifkin's description of the bull:

> The bull has always reminded us of our maleness—he represents generativeness, ferocious power, domination, and protection. He is the most territorial of beasts, passionate and aggressive, the embodiment of fertilizing power. The bull is pure unrestrained energy. A formidable force, he is fearless, unreconcilable, and purposeful.

Rifkin's archetypal bull is, as Nelson rightly points out, nowhere to be found on the open range: "The bulls I've known spend 99.9 percent of their time napping. They have no problem restraining their energy, and I've never seen them protect a single thing. Because of their size and weight, bulls do have power, but they seldom have it under control."

It does kind of make one wonder about just whose "maleness" is at stake in Rifkin's argument. And then there is his surreal description of the cow:

> The cow is one of the most gentle and sublime creatures, the embodiment of patience. Her enlarged udders are available for all the world to suckle. She is nurturer and nourishment, the giver of life. She is self-contained, peaceful, a serene image, grounded and tranquil. The cow is purity, and represents the forces of benevolence and good in the world.

"That one is especially funny," Nelson chortles. "It's obvious that Rifkin has been looking at too many four-color calendars of cows and doesn't really know the meaning of 'sublime.' . . . Cows don't let their milk down unless they want to, and a bawlin' old cow, slingin' snot and stretched out on her side in the rocks and cactus, probably doesn't want to. Unless you smell like a calf, you won't get any milk, and even then you dang well better smell like *her* calf. She's sublime, alright."

Still, Nelson can only make her point in backhanded defense of real-world beef cattle by knocking dairy cows: "You'll never see a Hereford milk cow. Those black-and-white refrigerator magnets and salt-and-pepper shakers ain't cows," she says. "I don't know what they are." And this is where her apologia pro beef cattle becomes both interesting and problematic, for me. I couldn't agree more with her, about the nature-faking—and the downright naïveté—involved in so much popular writing about the lifeways of animals, both domestic and wild. And, while our bison are wilder bovine cousins of her beef cows, her descriptions of herd structure and behavior generally ring true: the smarter, older cows are the real decision makers in any bison herd, and bulls lead a fairly peripheral existence, except during breeding season, when their peak activity occurs at night and they tend to spend the days apart from the herd, snoozing.

I also heartily agree with the central thesis of Nelson's book, that the conceptual distinction between "wild" and "domestic" causes all sorts of trouble. It has led us too readily to sort our experience of the natural world into oppositional categories of good versus bad (or, at best, not-so-good) animals and plants. Nelson says—and I know this feeling as well—that with "one foot in literature and the other on rural grazing land," she finds herself "continually trying to negotiate between cows and my fellow environmentalists." She holds the latter accountable for spreading a fundamental untruth: "The idea that domestic animals are somehow more destructive, less intelligent, and less valuable than wild grazers" which "seems to be rooted in the wild/domestic dichotomy I find rampant in the popular press, science, and American literature."

Well, yes, and no. After twenty-plus years in cattle country, fifteen of them raising bison, I have had ample opportunity to compare the two species. I can say for a fact that beef cattle are more destructive of stock wells, gates, and fences than buffalo. They are less efficient and more selective grazers, harder on the prairie, especially in dry years. They consume gallons more water per head. They require more chemicals, in the form of vaccines and dewormers and insecticides, to keep them reasonably healthy. They demand more veterinary care. They make more noise. I even think they may attract more flies.

And beef cattle are definitely less brainy than bison, by any reasonable measure. You will never see a herd of bison jammed into the gateless corner of a pasture, for no apparent reason, on a hundred-degree high-summer afternoon, madly fanning flies with their tails and, in the process, generating additional body heat. Nor, in winter, do bison stand in a few inches of snow, their unwavering gaze directed toward the anticipated hay truck; instead, they scratch the snow away to graze the grasses underneath. Bison calves have the sense to get out of the way of an oncoming vehicle; beef calves have a penchant for waiting until you're practically on top of them, then darting into your path. As to giving birth: bison cows do it on their own, without benefit (or need) of the mechanical "calf pullers" or C-sections upon which cattlemen routinely rely.

There *are* some meaningful distinctions between domesticated and wild animals. And bison are wild animals. The fact that they can be raised domestically does not mean they are, or can or should be, domesticated. They can be conditioned, to some extent, to tolerating a certain amount of interaction with humans, especially if a bit of compressed grain feed cake is involved. They can be "managed" up to a point. But the conventional wisdom among bison folk is that you basically can only get a herd of buffalo to do what they essentially want to do anyway—they like to let you think it's your idea. You have to learn to think like them, to work *with* them, and keep a respectful distance. It is a fascinating transactional relationship, really—much like that between falconers and their birds. The animals are, and remain, wild in relationship to their human partners. And they are smart, in the same ways that pronghorn antelope and mule deer and golden eagles and red-tailed hawks—other species that coevolved with them in this landscape—are smart. Ways, that is, which often differ vastly from what looks like intelligence to a lot of humans, particularly those modern humans who spend too much time indoors.

Barney Nelson holds—and here, in principle, I agree with her—that one problem with a strict dichotomy between domestic and wild is that it reinforces the distinction between human and nonhuman animals. Yet this distinction doesn't always play out so neatly, or invariably, as she suggests. In a very interesting study published several years ago and based upon extensive crosscultural data about societies less "developed" than our own, anthropologist Susan Kent found that among hunter-gatherers and hunter-horticulturalists, *all* animals are regarded as intellectual beings. They are, in fact, seen as having intellectual capabilities not unlike, and at times even superior to, our own. In these contexts, one hears stories of Trickster Coyote, Spider Woman, Raven, White Buffalo Woman: wise and canny creatures all, bestowers of knowledge and skill. Kent found, however, that once large-scale agriculture enters the cultural scene, and with it the differentiation between wild and domestic, people begin to make sharp distinctions between the intellectual capabilities of humans and animals. But these distinctions don't always work out in the same ways. People who maintain an active tradition of hunting, in addition to raising domestic animals, tend to regard wildlife as intelligent, and domestic animals as, well, stupid. People in societies like our own, in which human hunting plays no prominent role whereas the domestication of animals does, tend to strip *all* animals of their status as intellectual entities. In this light, Nelson's desire to "stick up" for beef cattle, cowshit and all, makes good sense.

But, hunter that I am, and to some extent I suppose bearing out Susan Kent's research, I cannot shake the idea that cattle are on the dim-witted side. You cannot blame them for it. In agricultural terms, domestication is the science of selective breeding, to ensure a more desirable end product. (There's that word again: product.) Desirability, to be sure, is a matter of perspective. Geneticist Helen Spurway coined a term for animals like today's beef cattle and battery hens, animals genetically engineered for feedlots and factory farms: "goofies." They are, in her view, pathetic freaks of nature, with all the wildness, and adaptability, bred out of them. They are the sad result of the millennia-long march of domestication. They are designed to be mere commodities. They are as we, humankind, have made them, victims of our manipulation.

Or are they? One of the more interesting trends in contemporary thinking about the evolution both of species and of cultures is the idea that we humans have been far less in control of things than we would like to believe. Or, at least, not in the precise ways we would like to believe. On the one hand it is true that, as Michael Pollan argues in *The Botany of Desire*, "that space, which is the one we often call 'the wild,' was never quite as innocent of our influence as we like to think," and, indeed, "even the wild now depends on civilization for its survival." Nonetheless, as he goes on to demonstrate, in the process of domesticating plants for our human use and enjoyment, we have been taken advantage of, for their own evolutionary ends, by those very flora we thought we were manipulating. Indeed, they have had their way with us. If they now depend upon us for their continued survival, that is in a sense an ironic form of historical payback. Read Pollan's book, and you will never look at a tulip or an apple in the same way again.

Science writer Stephen Budiansky mounts a kindred argument, regarding animals, in his *The Covenant of the Wild: Why Animals Chose Domestication*—the subtitle of which announces his intention to turn conventional wisdom about domestication on its head. That conventional wisdom looks something like the *Far Side* cartoon, in which three wolves in the Upper Paleolithic are spying on a human encampment, outside a cave entrance. There, by the fire, sits another wolf, along with three fur-clad cave men. In the caption, one wolf is saying to the others, "It's Bob, all right . . . but look at those vacuous eyes, that stupid grin on his face—he's been domesticated, I tell you!" Cartoonist Gary Larson is here playing off the notion, developed out of anthropological literature, that the process of domesticating animals—and the dog is the earliest, and therefore classic case in point—began when individual humans adopted wild canines as pets. This is known to happen, to this day, among various aboriginal and tribal peoples.

Eventually, or so the conventional thinking goes, these now-tamed wild things were bred for desirable qualities like docility and hunting prowess, and produced ever more accommodating offspring. You start with a wolf, exercise some patience over time, and voila!, end up with a Chihuahua. As the Soviet biologist D. K. Belyaev demonstrated some thirty years ago, you can literally turn a line of foxes into veritable lapdogs in the course of about twenty years.

But that this can be done, in a captive breeding situation, does not mean it is how it actually happened in the first place. Budiansky points to the "extraordinary high failure rate of man the domesticator." No matter how many individual baby raccoons, or orphaned fawns, or bear cubs Native peoples have for centuries adopted as pets, these species at large have not become the least bit domesticated. The ancient Egyptians had an economy based upon cattle herding. Nonetheless, adept as they were at hybridizing their herds to produce superior cows, they never succeeded in domesticating wild ibex, or hyenas, or gazelles—not that they didn't try. Yet, as Budiansky observes, several millennia before the rise of Egyptian culture, Neolithic agriculturalists, "people who had never built a fence or mowed a hayfield, succeeded in domesticating virtually every animal that even today, more than five thousand years later, occupies a place of importance in our homes and fields." How could this be?

The way out of this apparent historical conundrum is so startlingly simple that evolutionary biologists failed to light upon it until relatively recently: Some animal species clearly found domestication to be to their own evolutionary advantage. They, as Budiansky puts it, "chose us as much as we chose them." It probably began as an opportunistic, and more or less casual, relationship—wolves lurked at the fringes of human encampments, to scavenge the food waste that hunting parties left behind when they moved on, and eventually became cooperative members of the hunting band itself. Of course, it would take a special sort of wolf to do this, one not terribly troubled by close contact with a fellow predator, and who knew how to defer to human authority when either necessary or advantageous. As hunting began to give way to small-scale horticulturalism and previously nomadic people started to establish settlements, the stage was set not merely for the coexistence between humans and wolves-turning-into-dogs, but for the coevolution, along with human culture itself, of various hitherto wild species. Dogs were the earliest domesticated animals; they've been around for about thirteen thousand years. With the rise of agriculturalism ten millennia ago, other species followed: sheep and goats roughly nine thousand years ago, cattle roughly seven thousand, and horses—the most recently domesticated of large animals—about five thousand years ago.

During all that time, of course, wild bison were inhabiting the broad expanse of North America, as were Native peoples, some of them hunter-foragers, others agriculturalists. There were also bison in Europe, as well as aurochs, which after the last Ice Age were the progenitors of both dairy and beef cattle. There are still some wild bison in eastern Europe: wisents (*Bison bonasus*). Currently listed as a threatened species and living on nature preserves, they are somewhat smaller relatives of the American bison, or buffalo (*Bison bison*). The wild European auroch, which never roamed North American shores, has gone extinct.

Why did the aurochs "choose" domestication, while the bison did not? As Budiansky, and more recently Jared Diamond in *Guns, Germs, and Steel,* have suggested, some animal species appear simply more willing to trade off some of their wildness for the material advantages— food, shelter, security from predators—afforded by dependence on humans. Others do not especially need to. The same thing seems true of plants. Wheat, which derives from a species of hard grass (*aegilops*), seems to have been domesticated in the Near East ten thousand years ago. Oak trees, on the other hand, have for millennia foiled human attempts to domesticate them.

Taking the long view of history, of course, it is clear that the so-called march of civilization depended on the ever-more-efficient domestication of plants and animals, and this in turn took its toll on certain wild and human populations. Budiansky is worth quoting at length here:

Agriculture sowed the seeds that ensured the destruction of any competing systems. It did not matter if agriculture was a superior "invention"; by its very nature, it wrought changes in the surrounding environment and in the human social structure that guaranteed the elimination of other ways of life. The near extermination of the American bison by white hunters in the nineteenth century tends to obscure the fact that it was the arrival of European agriculture in the New World and the resulting appropriating of the bison's habitat for grazing and the destruction of its habitat for tillage that really sealed the bison's fate—and the fate of the Plains Indians who depended upon it. Even after what is universally considered a superbly successful conservation effort in the last century, the bison survives today on the merest fraction of its original range.

Domestication, on this level, is the enemy of the wild. It is not the same as taming. And among wild species resistant to it, even individually tamed babies will generally mature into wild adults. Marjorie Kinnan Rawlings's novel *The Yearling* tells that story more graphically, and eloquently, than any evolutionary biologist could ever hope to. Wild animals held in human captivity, like the endangered tigers some people seem to think they are doing a favor by collecting and keeping in cages, do not lead satisfying lives. And—just ask Siegfried and Roy—they can turn on even the most compassionate keeper. Wild animals interbred with domestics—the "wolf-dog" hybrids that surface occasionally in the West come to mind here, as do the weirdly uncoordinated offspring that result from the mating of domestic geese and ducks with wild waterfowl—these are nearly as "goofy" as Spurway's feedlot-bound cattle and factory-farm chickens.

I realize, of course, that it smacks of anthropomorphism to speak of any animal "choosing" domestication. Like so much of the language of science, it is a metaphor that aims to get at an objective truth. And yet, it may be both more and less than that, as well. I know it is dangerous, even lethal, for a wild animal, one not suited to domesticated life, to try to choose that life anyway. I know this, because one of our bison tried it.

THE BUFFALO WHO THOUGHT SHE WAS A HORSE

These things happen.

For the most part, once a bison herd has established its home range, it'll be content to stay on it. Buffalo are migratory animals, but assuming they've got a reasonable amount of room to move—a few square miles, say—they are generally content to stick close to home, especially once the cows have calved there. Nonetheless, when collective whim and/ or climatic circumstances allow, bison will on occasion exercise the prerogative to go visiting the neighbors.

The last time this happened with our herd was three years ago. Drifted snow from a late-season storm had brought down a section of boundary fence at the far end of the pasture where they had begun calving, in midspring. The season when the cows are dropping their calves is one time of year when we leave the herd pretty much to its own devices—in part because the mothers like a modicum of privacy while they bond with their new babies, and also because that is one time of year they generally don't range very far.

Note that I said "generally," there. After Doug had failed to make even a long-range bison sighting for two or three days, he began to suspect they might have breached that section of fence he'd been meaning to get around to repairing. He rode up on horseback, glassed the area, and sure enough spotted them not too far off, on our neighbor's land. He went back home to swap his horse for a truck, loaded up fence supplies and feed cake, returned to repair the busted fence, and, after a few foiled attempts, just as daylight was dwindling he managed to coax most of the herd back onto our place through the nearest gate. But the several cows that had calves on the ground had hung back. Every time he teased them close to the gate, they wound up circling back and spiraling away. This went on for another day or two, and Doug finally called the neighbor, Jerry, who said he'd be glad to help try to haze the mamas and babies back onto our place.

Jerry was riding a four-wheeler, and carrying a sidearm, just in case. Working in tandem, he and Doug managed to cautiously move the reluctant bison back where they belonged, cow-calf pair by cow-calf pair. However—and this, in our experience, is a common trait among cud-chewing quadrupeds of all kinds—there will invariably be one or two animals that don't want to get with the program. They'll hang back or wind up on the wrong side of the fence, or—worst case scenario—they'll become aggressive. Jerry found himself staring down one of our cows, who looked to him like she was fixing to charge. She may or may not have been, but unwilling as he was to give her the benefit of the doubt, Jerry shot her. Doug wasn't happy about this, but he didn't press the point with Jerry. Given the circumstances, and the need to maintain neighborly relations, that was the prudent thing to do. The cow's calf had darted away at the sound of the shot. Doug knew the baby would return later on, keep a vigil by its mom's remains, and probably be coyote bait before morning.

Ah, well. These things happen, too.

A day or two later, Doug got a call from our neighbor Erland, who had some cattle pastured nearby. "You missing a calf?" he asked. Well, yes, Doug responded; how did he know? "Because a little orange heifer turned up with my cows. You want to come over and pick her up, I've got her here in the barn." Doug drove over in the pickup, and after a good deal of scrambling about in the barn, he and Erland managed to capture the little heifer, whom Erland neatly hog-tied. They got her into the truck bed, and she made the trip back home, where Doug released her into a corral behind the house.

Now the question was, what to do with her? With her mother gone, she couldn't be released back into the herd right away. The other calves would likely beat up on her, and none of the cows would give her any milk. She was too young to make it on grass alone, and would either starve or be kicked or gored to death. Forget whatever you may have heard about there being no hierarchies in nature: every bison herd functions according to an elaborate and rigorously defined pecking order.

So Doug got a bag of cattle milk replacer. Attempts at bottle feeding didn't work, but she was happy enough to slurp the stuff out of a bucket. He reckoned that once she was a bit bigger, he could keep her in a back pasture that we call, for old times sake, the "Llama Pasture." There she could munch on good grass and have three horses—our two mares, Cali and Nina, and Cali's daughter Coya—for four-footed company. And he gave her a name: Sybil.

This much he told me on the phone, as I was still teaching in New York. "Sybil?" I asked.

"After the Sally Field character in the movie."

"So this bison baby has multiple personalities?"

"Well," he said, "no, I'm thinking more that she's a survivor, she's got tenacity to her, like that Field character." As things would turn out, the multiple personality diagnosis might not have been too wide of the mark, after all.

By the time I returned home for the summer a few weeks later, Sybil was adapted to her twice-daily buckets of milk, along with a mash made out of water and feed cake. She was a feisty little kid, and by no means interested in any close-up human contact. This, we felt, was very good. We wanted to keep the wildness in her. We weren't interested in creating a petting zoo specimen. The whole point was to get her to a developmental stage where she could safely be returned to the herd. In the meantime, the horses were good company for her. Nina dropped a foal in early June, and so Sybil gained a playmate in the little colt we named Unico. Spring slid into summer, and the little heifer continued to do well. We noted that she was developing a particularly close bond with the yearling filly, Coya, who appeared content to play the role of foster mother.

Sybil seemed plenty healthy, although she remained somewhat undersized. Nonetheless, by midsummer we thought she could safely be released. Our strategy for accomplishing this was fairly straightforward: Move the herd to a nearby pasture, where she could see and smell them on a regular basis. Recognizing her own kind would, we assumed, ignite a spark of recognition, and she would be eager to rejoin the herd. Coya, who by now had become rather protective of Sybil and who engaged in mutual grooming sessions with her, would quickly get over losing her foster child. Life would go on pleasantly, with the return of our "bum calf" (the colloquial term for bovine orphans) to the herd.

Sybil had other ideas. She expressed not a whiff of interest in the bison on the other side of the fence. At one point, we tried escorting her through a gate to join them. Doug opened the gate and with a bit of coaxing, she ambled through, ran right up the hill in the direction of two bulls who were sipping from a stock tank, got a good up close look at them, and came tearing back through the gate, before Doug had even had a chance to close it. Mission not accomplished.

We consulted Erland for advice. It appeared, we said, that our little heifer was under the impression that she was, in fact, a horse. How about isolating Sybil with one of the more docile members of the herd? we ventured, on the logic that once they "buddied up," they could be returned together to the larger group. Our cattleman friend said that made good sense to him. And so we waited for an opportunity to cut out from the herd one of the girls who was on the very bottom of the pecking order—a smallish young cow we had nicknamed "Rimfire," for her #22 ear tag (the reference is to .22 caliber rifle cartridges). We managed to separate her, and to put Sybil with her in a very secure corral.

Something of a lifelong runt, Rimfire had spent most of her time more or less alone, hanging about the fringe of the larger group, and always getting shortchanged when it came to hay in winter, or feed cake year-round. We figured that, in addition to some reliable good eats, Rimfire would be delighted finally to have a little friend to affiliate with. In fact, as we quickly learned, Rimfire was delighted finally to have another, smaller, lower-on-the-totem-pole heifer to pick on. Such is the dominance structure within the herd. Within a week, Rimfire was bored with Sybil and clearly annoyed at her reduced circumstances in the corral, while Sybil was obviously terrified of Rimfire, and miserable at being separated from Coya and company. We turned Rimfire back out with the herd, and Sybil rejoined her horse family. And we began to worry about whether we were creating a monster.

Sybil was cute, there was no doubt about that, a fluffy miniature buffalo running with the horses and frisking with the little colt. But there was also no doubt about the fact that she was beginning to fill out, and that she would continue to grow, horns and all. We considered alternative possibilities for her. We advertised her for sale—we were trying to sell Coya as well, and offered a two-for-the-price-of-one deal: Buy a Peruvian Paso filly and get a bison heifer for free! No takers. Seeing our flyer posted in town, someone called and suggested we contact a cowboy he knew, who trained cutting horses down in Broadus. He'd probably be happy to take Sybil off our hands. But we knew about this practice already: Cutting horse trainers love using bison calves to work their horses, because whereas a cattle calf will quickly tire, wilder bison calves will go at it all day long, never yielding to the chase. This struck us as a challenge for horse and rider, to be sure, but also as harassment for the bison calf involved. We didn't have the heart to subject Sybil

The bison who thought she was a horse: Sybil, Unico, and Coya. Photo by Doug Stange.

to it. We did get one other call, from a woman who said she'd always wanted to give her aging father a buffalo, for a pet. We passed on that one, too.

Fall, and then winter, loomed, and Sybil remained with the horses. We rationalized that at least with the horses, she would get her fair share of hay and feed cake, so her wintering-over with them probably wasn't such a bad idea in the long run. By the following spring Sybil, now a yearling, was beginning to catch up developmentally. And she was clearly convinced that she was a horse; indeed, horselike, she recognized her own name.

We still thought we stood one more good chance to reintegrate her into the bison herd. We were purchasing a small group of bison from a local breeder—twenty or so animals in all, mostly yearlings. This new miniherd would have to spend some time quarantined from the large resident herd. This was only superficially for health reasons. More especially, it was to acclimate them to the routine sights, sounds, and smells of our place, since this new group had been raised, if not exactly in a feedlot, nonetheless in fairly close quarters, and had been fed exclusively on hay. We wanted them to feel thoroughly at home, and get used to grazing our grass, before turning them out into a big pasture with the big herd, at which point the predictable pecking order readjustment would occur. So we put the newcomers in the Llama Pasture, with Sybil and the horses in a small adjacent pasture, to see how things would develop.

At first, the plan seemed to be working. We would often observe Sybil by herself at some remove from the horses, by the fence, with the other bison nearby on the other side. One little bull even seemed to be carrying on a flirtation with her. Bison only begin to breed at the age of two as a rule, but this looked like promising "adolescent" behavior. Yet as Sybil's second summer wore on, and as the time came when we would have to release the new buffalo into the larger herd, our heifer/horse lost interest in her Romeo, and drifted back into her daily routine with Coya and the other two mares (we had by this time sold the little colt). And, horse that she thought she was, she nonetheless began to exhibit some totally normal bison-aggressive tendencies. No longer was Coya her protector. Rather, when alpha mare Nina bit or shoved Coya (a totally normal horse-aggressive behavior), Sybil fought back. And Sybil by now had a good set of horns on her. This, we readily recognized, could get pretty ugly.

A second winter eventually set in, and with snow and cold the animals settled into a fairly nonviolent routine centered on day-to-day survival, chowing down on their daily allotment of hay and conserving energy. Meanwhile we fretted over what to do with Sybil, come spring. By that time she would be big enough to do serious harm, intentional or inadvertent, to any of the horses.

We knew, of course, what we would ultimately have to do. The only sane, and indeed humane, thing we could do would be to offer her to someone else for slaughter, or to kill her for meat ourselves. Neither prospect appealed. We had come to know this little buffalo gal as something of an individual. Shooting her for food felt as inappropriate, somehow, as does killing the deer that annually threaten my vegetable garden and Doug's apple trees, and pillage the horses' hay in winter, but that we nonetheless cannot help but regard as "home deer," neighbors of a sort, and somehow off-limits for our hunting. And we certainly didn't need the meat; we had an ample supply of bison meat, and venison from the previous fall's hunting season, in our basement freezer.

That last fact changed, however, in early May 2008, when a freakishly severe late-season blizzard dropped over two feet of wet snow on southeastern Montana, with high winds dragging down a few thousand power poles in Carter County. Doug was without electricity for eleven days (I was still in New York). We had often toyed with the idea of getting a good generator, but our rural electrical co-op has generally been so efficient in getting the power back on in a reasonable amount of time that we never really felt the need for it. This time was different; we lost the entire contents of our chest freezer. Suddenly, Sybil began to look a lot more appetizing.

A word is probably in order here, about the implications of naming animals one intends eventually to eat. Years ago, when I was teaching at St. Lawrence University in extreme upstate New York, I had a colleague who lived with his wife and two young children on a small farm. They raised chickens for eggs, and turkeys and rabbits for meat, and, annually, one calf for fall slaughter, to provide beef for the year. How, I asked them, did they help their daughter and son adjust to the idea that the cute little thing they bottle-fed in spring, and played with all summer long, would wind up on the dinner table come winter? By giving the calves names like "Meatloaf," they responded, or "Pot Roast," or "Taco." Of course, this wouldn't satisfy those animal rights proponents who like to ask "Does your food have a face?" But it made sense to me, as a way to accustom children to the fact that, well, yes, if you eat meat your dinner did at one time have not simply life and breath but also what can only, honestly, be called personality. In one of my favorite essays of his, "Survival and Sacrament," the poet/environmentalist Gary Snyder remarks, "If we do eat meat, it is the life, the bounce, the swish, of a great alert being with keen ears and lovely eyes, with foursquare feet and a huge beating heart that we eat, let us not deceive ourselves."

And so it would be with Sybil. The idea of consuming her ourselves made a certain emotional sense. The idea of killing her ourselves, however, did not. This was actually the second time we had confronted the prospect of dispatching a bison to which we had formed some personal attachment. The first time, it had been one of our original breeding bulls, named Favre. (Just as our llamas had Shakespearean names, our big breeding bulls have been named for NFL quarterbacks, with Marino, Montana, and Favre being our original three foundation bulls.) As bison bulls age, getting to around nine or ten years old, they tend to become more aggressive against both humans and each other, and potentially prey to younger bulls who are working their way up in the breeding hierarchy. Favre had been a magnificent bull: We could always tell his offspring in the herd, and they tended to inherit not only his size and good conformation, but also his tractable temperament. When he began to show that "I just want to be a buffalo" attitude, we didn't want to see him come to a bad end, gored in a fight with a younger bull. Nor did we want to see him deteriorate physically, the other likely fate of aging bulls.

We have a friend, Don, who is by profession a long-haul trucker, but by passion a hunter and rancher who skillfully butchers his own meat. Doug asked him whether he would do us the favor of slaughtering Favre. Don could have the hide, and the meat to make into his superb summer sausage; all we wanted was the head for mounting.

He agreed, and on the appointed day, Doug directed him to the back pasture where he had isolated our favorite bull. Don is an expert marksman. But he knew from experience—he also frequently contracts as the skinner for our bison hunting operation—that even a skilled shooter can have a tough time knocking down a buffalo, particularly a big bull that weighs in at roughly a ton.

"I just want to hear one shot, understand?" Doug told him. "A single shot." Don nodded somberly, and ventured out. Doug paced back and forth in our living room, his ears pricked. After a small eternity, he heard the crack of Don's rifle. Then, silence. A few minutes more, and Doug walked out to meet Don on the road back to our house. "Last time I agree to shoot somebody's goddamned pet!" Don muttered, as he cased his rifle and put it back in his truck.

We nonetheless called upon Don again in early summer 2008 about Sybil. He knew her story; indeed, he knew her, from frequent visits to our place. If he wouldn't mind shooting and butchering her for us, we would split her meat with him. And, unlike the much older Favre, this two-year-old would make succulent steaks and roasts. He said it would be a few days before he could make it out to our place. In that meantime, we treated Sybil to ample portions of feed cake, and put her on the best grass we had. The morning Don came out for her, we gave him a double portion of cake to lure her away from the horses. We waited behind. One moment, we knew, Sybil was contentedly munching, and totally focused on her favorite delicacy. The split-second of a rifle blast later, she was dead.

It was a bittersweet morning for us. Had we been able successfully to return her to her own kind, Sybil would have been among the cows that make up the resident herd. Because we had worked so hard to keep her alive after she was orphaned, because we had developed an attachment to her and felt a sense of responsibility for her, she would have joined the ranks of those favorites, like Rimfire, who—even if they are not our best cows, even if they don't reliably produce calves—would nonetheless never be targets for our hunters. We did the best we could to achieve that outcome, but our little heifer/horse chose otherwise. These things, sadly, happen, too.

And she subsequently proved delicious.

FACING NATURE HEAD-ON

I'd like to go back, for a moment, to that question: "Does your food have a face?" I don't want to jump the gun here, literally or figuratively, because I intend to take up the matter of hunting more specifically in subsequent chapters—but the hunter-forager in me has always found this cloying question to be profoundly annoying. There is, I believe, much to be said for having a face-to-face relationship with the sources of one's sustenance. There is, or at least there should be, some intimacy about our eating: about the fact that we live only by virtue of the fact that other beings die, some of them sentient and some not, at least as far as we can know. In the same essay I quoted above, in fact immediately before the line I cited, Gary Snyder reflects on the wonder of it all: "Innumerable little seeds are sacrifices to the food-chain. A parsnip in the ground is a marvel of living chemistry, making sugars and flavors from earth, air, water." The extent to which we cease to appreciate the awesomeness of this web of life reflects precisely the degree to which we, as individuals and as a society, have become alienated from the natural world upon which we depend for life and breath.

Of course, it is certainly easier to objectify our food, to turn it into a mere commodity, than to look nature squarely in the eye. There is more than one route to this kind of nature avoidance. The vegetarian or vegan gets there by posing the "food with a face" question (with its allied axiom that "Meat is Murder"), and assuming, thereby, a theoretically higher moral ground—although, and ironically, somewhat at the conceptual expense of Snyder's marvelous parsnip. The cattleman takes a different route, by focusing on generating "product" and regarding his "production" calves as, essentially, mechanisms for converting one form of protein (grass or grain) into another (meat). This is why branding bothers me so much: it is the ritual initiation by way of which the baby cow becomes meat-in-the-making, its first unwilling step on the road that ultimately leads, via feedlot, to slaughterhouse. While there are numerous points on which I disagree with animal rights activists, I can only concur with them on this one: the similarities between industrialized agriculture and slavery—including the role branding has historically played in both cases—are too obvious, and direct, to go unnoticed.

Hunting is often referred to as an intellectually honest way of being a meat-eater. I think this is true. Nonetheless, there is still some psychological sleight of hand involved in thus assuming one's conscious place, as a predator, on the food chain. I recall reading once, I do not now remember where, that in the process of upland shooting, there is a moment of concentration, a split-second when, in the hunter's mind, what initially was a bird becomes a target. I can certainly attest to the truth of this. Every pheasant season, without fail, I blow my first shooting opportunity because my breath is so taken away by the wildly cackling iridescent miracle winging skyward a few yards in front of me that I neglect to shoulder my shotgun to shoot it. But then, as the morning wears on and my focus shifts from scenery to sky, the pace set by the rhythm of the dogs scenting their way through the tall grasses,

I become part of a larger, fundamentally organic, process. The birds *do* transform themselves into targets. But that does not mean they cease to be birds. Or, dare I say it, food with faces. We are in this thing together.

The nonhunter might well ask, at this juncture, why I don't simply "hunt with a camera?" The answer has to do, in approximately equal parts, with Gary Snyder's parsnip on the one hand, and my own meat-eating sanity on the other. In neither case can I commodify nature so neatly. The pheasant expertly flushed by our springer spaniels would in some sense be objectified more decisively by being fixed in a digital image, than by being downed by a well-placed shot from my 16-gauge, retrieved by the dogs to great celebration, admired as a luminescent miracle of nature, and subsequently savored with a bottle of good wine, and cherished as the central character both of an oft-repeated story and of a perfect morning's memories.

Call this rationalization, if you like. In his marvelous poem, "The Heaven of Animals," James Dickey depicts an animal afterlife that is a hunting ground: not a "happy" one, necessarily, but a sacred, indeed a sacramental one, where predators revel in hunting with perfected skill as prey animals play their submissive parts without pain or fear, ultimately yielding themselves up to the kill, willing sacrifices in an eternal dance. That's rationalization, too, perhaps, but one in keeping with a tradition far older and deeper than the rituals of branding day—a tradition rooted in the rites and mythologies of humans who lived in closer harmony with the natural world around them, and with its painfully complex realities. A tradition that, to borrow Snyder's phrasing, links survival to sacrament.

It is a tradition that calls out the wildness in us. And it tells us that in seeking nature's face, we discover our own.

Bison bull in tall grass. Photo by Doug Stange.

CHAPTER 6
Hard Grass

ALL FLESH IS GRASS

For the cattleman, this is a literal truth, quantifiable in terms of the conversion of units of protein from vegetable to animal form. For the Biblicist, it is a metaphysical truth, an intimation of mortality and the eventual fate we all share. And for one attuned to the ghostly presences that coinhabit the eastern Montana landscape, the spirits of those here before us, it is perhaps a simple fact of life. In our beginnings are our ends.

Weather and work schedule permitting, I run most mornings. My customary jogging routes are the dusty two-track roads that lead in three different directions from our homestead. From time to time, something will catch my eye in the road ahead. Things sift to the sandy surface, fragments of the past over which we have walked or driven countless times. More often than not, such found objects are merely the detritus of earlier settlers or visitors here: antique rifle cartridges, rusted bolts and fence staples, bits of barbed wire, fragments of old Coke bottles, and suchlike. One would think, of course, that in this part of the country, the roadway might present the occasional Indian artifact.

But Bud, the former owner, bragged when he left: "Don't bother to go lookin' for any arrowheads on this place. Me and the kids already found 'em all!" He seems to have been pretty much right.

Nonetheless, the earth occasionally offers up a welcome surprise, as happened one sunny morning several years ago. I had barely jogged a quarter-mile south of our house when light glinting off a small, flat stone captured my attention. It had obviously not been shaped by natural forces. I bent down and picked it up. A semitranslucent waxy brownish color, the stone's sides had clearly been deliberately flaked to a fine edge. The fact that my right thumb nestled naturally in a depression on the stone's right side, and it fit my hand so comfortably, told me that I was holding a well fashioned scraping tool. I knew this more instinctively than intellectually, quite literally by the feel of it.

As I stood there, turning it in my hand in the July sunlight, I felt as if I had slipped through a seam in the human history of this place. I would subsequently learn that the stone that I held was a flintlike substance called chert, and that this little tool was between eight and ten thousand years old, dating well back into "Paleo-Indian" times. But from the moment I picked it up, I knew much more than that about it, and much more intimately. The person who used it was small framed and right-handed, as I am. It was almost certainly a woman's tool, since in hunter-forager groups women are generally assigned the tasks for which a small implement like this one would have been employed. On a similarly gorgeous midsummer day, she may have been using it to do some fine detailed finishing on a bit of bison hide she was working. Or she may have been using it to prepare for cooking some roots she had gathered for the communal meal later in the day. As she worked, she was serenaded by the same sounds I was now hearing—the whirring of crickets and grasshoppers snapping in the warming grass, the trill of meadowlarks and doves' coo-cooing, the occasional gurgling rush of a swooping sparrow hawk, the keening cry of a golden eagle. Leaves rustling in the light breeze comingled with the rhythm of her own soft breathing. The ancient soundscape of the prairie cannot have changed very much. Nor has the cerulean blue of its high-summer sky, nor the wafting scent of its wildflowers.

And this land was anciently inhabited. At the "Mill Iron Site," a piece of BLM land about twenty-five miles from our ranch as the crow flies, archaeologists have uncovered spear points and arrowheads from what has come to be called the Goshen Complex, a culture dating back to eleven thousand years ago, roughly contemporary with the more celebrated Clovis people of the Southwest. They were bison hunters, as bones recovered at the site attest. Doug has found on our place a slender flint arrowhead that might well be a "Goshen point." We have also, over the years, discovered a few more crudely worked quartzite knives and scrapers, their less artful construction suggesting either that they were made by very primitive artisans, or—more likely, to my way of thinking—they were fashioned quickly, for use on-site, and then discarded. My little scraper and Doug's arrowhead have about them more the look of carefully-worked tools, meant to be kept and reused.

Such artifacts are not the only traces of the past we find written into land that we, for the time being, call our own. Long before there were humans here—eons before there were humans anywhere—this was dinosaur country. Hereabouts they walked the shores of a vast inland sea. The Chalk Buttes are so named because of their whiteness. They are, however, actually comprised of sandstone, deposited here in the recession of that "Western Interior Seaway" roughly sixty-five million years ago. That was around the same time the dinosaurs were going extinct. The Carter County Museum in Ekalaka—the oldest county museum in the state—is one of thirteen stops on Montana's "Dinosaur Trail," and houses several fossilized skeletons and skulls, including that of a triceratops, collected in eastern Montana. Crews of paleontologists comb this region every summer, searching for the next big find. "Sue," the famous fully intact Tyrannosaurus rex specimen now in Chicago's Field Museum, was excavated in western South Dakota—a mere stone's throw from here, geologically speaking.

We have a hunk of rock the local museum curator verified is a dinosaur fossil. Whether the rest of the beast is lying out there, somewhere on our place, waiting to be unearthed is, alas, an open question. When Doug found it some years ago, he tossed the curious rock into the back of the pickup, where it had rattled around for the next few days until he thought to bring it inside to show me . . . by which time he had forgotten where, exactly, he had picked it up. We fantasize, from time to time, about discovering the next big T-rex or some such, and retiring on the proceeds.

But then again, I think we both believe, deeper down, that it's better to let sleeping dinosaurs lie. There is a rocky outcropping just to the north of our ponderosa pine woods, on the downslope where forest gives way to wooded draws and grassland. It serves as something of a landmark for us, and a sometime deer stand during hunting season. Early on in our tenure here, I named it the Dragon's Back, having in mind the Chinese mythic notion that dragons inhabit the earth, stirring just under its surface and sometimes irrupting through. Doug, for his part, dubbed it the Dinosaur's Back, and over the years, it is that name that has stuck. The logic is essentially the same, and historically closer to home. Spirits of great power lurk just beneath the surface here, sometimes breaking to light. They were here first, and they will outlast us. They deserve both remembrance and respect.

Montana-based nature writer Richard Manning thinks along similar lines in his *Grassland: The History, Biology, Politics, and Promise of the American Prairie*. Relative to the mass extinctions of prehistoric megafauna that roughly coincided with the end of the last Ice Age (around the time of the Goshen Complex folk), he remarks:

> Consider the wind of the West as inspiration, as that word lies tangled linguistically with wind, ghost, spirit, and breath. Understand that the wind carries ghosts that we should know. Understand that it carries the whiff of dead elephants.

Manning subscribes to the much-disputed hypothesis that it was human hunting that precipitated the extinction of the several species of giant bison, mammoths and mastodons, camels, horses, and big cats that formerly roamed this landscape. There is a mastodon tusk in the Carter County Museum, recovered not far from here. But whatever we might reconstruct in light of fossil finds and museum displays, a more powerful story is told by the millennia-old ghosts still haunting this living country. Just ask any pronghorn antelope.

WHERE THE DEER AND THE ANTELOPE PLAY

Antilocapra americana, the American pronghorn, is a unique species, the sole surviving members of the once numerous *Antilocapridae*, an ungulate family native to the interior West. They have no close contemporary relatives; although they are popularly referred to as "antelope," they are an utterly distinct species. The terminological borrowing arises from certain superficial traits pronghorns share with their African counterparts: grace, agility, endurance, and—most of all—swiftness. The pronghorn is the fastest, and arguably the sturdiest, land animal in North America. These wiry amber denizens of the open grassland can

The Dinosaur's Back. Photo by Mary Stange.

go from zero to seventy-plus miles per hour in a matter of seconds. And they can sustain a "cruising speed" of fifty or more miles per hour for two or three miles at a clip, without becoming visibly winded, thanks to heart and lung capacity comparatively large for their size. They are, in fact, faster than African antelope, and by some estimates second in speed, among all land mammals, only to cheetahs.

It's been established that an American pronghorn could easily out-run, and outlast, a Thompson's gazelle—an animal that inhabits an African ecosystem not too dissimilar from the High Plains rangeland. The question is, why? The gazelle has plenty of reason to pour on the steam, given that it counts cheetahs and lions among its likely preda-tors. Yet, as zoologist John A. Byers remarks in his groundbreaking study, *American Pronghorn: Social Adaptations & the Ghosts of Predators Past*, pronghorn are not simply fast, they "are ridiculously too fast for any modern predator." Countering the conventional wisdom among evolutionary biologists that assumes that any trait a species consistently displays must in some fashion be an adaptive response to contemporary selective pressures, Byers argues that pronghorns' speed and stamina (as well as a number of their social behaviors) can only be understood in light of the mass extinctions of the last Ice Age. "The behavior of pronghorn really cannot be understood," he writes, "without reference to the recently vanished suite of North American predators. The behavior of living pronghorn is, in part, a 'historical document' . . . that illuminates the fossil-written text of the North American savanna fauna."

In other words, I might be stalking a herd of pronghorn with my rifle in hand, in much the same way as a Paleolithic hunter would have, with his flint-tipped spear—which, technologically speaking, is on a direct evolutionary continuum with my Sako .270. But now, as ten thousand years ago (a mere blip on the evolutionary screen), when the keen-eyed pronghorns sense present danger in human form and explode into lightning-fast retreat, they are actually fleeing the sabertoothed cats, jaguars, giant bears, hyenas, and cheetahs that preyed upon their evolutionary forebears a million and more years ago. Today's pronghorn is, Byers finds, "a fair representative of its family," *Antilocapridae*. But, "In most respects, the pronghorn is not a specialized end product but, rather, the fortunate survivor of late Pleistocene extinctions that wiped out nearly all species of a specialized lineage."

Think about that for a moment. It lends an almost unfathomable depth to the pronghorn's wildness. Having evolved right here, pronghorn antelope are more truly native to this particular terrain than any other ungulate. Whitetail deer have, as a species, been around even longer, perhaps for four million years; but they didn't originate here. Mule deer, our other cervid species, are at best newcomers, having been around for a mere seven to fourteen thousand years—that is, on the outside, about as long as humans—in this neighborhood. Even our native buffalo is an import: the giant bison, *bison latifrons*, hunted by the Goshen Complex people, went extinct at the end of the Pleistocene. The somewhat smaller American *bison bison*, along with elk and moose, and by some accounts deer, are all Eurasian in origin, having migrated into North America along with the continent's first human inhabitants, across the Bering "land bridge" (more properly referred to as the landmass "Beringia") between thirty and fifteen thousand years ago.

Anyone who hunts these parts quickly becomes aware that pronghorn survival strategies differ markedly from those of their neighboring mule deer and whitetails. Each species adapts in its own way, of course. Deer's principal sense is smell, while pronghorns rely primarily on vision. Whitetails tend to occupy forest and wooded draws, whereas mule deer inhabit more rugged country. When it comes to flight response, both species of deer are wired for quick bursts of energy: mule deer stotting, pogolike, up rocky ridges and out of sight, whitetails gliding their way in long graceful strides down into creek bottoms, and to safety. Pronghorns, meanwhile, as dwellers on the open prairie, are built for speed and the long-term endurance required when, lacking cover, one has to outdistance danger. Deer, in other words, can afford to be sprinters, whereas pronghorns need to be marathon runners.

More striking still is another difference between the deer and the antelope that "play" in these parts. As anyone who spends much time in deer country can attest, it is not unusual to find oneself face to face with a deer, sometimes quite literally so, a mere few feet or yards away. The deer's gaze is direct, at once placid and alert, its body poised for flight, but not quite yet. The encounter may last a mere moment, or several, generally depending upon how long it takes the deer to get a good whiff of your scent. But in that sliver of time—those two or three pulses when time itself seems suspended—something is communicated in the deer's imperturbably fixed countenance. In those liquid eyes, a look both deeply knowing and impossibly remote seems to say *we are and are not of a piece, you and I*. Prey and predator, we comprehend each other's position in the scheme of this space we coinhabit, this space we share to the extent that we move just within the peripheries of one another's awareness. A look may take one's breath away, but it won't kill. We can look one another in the eye, if ever so fleetingly.

Beyond such magically charged moments, there are, of course, the more mundane encounters between humans and deer that have earned the latter the (disrespectful) title of "prairie rats," and that generally involve deer incursions into vegetable gardens and flower beds. Even as I am writing this, in the fall of 2008, the Ekalaka town council is weighing the wisdom of an "urban hunt" (in the case of a town of fewer than four hundred, something of a misnomer, perhaps) to decrease deer numbers within the town limits. Yet, as the ancestors of today's Ekalakians would be the first to tell them, deer depredation is hardly a new issue in these environs.

The old homesteads that dot eastern Montana—we have three on our place—are rich in more than human history. Even when no artifacts remain, their setting, the placement of the buildings relative to vestigial vegetable gardens and root cellars, speak volumes about what it must have been like to live, and frequently to suffer, the "pioneer experience." It is obvious to anyone who has seen these places, and perhaps more so to one who has felt through them the chill of a December blizzard or the heat of an August drought, or maybe thought they heard faint echoes of a scratchy gramophone mingling in the autumn breeze, that spirits seem to linger at homestead sites. Deer seem to linger there too, because these sites are important elements of *their* history, as well.

Abandoned homesteads, I think, attract deer for several reasons. The first is the most obvious. When it comes to choosing the sites for their dwellings, human beings tend to seek basically the same things deer do: shelter from the elements, a certain degree of seclusion to ensure some privacy, nearness to water, and a ready access route. The extent that human housing developments are gobbling up prime deer habitat across the country today surely attests to the fact that we pretty much think like deer when it comes to deciding where we prefer to bed down. In this regard, the original homesteaders may have represented, from a deer's point of view, anyway, the first outreaches of prairie suburbia. Whatever impact settled human habitation subsequently may have had, the deer, after all, were here first.

However, rather than sighing "There goes the neighborhood" and moving on, the deer decided to stay. They had good reason to. The kitchen vegetable garden, newly cultivated fruit trees and berry bushes and flower beds, salt and mineral licks put out for livestock: all were enticements to hang around the homestead. And even after the two-leggeds packed up and left, traces of these delectables remained. Poke around many an old homestead today, and you will discover juneberry and currant bushes, rhubarb, sometimes even volunteer squash or sunflowers that come back season after season. Years of putting out salt licks leave trace residues in the soil, and deer scrape the surface to get the salt. Old two-track roads and overgrown garden paths still provide relative ease of access, as well as escape. Robert Frost notwithstanding, some wild animals—like most humans—generally prefer the road more frequently taken, especially when winter snow sets in.

Deer are among those wild species that readily became habituated to sharing their space with humans. They then continued to reap the fruits of human habitation even after the two-leggeds left. Hence, another reason why deer tend to haunt abandoned homesteads, which became part of "deer history" as each generation of does passed on to their fawns the behavior patterns that led them back to the homesteads. The same is no doubt true for the deer—mule deer and, more recently, whitetails too—that frequent my garden and Doug's small apple orchard. Many deer may have no more rational reason than many humans do, to call a particular location "home," except that it has something to do with Mom. It is a primal place of shelter and security. And it is where you return, when what you need most is a place that feels safe, and where the eats are good.

On the other hand, I have never spotted a pronghorn in our yard, or even grazing within sight of our house. Nor, in a region where antelope numbers are high, and the fish and game department practically gives hunting licenses away to control the pronghorn population, have I ever encountered a story about "nuisance" urban antelope. It is certainly not uncommon, when driving the gravel roads and highways of eastern Montana and Wyoming, and the western Dakotas, to see herds of antelope grazing on the outskirts of towns—but always on the outskirts, always with some safe buffer zone between themselves and human habitation and activity. "Pronghorn history" is, as it were, deeper and older and less comfortably accommodating of encroaching human settlement. About as close as they are willing to come, in my experience, is hanging out with domestic cattle. They seem to have put it together that, during hunting season, they are less liable to be shot at when mingling with a group of Herefords.

By the same token, I have never gotten close enough to look an antelope in the eye—nor, I am certain, would the pronghorn hold my gaze, deerlike, were I able to. On occasion when hunting, I have startled a pronghorn into momentary stillness at reasonably close range. But the instantaneous flight response is so hardwired in these animals that it hardly takes anything to trigger it. All it takes, really, is to be in the animal's visual space. Hence their proclivity—especially, it seems, among bucks—to be set in motion by vehicles passing on the road, often racing parallel to them, keeping the threatening presences in their field of vision until they get to a place where they can angle off to safety, apparently knowing from experience that the offending vehicle will stay on the highway.

Perhaps it's a game the pronghorns are playing, or a way of keeping in shape. But when startled into flight, whatever the cause, they invariably look, for all the life of them, as if they have just seen a ghost. Because, of course, they have. Whether in the form of a hunter walking a ridge or a Ford F-250 on the county road, a modern predator invariably conjures up, for them, those "ghosts of predators past." In turn, these anciently evolved denizens of the prairie take on a phantomlike quality of their own.

There are yet other spirits weaving their way through these prairie grasses, very close to our home.

SITTING BULL SLEPT HERE

> I will remain what I am until I die, a hunter, and when there are no buffalo or other game I will send my children to hunt and live on prairie mice, for where an Indian is shut up in one place his body becomes weak.
> —Sitting Bull

Those Native Americans to whom archaeologists refer as "historical Indians," the tribal peoples whose life here postdated Paleo-Indians and preceded Euro-American settlement, recognized both the natural richness and the spiritual power of this place. For the Lakota peoples, southeastern Montana is sacred land, within the Hoop of the Nation, those lands in eastern Montana and Wyoming, the western Dakotas and Nebraska, that constituted their historical territory. The Carter County Museum literature describes the Hunkpapa chief and holy man Sitting Bull as a "frequent visitor" to this area, where he ostensibly enjoyed hunting. This, of course, vastly understates the case, but is a common enough governmental ploy for rewriting the human history of the West. U.S. Park Service brochures similarly characterize Native Americans as early "visitors" to Yellowstone Park, which they say was "virtually uninhabited" at its founding in 1872—as if the Nez Perce who regularly hunted and camped and engaged in vision quests there were merely proto-tourists.

In the winter of 1876, tensions were building between the U.S. Cavalry and those Indians declared by the government to be "hostiles" for their refusal to retreat to reservations. Sitting Bull and his village were then camped along the Powder River, just west of what is today Carter County. Toward winter's end, when soldiers raided another Powder River encampment of Lakota and Cheyenne farther to the south, breaking what had been an uneasy cease-fire, Sitting Bull and his people migrated eastward, toward a place of power. According to historian Robert M. Utley, working from contemporary accounts in his biography *The Lance and the Shield: The Life and Times of Sitting*

Bull, "Sitting Bull's village stood at the head of Spring Creek near the foot of Chalk Butte [*sic*], an elevation on the divide between the Powder and the Little Missouri. One hundred lodges sheltered Hunkpapas and Miniconjous."

Spring Creek has several branches, two of which have headwaters at either end of the Chalk Buttes. Depending upon how you read the above account in light of Forest Service and BLM maps, Sitting Bull's encampment was either on the divide that marks our ranch's southern boundary, or on neighboring land immediately to our northeast. Sitting Bull had by then been declared the leader of the combined forces of Sioux and Cheyenne warriors. From his encampment here, he and his growing number of followers, joined by Crazy Horse and his band of Oglala warriors, proceeded westward once again, hunting and gaining in both physical and spiritual strength throughout the spring. Early that June, Sitting Bull, in his role as medicine man, presided over what is believed to be the largest Sun Dance ever held, involving ten thousand participants from various Plains tribes. Three weeks later, he and his combined Sioux, Cheyenne, and Arikara forces defeated Custer's Seventh Cavalry at the Little Bighorn.

Of course, it is my assumption that Sitting Bull and his people came here late that winter because they were drawn, in a time of trouble, to a place of spiritual power. That assumption is borne out by the fact that he is known to have frequented the Medicine Rocks—ten miles north of Ekalaka and, as the crow flies, twenty-odd miles northeast of our place. It is further supported by the special status of the Chalk Buttes and Medicine Rocks in the religious imagination of the Northern Cheyenne people, the other Native American tribal group who primarily lived here.

Ironically enough, that status is perhaps most clearly set forth in a document published by the Bureau of Land Management in 2002, titled *The Northern Cheyenne Tribe and Its Reservation,* the purpose of which is to educate land managers as to the differing ways in which local indigenous populations regard land "use" (and, by extension, land abuse). The BLM report was actually authored by a committee composed of members of the Northern Cheyenne tribe, along with academic specialists on Native American culture and economy. Among the latter, archaeologist Sherri Deaver, in consultation with Cheyenne elder Joe Little Coyote, authored the chapter "Northern Cheyenne Cultural Resources," which outlines the religious function of the land for the Cheyenne people. Regarding the area around the Chalk Buttes, which are today demarcated as a section of the Custer National Forest, and which are, simultaneously, a Cheyenne pilgrimage site, the BLM document states:

> The Northern Cheyenne recognize that the Custer National Forest has defined a management boundary around Chalk Buttes, which essentially conforms to Forest Service land boundaries. However, the Northern Cheyenne recognize a much wider area including all the area from which Chalk Buttes is visible and includes Medicine Rocks State Park. This entire area from which Chalk Buttes is visible is viewed as a powerful spiritual area that must be respected and honored. Fasting at Chalk Buttes and leaving offerings at Medicine Rocks is part of a living religious tradition where participants make both a spiritual and physical journey. During the entire journey the spiritual aspects of life are dominant. The Forest Service management boundary is irrelevant to their cultural responsibility to honor these spirits in this place and to act respectfully.

The BLM document goes on to detail how, "in contrast to the scientific-academic view of history," the spirituality of the Native peoples to whom this area is holy collapses such distinctions as those between living and dead, human and nonhuman environment, spiritual and physical life, present and past. In this context, the past becomes not less but more relevant: it "provides a template for the proper way of life. It legitimizes the present by showing it is related to things that have gone before."

The Northern Cheyenne view is grounded in their myth and cosmology, "the things that have gone before" being aspects of those mythic beginnings which both predated, and provided the foundation for, human existence. In the Cheyenne scheme of things, space itself has several dimensions or layers. There is the dome of "Blue Sky Space," the heaven above, and the Earth, between which eagles, hawks, dragonflies, and butterflies serve as intermediaries. Closer to earth's surface is "Nearer Sky Space," the realm of clouds, birds, dust devils, tornadoes, and high places—these last being regarded as sites of increased spirituality, most notably Bear Butte and the Black Hills in South Dakota, Devils Tower in Wyoming, and southeastern Montana's Chalk Buttes. The earth itself, comprised of forest and grassland is, in this view, animate: hills are home to the spirits of animals and people who have gone before or are yet to be born; springs are spirits emerging from the living earth; rivers and streams are full of inspirited life. Rocky badlands, on the other hand, are held to be spiritually inert "Deep Earth" . . . although, dragonlike, great animal spirits like bison may, on occasion, emerge from them.

As space is divided in this world view, so too is time, into five distinct phases. First came that sacred time of beginnings, when the Creator Maheo—the "Great Spirit"—and other spiritual beings created the world and everything that is good and holy in it. Such spiritual sites as Bear Butte and the Chalk Buttes date back to that time, when the world was first imbued with sacred qualities. There was then the time when ancient Indian peoples lived here—people for whom the boundary between spiritual and physical did not exist, and who freely interacted with powerful spirits. There followed historic time, when the ancestors of present-day peoples lived, their stories preserved in oral traditions. This brings us to the present and—no less relevant, as a unit of time—the future.

One fascinating element of this chronological scheme is how similar it is to the anthropological account of the history of this place. Scholars have noted striking narrative similarities between the Cheyenne creation stories and the Cheyenne nation's history: the split between northern and southern tribes, their displacement from their original lands, the coming of the white man, and so on. But one cannot also help but wonder whether, in flint arrowheads and spear tips, their visionaries and storytellers discovered ancient heroes where archaeologists see Paleo-Indians, or in fossilized fish and seashells they saw the evidence of a still-formless primordial ocean where geologists speak of a "Western Interior Seaway." Similar questions are, of course, raised by a variety of mythic systems: there's geological evidence of the Great Flood of the Hebrew Bible, for example, and archaeological traces of the Trojan War. But, from the point of view of Western religion and culture, these echoes of the past—resonant though they be in myth and legend—are reliably "prehistoric," relegated to a "then" comfortably distant, and distinct, from "now." From the Native American point of view, by contrast, the sacred past is happening right now, and the landscape itself attests to its reality, its presence.

Some years ago, the Kiowa novelist and Pulitzer Prize winner N. Scott Momaday was asked to expound upon what distinguishes the Native American way of seeing and experiencing the physical environment. He responded, "first that the Native American ethic with respect to the physical world is a matter of reciprocal appropriation; appropriations in which man invests himself in the landscape, and at the same time incorporates the landscape into his own most fundamental experience." Momaday took pains to explain that what might look, to a non-Native, like a dichotomy between landscape and experience is better understood as a "paradox," which might only be resolved through an act of imagination—a way of seeing, and of experiencing, that is rooted in deep cultural memory: "his attitude toward the landscape has been formulated over a long period of time, and the length of time itself suggests an evolutionary process perhaps instead of a purely rational and decisive experience." The implications of this worldview, he suggested, are broad and deep:

> I think we should not lose the force of the idea of seeing something or envisioning something in a particular way. I happen to think that there are two visions in particular with reference to man and his relationship to the natural world. One is physical and the other is imaginative. And we all deal in one way or another with these visions simultaneously. If I can try to find an analogy, it's rather like looking through the viewfinder of a camera, the viewfinder which is based upon the principle of the split image and it is a matter of trying to align the two planes of the particular view. This can be used as an example of how we look at the world around us. We see it with the physical eye. We see it as it appears to us, in one dimension of reality. But we also see it with the eye of the mind. It seems to me that the Indian has achieved a particularly effective alignment of those two planes of vision. He perceives the landscape in both ways. He realizes a whole image from the possibilities within his reach.

Momaday concluded that, "The moral implications of this are very far reaching." Indeed they are. So, too, is the question whether this Native way of seeing is destined—some would no doubt say doomed—to be at odds with the Euro-American view of land and its appropriate uses.

It all comes down, as Momaday suggests, to a particular way of seeing, as well as to the stories that arise from it. I earlier told one story of Starvation Butte. Here is another, recounted by the late Northern Cheyenne holy man Bill Tallbull:

We call it "where the white stone stands." In the past the roaming bands of people have camped in the area for many generations. During these times my people would go there for vision questing and camp on both the west and east sides of the buttes. Blue clay was obtained there. Vision quest and eagle trapping sites are still there. Wild horse spirits guard the east slopes. I witnessed this phenomenon when I was parked on the east slope. I had to move away from that location. Without the pickup, I later went back to give proper offerings. One of the sandstone towers has been in our history. (This is) where long ago a young married woman sang a song and danced backwards off of a high sandstone rock and fell to her death. Her young man had been killed in battle. She was buried beneath the towering stone. When I visited the stone tower, a woman appeared on top of this stone. She watched me approach; I stopped and she disappeared. I had reconnected myself with this powerful place.

So Tallbull recounted in a 1994 report issued by the Northern Cheyenne Cultural Commission, which he headed and which was working toward special Forest Service designation of the Chalk Buttes— "where the white stone stands"—as a "Traditional Cultural Property" (TCP) protected from development and preserved for Native use. He told Doug the same story of his vision of the woman atop Starvation Butte around the same time when Doug and a group of local activists, concerned about a Forest Service plan to stage a "prescribed burn" in the Buttes, brought Tallbull in to do a spiritual mapping of the place. The tactic seems to have worked. The burn—a forest fire intentionally set, ostensibly to maintain the health of the forest, but often with unfortunate unintended consequences—never occurred.

The problem with achieving TCP status for the Buttes—as well as for their wider environs, referred to by the Cheyenne as the Blue Earth Hills and occupying much the same area as the Lakota Hoop of the Nation—has to do with opposed visions of humans in relationship with the land. Tallbull, working with anthropologist Sherri Deaver, outlined the problem in a 1996 article, "A new way to study cultural landscapes: the Blue Earth Hills assessment." The framework of National Forest Service decision making, they wrote . . .

. . . is based in the Euro-American world-view which assumes that humans are separate and qualitatively distinct from places. A person may use a place, buy or sell a place, or live in a place, but it is strictly a physical relationship between the person and place. Many Native American traditionalists do not make the same assumption. Rather, their world-view assumes there is always a spiritual as well as physical aspect to the relationship between person and place.

In the same article, Tallbull and Deaver acknowledge that the Euro-American descendants of homesteaders in this area have their own deep connection to the land on which their families have lived for generations, their own personal relationship with that "vast prairie . . . sea of grass" that has sustained them, on which their children have frolicked and where their dead are buried. The rancher's "landscape is meaningful and cherished because it supports his chosen way of life." So, too, for the Northern Cheyenne, whose "cultural landscape" traditionally is marked by birth bundles and medicine offerings and graves and other sites, and where "spirits living in the hills, springs, and streams provide them a network of meaning that sustain their chosen way of life."

It was in 1910 that today's National Forest lands in southeastern Montana were set aside to be held in the public trust, with the more arable land around them designated as suitable for homesteading. But this hardly made the forest a sanctuary. It is useful to recall, in this regard, that the Forest Service is a division of the U.S. Department of Agriculture. Forests are resources, to be cultivated (as via the occasional prescribed burn) and exploited for human uses ranging from commerce to recreation. A similar pattern emerges among all the sites most sacred to the Lakota and Cheyenne: Wyoming's Devils Tower is a national monument, administered by the National Park Service and in recent years the site of hotly contested development (including a golf course/resort and covenanted housing development) and tensions between rock climbers and Lakota, Cheyenne, and Kiowa traditionalists whose springtime observances the climbers disrupt. The Black Hills in South Dakota—for the Lakota "the heart of everything that is" and historically regarded as a place for ritual use only—are today a patchwork of federal, state, and private land, where Mount Rushmore and the still under construction Crazy Horse Monument compete for tourist attention with the likes of Reptile Gardens and the gambling casinos in Deadwood. Bear Butte—on the plains outskirts of the Black Hills, and especially sacred to the Cheyenne—is a state park, the area around which has seen massive commercial and recreational development in recent years, largely as a result of the huge annual motorcycle rally in nearby Sturgis.

Viewed in light of these other sacred sites the Chalk Buttes, and the nearby Medicine Rocks, become that much more precious, and in need of preservation. As the BLM report observes, these areas have, thus far, escaped development largely because of their geographical isolation. But, as the West continues to be carved up into ranchettes and resorts, it is reasonable to fear for their future. And, as the years pass, Doug and I become ever more conscious of our own responsibility to this place.

The Cheyenne have a saying: "We are just moving through, don't tarry long." It is a sentiment born of a hunter-forager mentality, of a people who seasonally follow wildlife populations, and successions of bloom and fruition, who move through the landscape with an attitude of reciprocal respect. Yet before they migrated west early in the nineteenth century and adopted the hunting lifestyle of the Plains Indians, the Cheyenne had been agriculturalists, living more settled lives farther east of here in the northern Great Lakes region and, subsequently, Minnesota. The same had been true of the Lakota, who also migrated to the High Plains from Minnesota. Their lifeways changed with the shifting landscape, although in keeping with a view of the land of which the concept of "ownership" was not readily a part.

Might something similar happen to non-Indians moving here? I wonder.

SENSING A PLACE

The first time Doug and I set foot on this ranch as its new owners was shortly after we had closed on its purchase. It was a splendid early spring day and coincidentally our wedding anniversary, and we were in high spirits. I had packed a picnic lunch. We drove the unimproved road down into our "beautiful valley at the edge of the forest," parked the pickup and hiked a short way to the edge of the woods, near one of the old homesteads which we would subsequently learn bore the name "Smith-Davis Place," after the last families who had lived there into the mid-twentieth century. We spread an old quilt on the ground, unwrapped our sandwiches, and drank a toast of cold beer. After a few minutes' excited chattering about our new home, we both fell silent.

"We *own* this?"

One or the other of us finally managed to put into words the thought we were so obviously sharing. "*We . . . own . . . all . . . this?*"

How could it be possible, that anyone could claim ownership of this vast nature, all wonder and wildness and complexity? In part, no doubt, it had just hit us both how little we comprehended what we had gotten ourselves into. That realization came in the form of a powerful burst of humility, along with an intimation of how absurd was the very concept of owning wild land at all. Academics that we both were, we readily enough shifted gears and began talking about the idea of "stewardship" as a more fruitful model of what we were about. Having thus collected ourselves, we collected our picnic things and hopped into the truck to drive down to the house where we were to meet with Bud and Betty, to spend the afternoon learning various things we needed to know about the place.

When we arrived at the house, Betty assumed that we must be hungry and offered us leftovers from their noon meal. We declined, explaining that we had picnicked on the way. "Oh, a picnic. That's nice. Where?" they asked.

"Up by that old homestead, on the road coming off the divide," we answered.

"You had your picnic *on the place*?!" they exclaimed, seemingly aghast and giving us the stern, level look customarily reserved for trespassers and poachers. What, that look explicitly said, made you two think you had the right?

It was, of course, a sensitive moment. The closing—at which neither they nor we were actually present—had occurred a mere three weeks earlier. They were having as much trouble letting go as we were having getting accustomed to our new status vis-à-vis this land. That they felt on some level violated was understandable. So too, perhaps, was their reflex response, taking umbrage at people invading their space. That much was clear.

But what was equally clear was the fact that their space had been mapped differently than ours would be. I am quite certain the question of what, exactly, ownership means had never occurred to them, as it did, and would continue to, for us. Along with a few ruined homesteads on "the place," they had inherited the homesteading mentality that said the land was there to be platted and utilized. And utilize it they had, grazing every available acre of rangeland to the nub, season after season. They had taken much from the land, without visibly giving much of anything back.

The placement of the log house, in a way, epitomized their

relationship to the land. It was comfortably enough sited, nestled in a crook of Spring Creek. Such flora as there were around it had been there before its construction—chokecherries, juneberries, yellow currants, buffaloberry bushes, mostly overgrown. One could say this was a naturalistic setting. One could equally say it was a setting that took advantage of what nature offered, and spared no expense—quite literally none—on any enhancements. There wasn't even a shelter belt, the customary planting of rows of evergreens, deciduous trees, and shrubs that protects homesteads from winter winds and summer storms. So common are these plantings in the West that they often outlast the dwellings they were intended to protect. It's not a stretch to say this was probably the only ranch in Carter County at the time to lack even the rudiments of one.

One might account for this oddity by observing that a shelterbelt could have obscured the magnificent view of the Chalk Buttes from the house . . . except for the fact that the house isn't oriented to afford a good view of the Buttes. Rather than facing eastward toward them, it faces south, toward the two-track connecting the house to the county road, as if the road were a five-mile driveway. Before we re-routed that road and did a series of plantings to create something of a "local" landscape, the view through our living-room picture window was nondescript indeed, of a dirt road coming up over a then sage-covered hill. One can only capture a vista of the Chalk Buttes by standing right at the window, peering out leftward toward the east. Nice, when savoring one's morning tea or coffee, but not terribly practical—especially when the winter winds shift, often bringing some of the most bone-chilling cold we get from out of the south, with the broad side of the house having the most windows and most exposure to the elements. In this setting, an eastern exposure would have made better climatic, as well as aesthetic, sense.

Of course, we didn't exactly buy the ranch, with its modest cabin, for "the view." Yet it is completely fair to say that, had all else been equal, we would not be here had it not been for the Chalk Buttes. We felt drawn both to their presence and this place. And we felt this place needed us in ways other ranch properties we had looked at did not. As we would learn—as we are continually relearning—righting the wrongs that had been done to this land, and getting truly in tune with its wild nature, would require much more than could be accomplished merely by re-routing a road or planting some trees.

LIVING IN ENEMY TERRITORY

From the outset, both Doug and I were struck by the force of what it means to live in enemy territory—when it happens that you yourself are the enemy. The reminders are everywhere here in "Custer Country," as the southeastern part of the state is called in the *Montana Travel, Tourism and Recreation Guide*, which coincidentally featured a photo of the Chalk Buttes as its frontispiece at the time we moved here. One look at a Montana state highway map tells you that history is written, and the terrain mapped, by the winning side. The racism that fueled the Indian Wars is thus encoded in the landscape. Naming, after all, is power.

And so many of the towns in these parts are named after military "heroes" who enforced the federal government war policy against the "hostiles." Custer, Montana, is a dreary little town right off Interstate 94, a few miles east of the turnoff for Sheridan, Wyoming—named for Philip Sheridan, for whom the only good Indian was a dead one. Drive farther east, and one encounters Forsyth, named for Colonel James Forsyth, under whose command Custer's old Seventh Cavalry avenged the soldiers who died at the Little Bighorn by massacring Big Foot's band of over three hundred Oglala Lakotas, most of them old people, women, and children, at Wounded Knee in 1890. Still farther east lies Terry, Montana, named for General Alfred Terry, who had arrived at the Little Bighorn too late to help Custer but hounded Sitting Bull and his people to the Canadian border. Closer to our home is Camp Crook, just over the South Dakota line, named for General George Crook, who forced the surrender of the Apache chief Cochise.

About midway between Forsyth and Terry on I-94 lies Miles City, named for General Nelson Miles. After Custer's death Miles assumed command of approximately one-fourth of America's standing Army, and pitched all its strength against the Indians of the Plains and Southwest. He is generally regarded as the mastermind behind the reservation system, although for many Native Americans under his direction being relocated to a "reservation" often actually meant being sent to prison, usually many hundreds of miles from their homes. This was in fact the intended fate of Big Foot's band, before they were killed at Wounded Knee. Ironically regarded by some historians as among the more "benign" of Indian fighters, Miles was at least indirectly responsible both for the murder of Sitting Bull and for the Wounded Knee massacre that followed a few days later. He also exiled the Chiricahua Apache warrior Geronimo to Florida, and forced the surrender of the Nez Perce under Chief Joseph through a brutal winter campaign.

Miles City is the county seat of Custer County. Intersecting its main drag is a street called Garryowen Road, after the Irish pub song that Custer adopted as his regimental march. The regional office of the Bureau of Land Management is located near the edge of town, on Garryowen Road.

Over our years here, Doug and I have worked with various entities, public and private, on wildlife habitat restoration and enhancement projects. When we took "possession" of our place, whatever that means exactly, our rangeland was categorized by the BLM as so degraded as to be "of no productive value." Forty and more years of abuse will do that to a place. Today our rangeland is classified "pristine," and the biologists and range managers who work with the BLM and the Natural Resources Conservation Service (NRCS), the two major agencies with which we have worked, point to our place as a success story. We could not, of course, have managed this without some expert help.

One of the experts with whom we have collaborated most closely is a wildlife biologist who works for the BLM in Miles City. He traces his ancestry to the Mandan and Hidatsa people, tribes located today in North Dakota, and linguistically and culturally related to the Lakota of South Dakota and Montana. Every day Bobby drives in to work on Garryowen Road, every time he gives someone his address or his business card, it cannot help but provide an explicit reminder of the near-genocide of his people. We summoned the courage to ask him, once, what he thought about that. "Obviously," he said, "I don't like it. Some of my people get crazy about it, but I suppose my anger is more subdued."

The conversation was awkward on both sides. After all, there we were, a white couple engaging with a university-trained Native American environmental specialist, employed by the federal government that had stripped his people of their land, working to restore the ecological integrity of wildlife habitat that had flourished before Native hunting and foraging patterns were displaced by farming and ranching. And this, in a county where some of our older neighbors still refer to Indians as "Prairie Afros" and call curly buffalo grass "nigger wool," and where the *Ekalaka Eagle* once ran an ad for part-time help that unblushingly solicited an "Indian" to do some low-paying menial chores.

Ekalaka is one of the few nonreservation communities in Montana to bear a Native-inspired name, doubtless thanks in no small part to

Ijkalaka's having married a white man. In recent years, efforts have been afoot among such Native groups in the area as the Northern Cheyenne and the Crow to recapture their original place names, or failing that, to reinvent them. Busby, on the Northern Cheyenne Reservation, is for example named after a rather unsavory homesteading store owner; Native residents have recently taken to calling it White River. The I-94 rest area between Hardin and Billings, marked "Mission Creek" on the Montana state highway map, is known by the Crow people as "Where the Whole Camp Mourned," because it was to this spot that a decimated Crow war party returned from battle at Rainy Buttes in North Dakota in the 1860s.

When it comes to natural topography, a number of area place-names actually are of Indian origin. One of a pair of maps drawn by the Northern Cheyenne scout John Crazy Mule in 1878 depicts the area around Fort Keogh (present-day Miles City) and westward. The map uses pictographs to indicate several place names, common among Native Americans and still in use today. A small shell marks the Musselshell River; a bighorn sheep's head indicates the Bighorn River; a bison head with tongue extended marks the Tongue River. The Bear Paw Mountains are indicated by a bear with exaggerated stretched claws. The Yellowstone River, on the other hand, which was known by the Indians as Elk River, is designated by a picture of an elk head. Today's Little Missouri River was known by the Cheyenne as Antelope Pit, for its function as an ancient pronghorn hunting area.

In *The Island Within*, ethnographer Richard Nelson comments on the Euro-American penchant for naming places after either their discoverers or their conquerors:

> All of these landmarks . . . originally had Indian names that described their appearance, related them to other natural phenomena, associated them with historical events, or had no meaning except as personal names for features of the terrain. These names emerged from the places themselves, became a part of their uniqueness, and enriched the tradition that bound people to their home territories. But few European or American chart makers wrote them down. Instead, the latecomers took this as a vacant terrain and filled it with the names of political figures, financial backers, friends, relatives, and fellow travelers.

Nelson is talking about the conquest-by-naming of the Alaskan frontier, but his remarks are equally true regarding Indian lands in the lower forty-eight—as well, for that matter, as the naming of meteors and topographical features on the moon or Mars. His remarks also point toward the ultimate futility of thinking a person or group can, by naming, bottle up nature for their own consumption.

The same, Nelson suggests, is true for the naming of plants and animals. "Whose idea," he asks, "was it to call a whole species of animal after a man, as if its earthly existence was intended as a memorial to someone's career?" We might, I would add, ask the same about the naming of diseases after their "discoverers"—which points to our oddly twisted sense of gaining control, and potentially immortality, through naming. Nelson makes a plea to free such beings as Anna's hummingbird, Swainson's thrush, Barrow's goldeneye, et al.:

> I wish these names could be quietly abandoned, filed away as remnants of an archaic, human-centered attitude toward nature. For replacements, I would choose names given by Native American people, reflecting generations of physical and spiritual intimacy with the animals. Failing that, I would search for names among farmers and backwoods people, drawing on their commonsense observations and the poetry of vernacular speech. As a last resort, I would ask the biologists and birdwatchers, hoping for better luck this time.

Of course, rely on a "backwoods" name, and you might come up with "nigger wool"; so much for "the poetry of vernacular speech." Erase the names of conquering heroes from the landscape, and you risk erasing, for future generations, the darker history of these places. Leave the naming process to random chance, and you may well bump up against the problem of sheer banality outlined by Carrie Moran Cleary, a member of the Little Shell Band of Chippewa who lives and works on the Crow Reservation, and is involved in an effort to recover and preserve traditional Crow place names. "For the younger generation of Crows," she writes, "the journey from Crow Agency to Bozeman, Mont., might be marked by the amount of gas money needed for the trip and by remembering where so and so's apartment is; 'You know the place we stayed that one time on the way to the pow wow.'"

We need names, of course, and the stories that are embedded within them. We need ways—some of them sublime and others quite mundane—to orient ourselves and map our surroundings. Perhaps what we need, ultimately, are more names for the places, plants, animals with which we find ourselves in complex networks of relationships—names that point to, or better yet arise from, the multifacetedness of our world and its history. Names, as well, that recall to us the fact that we are all on some level visitors to the places we adopt as our own and call home.

"WE ARE JUST MOVING THROUGH, DON'T TARRY LONG."

Before the BLM turned Bobby's primary attention to clearing leases for mineral extraction on public land in the Powder River Basin (more about this in a later chapter), we consulted with him about various strategies for wildlife habitat restoration, and about the desirability of specific grasses and forbs. So, too, with the biologists and range managers at the NRCS office in Ekalaka. When we arrived here twenty years ago, we could between the two of us name on sight a handful of prairie wildflowers, and fewer grasses. This, in an area celebrated by High Plains grassland ecologists for its biodiversity. It was one of those cases where we had so much to learn, we didn't even realize how much we had to learn. We are still learning two decades later, but—thanks to Bobby and Gary at the BLM, and Wayne and Rebecca and Jackie at NRCS, and Georgia who heads the county Conservation District—we have a much better handle than formerly on the implications of the fine art of range management.

Styles of, and attitudes toward, land management change over time, of course. As Texas rancher Barney Nelson notes, "Yesterday's uncleared land is today's old growth forest. Yesterday's bog, which only a lazy, uneducated manager did not drain, is today's priceless wetland. Yesterday's range improvements, like the productive varieties that replaced thin native meadow grasses, are today's introduced and demonized nonnatives." I'm as much a fan of old growth forests and wetlands as the next environmentally concerned person, but I think her point here is well-taken—particularly with regard to the relative merits of introduced versus native species.

I have a friend and colleague, a fellow environmentalist and passionate hunter who teaches at another northeastern college not far from where I work. We've carried on a decade-long disagreement over the question of environmental restoration, about which he is a decided purist. He has written scholarly papers arguing for not simply the preservation of wild lands, but their planned reversion to as pristine a state as possible. This means getting rid of nonnative species—all of which seem, by definition, to fall under the category of the "foreign" and/or "invasive." Drawing on the local Carter County parlance, one might regard them as the "eco-differnt."

Now, on one level, I am in perfect agreement with his essential argument: Our range could certainly do without such introduced plants as cheatgrass and Japanese brome, Canada thistle and Russian knapweed and leafy spurge. But banish the Russian olive, in the branches of which our native sharp-tailed grouse love to winter? Do away with crested wheatgrass, introduced over a century ago from Siberia and during drought years one of the few palatable forages available for our native bison? Preserve such native flora as bluestem and witchgrass and sunflowers and wild plums, but eliminate the Hungarian partridges and Chinese ring-neck pheasants that thrive on their seeds and fruits? And what about those charmingly native prairie dogs, whose network of burrows and hills turned a once lush sharp-tailed grouse drumming ground into, essentially, a wasteland? I'd be more than happy to repopulate that pasture with black-footed ferrets, the prairie dogs' natural predator. But alas, the ferrets are an endangered species, thanks primarily to sylvatic plague, which was introduced to North American shores from China around the turn of the last century.

Attitudes toward flora and fauna tend to replicate our notions about human populations. This is perhaps particularly ironic, against the backdrop of current trends in environmental theory. "Eco-regionalists" talk about learning to become native to the place where you live. Slow food adherents celebrate becoming "locavores," and relying on such food and drink as is available within one's home ecosystem. I find both ideas, in their own ways, attractive if problematic, and will return to them in pages to come.

But in the Blue Earth Hills, questions of the local, of home, of ownership or stewardship, of how we orient ourselves to our world, of how we adjudicate the competing claims of those various individuals and groups, Native and Anglo, who—in Bill Tallbull's words—severally experience this land in terms of their "chosen way of life" . . . all these questions need to be asked in light of the wisdom of the Cheyenne saying, "We are just moving through, don't tarry long," as well as of the Biblical intimation that all flesh is grass. Doug and I, Betty and

Bud, their homesteading predecessors, the Cheyenne and Lakota and Crow who inhabited this region for two centuries prior, their historic forebears reaching back ten thousand years and more: We are all sojourners in this powerful place. So, too, the plants and animals that chose to make their grassland home here after the last Ice Age.

In the end, the only true natives here are, perhaps, the pronghorn antelope: prairie phantoms themselves, fleeing the ghosts of an ageless past.

Mule deer buck in autumn. Photo by Doug Stange.

CHAPTER 7
Hunting Nature, Hunting Culture

PICTURE IT . . .

An early October dawn, the atmosphere a rosy commingling of fog and frost. That's not particularly uncommon in this part of southeastern Montana. Summer here frequently resists fall's onset, and that's the scenario for this particular day. By noon, the sky will be clear, and the morning chill will have turned downright sultry. But for now, it feels like a perfect time to intercept a few unwary turkeys threading their way between the mown hayfield and the ponderosa pine forest bordering it, on the top of the divide that forms the southern boundary of our place. And so I am still-hunting the edge of the woods, shotgun in hand, my ears alert to sounds of soft clucking from those woods, my eyes blinking away droplets of frosty mist.

Suddenly, I hear from the hayfield sounds of a different sort, first muffled then more distinct, and not at all birdlike. *Click! Clack!* . . . *CLACK!* . . . *Chock* . . . *Click. Click* . . . *CHOCK!!! Chock!* Punctuated by a snort, then a stomp, then silence. Then repeated. Nature's version of a John Cage percussion piece. I nestle behind a ponderosa sapling and wait.

Some minutes pass. Then, gradually, I see them—a procession of mule deer bucks, thirteen in all, emerging ghostlike through the veil of fog. They have been feeding, overnight, out on the hayfield. Now they are meandering back toward the forest, to eventually filter down to the wooded draws and grassland where they tend to spend their days. The buck in the lead is the largest, sporting "nontypical" antlers, with a dropped tine on each side. The other deer range from spikes and forked-horns to impressive young males. They are taking turns casually roughhousing with one another—hence the snorting and stomping, the clashing of antlers—although none of them challenge the drop-tine, who maintains an aloof disinterest in their adolescent displays of dominance. The rut is a lunar month away, so this sparring is simply practice. Eventually the fighting will become more contentious, but they still will not confront him.

Deer season isn't open yet. Even if it were, the number 4 loads in my shotgun would not be sufficient for deer. Turkeys, if not exactly the farthest thing from my mind, have nonetheless lost their relevance. If I were to stand up, the deer, now a mere forty yards away, would disappear in two heartbeats. Meanwhile, as minutes pass, any turkeys that may have been in the neighborhood will have filtered down into the daytime shelter of the understory.

Eventually, in their own time, the mule deer also fade into that dense forest. I tell myself that I wasn't all that serious about turkey hunting this morning, anyway; I've got ample time to try to bag a bird named "Thanksgiving." The mule deer, meanwhile, who in two weeks will become legal prey, were this morning purely a gift, and a vision of grace. Perhaps I am, like this October day, not quite ready to be autumn yet. Perhaps this is also what it means to be one with nature.

But does being one with nature necessitate killing? Would a camera, had I had one on me, not have been enough? Hunting writers love to cite—to the point of rendering it cliché—the Spanish philosopher José Ortega y Gasset's remark that one does not hunt in order to kill, one kills in order to have hunted. As one who in the last twenty-plus years has had much blood on her hands, I know that the killing I have done as a hunter is hardly beside the point. But neither is it the point. We humans evolved as predators; it is in our very nature. We have eyes in the front of our heads, well developed distance vision, and excellent depth perception: all crucial for stalking and capturing prey. We see a rainbow of colors. We have hands designed to grasp, and while our fingernails are poor excuses for claws, these same hands can make tools—from slingshots to bows and arrows to high-powered rifles—that more than compensate our lack of talons. Tools, as well, like that simple stone scraper that, when I found it in our road one sunny summer morning, transposed me, in imagination, to a prehistoric landscape that felt startlingly familiar.

I have come, over the years, to treasure the connection that my own hunting forges with that primordial past. I enjoy that I have more in common, in some essential ways, with those artists who created the great Paleolithic masterpieces in the caves at Lascaux and Altamira than I do with colleagues in the art department at the college where I teach. At the same time—the present time, when arguably far too few of us are carrying on the hunters' traditions that originally forged our cultures and our psyches alike—I also appreciate the ways hunting unites me with other outdoorsmen and women.

This special sense of communion struck me several years ago, when Doug and I were pheasant hunting on the Medicine Lake National Wildlife Refuge in northeastern Montana. It was a weekday, early morning, in midseason. I was, to be frank, playing hooky from teaching for a couple of days, and calling it "field research." The other hunters wandering those same fields were mostly local people, pursuing an hour or two of brush busting with their dogs, before heading off to their day jobs as hands on area ranches, or as clerks or mechanics or waitresses in nearby Plentywood. We probably had nothing substantial in common, in terms of education, politics, or life experience. Were we to encounter one another in virtually any social context, we would likely be hard-pressed to move beyond simple pleasantries. Yet we were all there, in that golden morning, breathing in the same pungent autumn air and being, no doubt, equally dazzled by the poetry in motion of every bird that launched itself skyward at our approach. Although our paths never crossed, we shared a commonness of purpose, and of understanding, that ultimately perhaps hunters alone can appreciate.

SISTER PREDATOR

This commonness of purpose extends across species boundaries, as well, in subtle and not always conscious ways. I have long relished the fact that, according to the Chinese astrological calendar, I was born in a Tiger year. It was with considerable pleasure that I first encountered a remark of Aldous Huxley's: It's a good time to be alive, he said—it's still possible to be eaten by a tiger.

Man-eaters—and as a feminist, I use the term advisedly—man-eaters, current anthropology suggests, have been a preoccupation of the human species ever since we have been a species. We human animals are both predators and prey, and endowed—though at times it feels more like a curse—with the capacity to reflect upon our complex situation. For the most part, we do such reflecting on demand, as it were: when a cougar pounces on a Colorado jogger like a house cat on a mouse, or a Yellowstone grizzly bear turns a camper in his sleeping bag into something like a human burrito. On the face of it, stories like these make the headlines because they are sensational. Yet they command our attention because they resonate with something deeper within us: the intimation that we participate in a natural process that, despite all our fantasies to the contrary, we ultimately do not control.

Historically, of course, the advance of civilization has been all about gaining control. In his elegantly written book *Monster of God: The Man-Eating Predator in the Jungles of History and the Mind*, environmental writer David Quammen demonstrates the intimate link between the subjugation of a land and its native people on the one hand, and on the other the eradication of its indigenous alpha predators, that is, those large carnivores that are at least capable of preying on humans. Lions and tigers, bears and wolves.

Of course, it's easy to look at the near-extinct state of, say, the Bengal tiger and chalk it up to the excesses of British imperialism; we Americans like to think of ourselves as nature-loving folk, after all. But in his book *The Beast in the Garden*—which chronicles the resurgence of mountain lions in the Boulder, Colorado, area in the 1980s—David Baron notes the bloody historical record on this continent. Baron writes:

> It is difficult to overstate the animosity Americans have exhibited toward large carnivores. We have poisoned wolves with strychnine, dynamited grizzlies, shot coyotes from helicopters, and lured mountain lions to steel-jawed traps with catnip oil. We have invented ingenious devices of death such as the "coyote getter," a contraption similar to a Roman candle that shoots cyanide crystals into the mouth of the animal that tugs at the bait. We have tortured predators—wired their mouths shut so that they starve; doused them with gasoline and set them on fire; sawed off their lower jaws and thrown them, crippled, to packs

of dogs. We have gassed their dens and strangled their young. All of this in an attempt by humans, the ultimate predators, to eliminate the competition.

As a hunter I am compelled to remark here that none of the atrocities Baron lists are acts that the majority of hunters would either perform, or condone. Still, our eastern Montana ranch neighbors—many of whom hunt, as well—were more than a little put out by the fact that one of the first things we did when we took over the ranch was rescind permission for the county predator control agent to fly over our place, shooting coyotes from the air. And it is not uncommon, in these parts where cattle remain king, to see a coyote carcass impaled on a barbed-wire fence, as if in warning to its fellows that they could be next: a kind of cross-species prairie lynching.

In point of fact, the awful things that farmers and ranchers—as well as urban and suburban developers—have done to cougars and coyotes, grizzlies and wolves, are twisted antitheses of what really being a predator is all about. And the extent to which many people regard these measures as valid alternatives to hunting is, I would say, precisely the extent to which we have lost touch with our own predator nature.

Our language reflects this estrangement. Predation is invariably cast in a negative light. We talk about "predatory lending," "predatory criminals," and "sexual predators."

And yet, in a historical irony numerous writers have pointed out, the more we have exiled our fellow and sister predators from our civilized world, banishing them at best to the edges of our human settlements as well as of our consciousness, the more we crave the assurance that they are still out there somewhere. Deep down, we know they are our kindred spirits. Just look at the history of the American West. No sooner had Euro-Americans "conquered" the frontier, than they set about demarcating parcels of it and setting them aside as "wilderness areas."

The word "wilderness" is from the Old English *wilddeornes*, "the place of wild beasts." The National Park Service, which administers our wilderness areas, defines wilderness as "an area where the earth and its community of life are untrammeled by man." And yet humans—some of them hunter-foragers, others horticulturalists—had "trammeled" this entire continent long before European settlers arrived and displaced them. As feminist literary scholar Annette Kolodny has shown in her classic study *The Lay of the Land*, those indigenous peoples themselves were classed among the "wild beasts" settlers saw it as their divinely ordained mission to overcome. And that dangerous, native wildness of those people and that land was itself gendered feminine: a land of virgin territories ruled over by a capricious Mother Nature.

The late ecofeminist philosopher Val Plumwood, who traced in her native Australia a conceptual scheme quite similar to our own in this regard, noted that in the patriarchal imagination virgins exist as empty spaces to be filled—by men. And to be fulfilled, by becoming wives and mothers. Patriarchal culture is all about the taming of female nature, human and nonhuman. That is to say, it's all about domestication. In this light, I especially appreciate the access to female wildness that hunting affords me.

Hunting not only makes me human; more to the point, it keeps me human. It teaches me that I am part of a natural process which I do not ultimately control—not all mornings afield are, after all, all that perfect. And it reminds me that full participation in that process cannot be accomplished by hiking or bird-watching or rock-climbing or mushrooming. This is not to denigrate any of these activities, all of which may constitute outdoor recreation in the best sense of that term: re-creation, the restoring of one's native sense of self, and soul. But hunting goes deeper still, to what we humanly have at stake in the process of life and death, in which some beings live because others die. It is in this sense that the late environmental philosopher Paul Shepard designated the hunter an "agent of awareness" for society at large. The hunter's story, he suggested, brings us back to ourselves, to the truth that the boundary between life and death is tissue-thin, and that the thread of mutual mortality is deeply interwoven in this green world of ours.

It is too deceptively easy to intellectualize all this, as has been the fashion in much writing both for and against human—and particularly women's—hunting. So why not just say it plainly? I hunt because I enjoy it. And because I am good at it. And because I can.

I also hunt because my mother could not. She was born of a generation, and in a time and place, where the very thought of her daring to challenge conventions was, well, unthinkable. A first-generation college student in her New England family, she became a registered nurse.

I only began hunting as an adult, and toward the end of her life. We had had a sometimes difficult relationship, not unlike other daughters and mothers. As my mother lay dying of terminal cancer, it turned out there was one thing we could talk freely about: my hunting adventures. Not about the killing—our shared awareness of the imminence of her death precluded that. But the humor: a connoisseur of sight gags, she chuckled at the image of my sinking into waist-deep slush on a frosty November duck hunt. And the toughness: as when I recounted sustaining a "scope bite" (a crescent-shaped scar above my right eyebrow, from rifle recoil), without shedding a tear. And the pride of accomplishment: as when she insisted I show all her friends the photo of my "huge" (to their New Jersey eyes) first mule deer kill. And the bounty: she savored the venison I brought home to her, until her illness rendered all food flavorless.

Mostly, though, we talked about the beauty of it all: A beaver sunning himself on a riverbank, looking like a small furry Buddha. The Northern Lights shimmering above deer camp. The sunlight glinting off the wings of wave upon wave of snow geese, flying in formations like undulating diamond necklaces strewn across the sky. "Thank you," my mother would smile, assured in the end that her daughter had inherited her strength. "Thank you for that story."

In *The Others: How Animals Made Us Human*, Paul Shepard observed, "The animals within us—and perhaps the plants—are like the beings of a larger and older reality. They exist within us in much the same sense that our parents and our ancestors are in us, not as ghosts but as shared form, a continuum of which we are only the present expression." So too, I would argue, about the animals with whom we share our space. On more than one occasion since we moved to the ranch, a great horned owl has taken up a perch on a power pole that happens to be near one of my favorite deer hunting stands. I have appreciated the symmetry of these shared moments: Sister predators we have been, she and I, intent on different quarry to be sure, but equally and mutually alive and alert, in the way that all predators are.

"THE BEST OF FOODS"

Hunting, of course, is not only about stalking and sometimes killing; it is also—and for Doug and me, necessarily—about procuring meat. As I was drawn into the world of hunting, which he had inhabited since childhood, I immediately recognized it as being on a continuum with the vegetable and herb gardens I have maintained throughout my adult life. And, as we both have discovered after twenty years of living and hunting here on the ranch, there is something profoundly nourishing, in manifold ways, about consuming the meat of those animals with whom we share this ecosystem.

I had first encountered the idea of hunting as a way of becoming native to the place where one lives in the early 1990s, in outdoor writer Ted Kerasote's *Bloodties: Nature, Culture and the Hunt*. For him, the primary hunt each season was for elk, and his home hunting ground was the Teton National Forest virtually outside the front door of his cabin near Kelly, Wyoming. I found the idea immediately compelling, and readily translatable to our annual hunts for deer on the ranch. The more deeply one comes to know a species and its home territory, the more attuned one becomes to the intimate life connections between these animals and these plants, the quite literal wisdom of the intimation that "all flesh is grass." In Kerasote's phrasing, reflecting on a simple meal of elk steak:

> From my gut the elk begins his slow combustion, the physiological sense of warmth and well-being that those who live in cold climates note and which fills me with a sense of indebtedness to him. He gives me this place, my strength, and I like to think that someday my bones will fertilize the grass that will make his grandchildren fleet.

One learns, as well, that animals' patterns of diurnal and seasonal movement—their "lifestyles," you might say—that every "Hunt the Big Bucks" article in every hook-and-bullet outdoor magazine presents as conforming to static and predictable patterns, are in fact intricately complex, and, like the landscape itself, ever-changing.

The idea of becoming native to one's home locale—or "ecoregionalism," to use what our Carter County neighbors would call the more highfalutin term for it—caught on like wildfire among environmentally concerned thinkers and writers at the close of the twentieth century. And not without good reason, given the manifest realities of global climate change, the carbon costs of a worldwide food market, the mounting evidence of both animal and human abuse in corporate meat production, and the demonstrably negative health consequences, both for adults and for children, of a national diet based on corn, soy, and supersizing—all well documented in a series of best sellers: Eric Schlosser's *Fast Food Nation*, Michael Pollan's *The Omnivore's Dilemma*, Barbara Kingsolver's *Animal, Vegetable, Miracle: A Year of Food Life*,

Pollan's *In Defense of Food: An Eater's Manifesto*, Bill McKibben's *Deep Economy: The Wealth of Communities and the Durable Future*. Add to this bioregionalist mix increasingly troubling stories of outbreaks of E.coli, salmonella, listeria, and a slew of other unpleasant—and sometimes deadly—infections from food-borne contaminants directly traceable to industrial agriculture. When spinach trucked in from California, or jalapeños from Mexico, begin to take on a downright sinister taint, it only makes sense to look for solutions closer to, if not exactly in, one's own backyard.

Hence the birth of a "food awareness" craze variously called locavorism, localism, or the localtarian movement: the idea of eating from one's own "foodshed," typically defined as that ecosystem that lies within roughly a hundred-mile radius of one's home. The Oxford University Press declared "locavore" its 2007 "Word of the Year." In February of that same year *Food & Wine Magazine* ran a feature on "How To Eat Like a Locavore." "Locavore's Guides"—to New York, Montreal, Philadelphia, San Francisco, Cincinnati, Miami, Palm Beach, and so on—proliferated, both in print and on the Internet. So did localist Web sites, like LaVidaLoca.com, a Green-leaning forum ("Come for the food, stay for the politics"). And the quasi-ascetic Locavores.com, where a support group of aspiring California locavores pledge their allegiance to the movement, setting their long-term goals, recognizing obstacles to be overcome, and also specifying their "exemptions"—that is, those must-haves that are generally impossible for most people to procure locally but that they cannot do without, like salt, pepper, spices, tea, coffee, or chocolate— although locavoristic purists on the site promise to eschew any exemptions and "go all the way." The locavore idea is so hot in Vermont that community-based "localvore challenges" are becoming statewide annual events, to which a Web site—vermontlocalvore.org—is dedicated.

The localtarian movement depends primarily upon the home vegetable garden, and the growing number of local or regional farmers' markets, that offer meat, poultry, eggs, and artisanal cheeses, as well as vegetables and fruits. Additionally, areas where there are a sufficient number of small farms practicing sustainable methods—as well as a sufficient number of people willing to contract with farmers for a steady, seasonally varying supply of the fruits of those farmers' labors—have witnessed the rise of "Community Supported Agriculture" ("CSA"), in which food moves directly from the individual farm to the individual consumer.

As to the preparation of that food, the movement takes its inspiration from "slow food" guru chef Alice Waters, whose Berkeley restaurant Chez Panisse revolutionized American haute cuisine a generation ago, and who in recent books like *The Art of Simple Food: Notes, Lessons and Recipes from a Delicious Revolution* and *Slow Food Nation's Come to the Table: The Slow Food Way of Living* alerts her readers to the need to "remake their relationship" with food. Waters is not alone in the field of how-to books for this lifestyle shift: in advance of Christmas 2008, Amazon.com featured a list of no fewer than forty "Seasonal, Mostly Vegetarian Cookbooks for Budding Locavores." Summing up the primary principles of locavorism, the compiler of that list, one J. S. Boyd of Churchtown, Pennsylvania, wrote: "So you've signed up for a farm share, hit the local farmer's market, and committed to cooking from scratch and eating a mostly plant-based diet that's better for you and for the planet. Congratulations! Now what do you do with all that kohlrabi? What the heck is kohlrabi, anyway?"

I haven't polled any of my Carter County neighbors as to their views on locavorism, and transplanted Easterner that I am, and cognizant of the movement's implicit cultural elitism, I'm not liable to any time soon. But I can imagine their likely responses to the idea. They would surely invoke the local mantra about mostly coastal city-folk: that they don't understand where food comes from, they think milk comes from a refrigerator case, and burgers from the McDonald's drive-through. They would probably object that relying on the Carter County "foodshed" would entail too many "exemptions"; in addition to spices and coffee and such, they'd have to add those little marshmallows that are so good in Jell-O salad, not to mention the Jell-O itself, along with Mountain Dew to wash it down.

They might well also contend that it was folks in these parts who invented the concept of eating locally in the first place, back in the "dirty thirties," when nobody had any money, but most folks had a garden and a few hens or pigs or a milk cow, and people bartered venison for eggs, and vegetables for bacon, or performed odd jobs in town or a few hours of ranch labor for bread or milk or a bit of beef. And they would object—rightly, I believe—that when it comes to genuine self-sufficiency, and the physical and mental stamina required to merely survive in a climate like ours, people who have sufficient time on their hands to muse about creative ways to present kohlrabi probably don't know squat.

I don't mean to sound dismissive of the localism idea—or ideal—here. In fact, I find it in many ways intriguing, and constructive, particularly with regard to its emphasis on becoming an educated consumer, promoting sustainable local agriculture, and taking an active role in producing and preparing real, good, additive-free food. My own can't-do-without "exemptions" would differ from my Carter County neighbors', running more toward wild-caught Gulf shrimp, un-oaked Australian Chardonnay, Irish black tea, and French vodka. But in addition to the movement's cultural elitism—with which, obviously, I could, given the right circumstances, pretty readily identify—there is the perhaps even more problematic matter of its *regional* elitism. It is, after all, not that difficult for Alice Waters or Michael Pollan, both of whom live in the San Francisco Bay area, to celebrate the rewards of eating locally. To be fair, there isn't much—from fresh seafood to fine wines to year-round farmers' market produce—that isn't readily available within a hundred-mile radius of Berkeley. Barbara Kingsolver's yearlong experiment in locavorism, recounted in *Animal, Vegetable, Miracle*, was surely facilitated by her family's move to the temperate southern Virginia climate, where they had inherited a farm with a long growing season. Her doubtless hefty publisher's advance for the book project probably didn't hurt either, when it came to freeing up time for the endless hours of canning, pickling, preserving, freezing, slaughtering, butchering, and cheese-making she describes as essential to her family's cuisine.

Writers like these tend to bemoan the fact that certain food items—bananas are usually invoked as a convenient example—must simply be done without, for the sake both of locavoristic consistency and the health of the planet. Yet as earnest and forward thinking and deserving of serious attention as they are, they seem nonetheless ill-situated—both culturally and geographically—to comprehend how, in the depths of an eastern Montana January with a blizzard howling outside, a clementine imported from Chile or Spain can seem like a miracle of nature. Nor do these writers necessarily appreciate that in terms of "food-miles"—the carbon cost of transporting food globally—the environmental price of those clementines shipped in or imported by rail to our neck of the woods is actually less than that of, say, tomatoes grown hydroponically and trucked into their own local farmers' market by a regional producer. A widely reported study in the United Kingdom found that, in terms of its carbon footprint, New Zealand lamb was pound for pound far more environmentally friendly than that produced in England for local consumption. And nature writer Jan Zita Grover, in a review of Kingsolver's *Animal, Vegetable, Miracle* astutely pointed out that in exempting things like coffee and chocolate from their locavore diet, her family was actually working against the interests of those "Fair Trade" producers in South America and Africa who frame the sustainable production of these crops as an issue of social, as well as environmental, justice. In a global economy, remaking one's relationship with food can prove fiendishly complicated.

From the vantage point of the hunter, of course, there is a delicious—if saddening—irony in the locavore's drive to become reacquainted, in meaningful if sometimes insufficiently thought-through fashion, with the sources of his or her daily sustenance. In "Locavore, Get Your Gun," an op-ed essay that ran in the December 14, 2007, *The New York Times*, Alaska outdoor writer Steven Rinella cannily observed of venison: "In the traditional vernacular, we'd call that 'game meat.' But, in keeping with the times, it might be better to relabel it as free-range, grass-fed, organic, locally produced, locally harvested, sustainable, native, low-stress, low-impact, humanely slaughtered meat."

Exactly so, but with a vital difference. The hunter's experience of his or her food begins with an awareness of participation in, not alienation from, the workings of the natural world. In this sense, the meat the hunter brings home is, as Paul Shepard remarked at one point, "the best of foods," because it embodies the encounter of life and death that reconnects us to the rhythms of nature. It is surely no coincidence that among the traditionally bison-hunting Blackfoot Indians, the word for bison meat means "real food."

Nor was it any coincidence that Doug and I, as hunters, decided to raise bison rather than cattle and, eventually, to offer bison hunts on the ranch. It was, if you will, one facet of our own becoming native to this place. It was, simultaneously, a way of returning the place to its own natural history.

BACK TO THE FUTURE

Ecologist Richard Manning remarks, in his *Grassland*, that "Saying the bison are back is only another way of saying the prairie is back. . . . All of the grassland west is a candidate for restoration ecology, a candidate for resurrection, and that resurrection must include bison. The prairie between the Rockies and the Mississippi River was held by three pillars:

bison, fire, and grass, and the place cannot live again until all three return." Our aversion to "prescribed burns" notwithstanding, Manning is here offering a fair description of the environmental philosophy underlying our Crazy Woman Ranch. And while, as I shall describe later on, our decision to offer bison hunts was spurred by economic as well as ecological considerations, it immediately felt not only appropriate, but inevitable. After all, hunting has figured prominently throughout the history of human interactions with the North American bison. To Manning's triad of bison, fire, and grass, we would add hunting as a fourth necessary component of the reawakened prairie.

The original locavores in these parts, Paleo-Indians were hunting the buffalo communally by the close of the last Ice Age, and their descendants saw in the bison not only the source of their sustenance, but their most heavily vested religious symbol. Down through the mid-nineteenth century, human hunting bore no ill effect on bison herd health or numbers, even though, as is widely acknowledged, far more bison were killed than the Plains Indians were actually able to use. It took Euro-American market hunters to bring the bison to the brink of extinction. Yet the atrocity of market hunting itself spurred the likes of Theodore Roosevelt and Gifford Pinchot on the one hand to inaugurate the conservation movement, and on the other to promote the ideal of sport hunting as founded in an ethic of fair chase. The movement they spawned laid the foundation, in turn, for Aldo Leopold's creation of the science of wildlife management, and his holistic vision of a land ethic. Today's heightened awareness about the impact of humans on the nonhuman environment is evidence that we can, and need to, learn from our mistakes. As the hunter and holy man Sitting Bull might have remarked, this lesson is a gift of the buffalo.

Some critics would counter, of course, that any Euro-American appeal to Native American lifeways in this regard rings hollow, even hypocritical. I agree, and I am alive to the danger of construing the notion of "becoming native" too broadly, or facilely. A quick Google of that phrase turns up links like the one to the Earth Heart Sanctuary, founded by late–middle-aged Caucasians Sunny Baba and Brooke Medicine Eagle, whom the site describes as "a modern-day couple living simply in elegant beauty, symbiotic with the earth," and preaching the process of "reindigenation," which evidently involves a lot of feathers, buckskin fringe, beadwork, and drumming.

I was at a conference at the University of Nebraska a few years ago, where Gerard Baker, the Mandan-Hidatsa park superintendant of Mount Rushmore, was a keynote speaker on the role homesteading had played in the destabilization of High Plains Native tribal and family structures. There was a white woman in the audience, who may well have been outfitted by Earth Heart Sanctuary, and who raised her hand throughout the postlecture question period. Baker had a plane to catch, and his aides were pressing him to bring the Q&A to a close, but he waved them off and gestured to the woman: "You've really been wanting to ask a question," he said. "Go ahead. I have time for one more."

Taken aback by the sudden attention directed her way, the rather birdlike woman demurred. "Oh no, I don't really need to, that's all right."

Baker, sensing her nervousness now that all eyes were on her, smiled encouragingly. "No, really," he said, "I can tell you really want to ask something."

"Oh, no, no, I don't want to ask it. That's all right," she jittered in response. They went back and forth this way for three or so more rounds, and she finally summoned the courage to rise and pose her question: "Don't you think," she ventured, "that . . . well, we all know terrible things happened in the past . . . but don't you think that today,

Our bison herd in summer. Photo by Doug Stange.

the important thing is for us all to live together in peace and harmony, and to do that it doesn't really matter what color you are or what your ethnicity is, because we are all, after all, human. And, that being the case, does it really matter whether Indians and whites intermarry, or whether individual Native cultures survive? Isn't the point really for us to survive as a human family? And aren't we all—all of us who were born in this country—'native Americans' anyway? Isn't it really more important to get back to the earth—to practice vegetarianism, things like that . . ." Sensing she had spoken long enough, and perhaps sensing as well that the rest of the audience was in a collective state of suspended animation, she abruptly sat down.

"You were right," Baker deadpanned. "You didn't really want to ask that question." He then managed to find a way to respond graciously, and to the general effect that the woman was embarrassingly clueless.

So I want to make it clear here that I am not talking about "appropriating" Indian lifeways, or "going Native" with regard to the Native American ethic of the hunt. As a Euro-American, I do not need to, since the same blood runs anciently in my own veins. We Anglos and the Indians have the primordial bison hunt in common. There is evidence that as early as seventy thousand years ago, Neanderthal hunters in what is now southwestern France were driving bison and other large game over cliffs similar to the pishkuns (that is, buffalo jumps) of the American West. Paleolithic cave art attests that our Cro-Magnon forebears were communal bison hunters, too. Bison are among the most prolific figures adorning such celebrated caves as Lascaux in France, and Altamira in Spain. The first cave drawing discovered in the Alps, dating to twenty thousand years ago, was of a bison cow. The first examples of Stone Age art discovered in the British Isles were rock engravings of bison, thought to date back fifteen thousand years or so, to the time when Britain was still part of the European landmass.

Archaeologists have long debated the meaning and function of these prehistoric art works. The dominant line of thinking used to be that the images related to sympathetic hunting magic ("If you draw them, they will come"), and/or to sexual symbolism connected perhaps with fertility rituals. More recent scholarship has thrown these classic theories into question. Are the paintings indicative of the birth of human cognition? Or are they, in fact, sophisticated pictures of complex cosmologies? Alternatively, do they reflect an observant human mind that has learned, through long hunter-forager acquaintance with the surrounding world, to depict that world in what can only be called naturalistic fashion? That is—to raise a question my art historian colleagues surely would at this juncture—are we talking about a combination of something like nature drawing, and something like art for art's sake here?

Take the ceiling of Altamira's "Great Hall," for example. A herd of twenty bison—some female, some male—wanders its expanse, in what appears to be a unified composition. It is clearly a particular herd, at a particular moment. As evolutionary biologist Jared Diamond describes it:

> [M]odern studies of the mating behavior of bison strongly suggest that the Great Hall depicts, with stunning accuracy, a herd of bison during their brief late-summer rut, the sole time of year when adult male and female bison associate closely. Biological understanding can even explain a scene of which art historians have been unable to make any sense: a depiction of a female bison mounting a male! As farmers and animal behaviorists are aware . . . sexually receptive cows and female bison often do mount bulls to arouse them if they are not quite ready to copulate. Thus, the Altamira Great Hall may be neither a collection of individual paintings that happen to share the ceiling nor a symbolic expression of male/female duality, but a unified realistic composition by an artist or group of artists familiar with bison habits.

Of course, these artists—working about twenty thousand years ago—were neither farmers nor biologists: they were hunters. And of course their art expresses a meticulous knowledge of animal behavior and anatomy: some of the bison at Lascaux are so finely detailed as to have tear ducts. The reason for this is simple, as any serious modern hunter could tell you. One cannot successfully hunt an animal one does not know, and know intimately.

What is so striking about so many of the European cave paintings is, ultimately, the way they speak to us today. Indeed, they are so deeply powerful because they are so startlingly familiar. The late paleontologist Stephen Jay Gould reflected, at one point, on how ironic it is that archaeologists have mostly consigned these images to the realm of the "primitive" or "precognitive." We are, he observed, "surprised, even stunned, to discover that something so old could be so sophisticated. Old should mean rudimentary—either primitive by greater evolutionary regress toward an apish past or infantile by closer approach to the first steps on our path toward modernity . . . The first known expressions of representational art should therefore be crude and primitive. Instead, we see the work of a primal Picasso—and we are dumbstruck."

And yet, Gould points out, we are far closer in time to these Pleistocene painters, than they were to those first Homo sapiens who evolved on the African savanna two-hundred-thousand-years ago. "These paintings," he observes, "speak so powerfully to us because we know the people who did them; they are us." As to the artists being "primal Picassos": upon visiting the cave, that great revolutionizer of modern art himself is said to have proclaimed, "After Altamira, all is decadence."

Aesthetically, then, images like these prehistoric representations can return us to our ancient selves. The question is, can we take the next step, back to the future as it were? Can we reinvigorate the hunting sensibility that brings these images to life? Some, like Paul Shepard, have suggested that we not only can, but must. In his last book, *Coming Home to the Pleistocene*, Shepard notes that to answer the question "How do we become native to this place?" we ought not look to history because "history itself is the great de-nativizing process." No, he suggests, we need to look beyond—or before—history, to experience the world as our prescientific and preliterate forebears might have experienced it:

> Ecology is largely conceptual. One sees plants and animals, the terrain, water, and sky, not an "ecology." Animals and plants are the language of nature, together participating in human perception in a great semiosis, a principle of analogy and a gift to human society. Before the signs turned into an alphabet, we read the world as the hunter/gatherers read tracks in a world of metaphors of human society, a special analogy to ecology.

Shepard cites archaeologist N. K. Sanders, who observed about the immediacy of Paleolithic cave paintings that "though man was seldom shown, he was the invisible participant in everything portrayed." One thinks here of the handprints on the walls of Altamira, and elsewhere. Only much later does art become an exercise in detachment, mirroring the human objectification of and alienation from the natural world. And as that happens, the familiar becomes strange.

We end up in the alienated situation described, in another context (that of his own 1933 memoir), by Lakota actor and writer Luther Standing Bear:

The white man does not understand the Indian for the reason that he does not understand America. He is too far removed from its formative processes. The roots of the tree of his life have not yet grasped the rock and soil. The white man is still troubled with primitive fears; he still has in his consciousness the perils of this frontier continent, some of its vastnesses not yet having yielded to his questing footsteps and inquiring eyes. . . . The man from Europe is still a foreigner and an alien. And he still hates the man who questioned his path across the continent. But in the Indian the spirit of the land is still vested; it will be until other men are able to divine and meet its rhythm. Men must be born and reborn to belong. Their bodies must be formed of the dust of their forefathers' bones.

Shepard, however, suggests that we can indeed be reborn, and heal ourselves of our alienated state, by somehow crossing that bridge back to the Pleistocene:

White European/Americans cannot become Hopis or Kalahari Bushmen or Magdalenian bison hunters, but elements of those cultures can be recovered or re-created because they fit the heritage and predilection of the human genome everywhere, a genome tracing back to a common ancestor that Anglos share with Hopis and Bushmen and all the rest of *Homo sapiens.* The social, ecological and ideological characteristics natural to our humanity are to be found in the lives of foragers. . . . [T]hey are our human nature.

In other words, we are still hunter-gatherers; the trick is to bring this awareness back to the surface, and to life.

And this means that while not all of us can, or will want to hunt, some of us must. In an important early article titled "A Theory of the Value of Hunting," Shepard observed that the hunter plays the important role of "agent of awareness" for culture at large:

What does the hunt actually do for the hunter? It confirms his continuity with the dynamic life of animal populations, his role in the complicated cycle of elements . . . and in the patterns of the flow of energy. . . . Aldo Leopold postulated a "split rail value" for hunting, a reenactment of past conditions when our contact with the natural environment and the virtues of this contact were less obscured by the conditions of modern urban life. . . . Regardless of technological advance, man remains part of and dependent on nature. The necessity of signifying and recognizing this relationship remains. The hunter is our agent of awareness.

In an important study of the attitudes of modern hunters and anti-hunters, social psychologist Stephen Kellert of Yale University quotes the above passage as an illustration of what he terms the "naturalistic hunting attitude," which he writes "more than any other motivational source for hunting, is compelled to confront and rationalize the death of the animal," and the "essential paradox of inflicting violence on a natural world cherished for its quiet beauty."

Shepard remarks about hunting: "Wildness is what I kill and eat because I, too, am wild." Such a hunt yields "the best of foods," or "real food." In a culture so disastrously out of touch with the natural processes of living and dying as our own, we need more of this kind of food. Might bison hunts, in particular—the consciousness they engender, the food they yield—therefore provide deeply enriching opportunities to reconnect with our anciently rooted selves? Might affording this experience to hunters and other sojourners here not perhaps be the best role we could play in the genuine reintroduction of the bison to their original home range? Carefully designed and well regulated bison hunts could and should be a part of the return of the bison to the Great Plains. If they are not, then that return will remain incomplete: If we let bison become mere livestock, and ourselves be mere consumers—whether of buffalo burgers or buffalo-as-scenery—then we will have done the bison, and ourselves, a greater disservice than did the market hunters of a century ago. We need the bison to be wild, so they can teach us about our own inner wildness. Hunter-environmentalists, working with conservation-minded ranchers, could help assure bison live a good life and die a good death. Both animal and human communities would be the richer for it. And the humans would be wiser, as well.

So Doug and I found ourselves speculating, for a variety of reasons both theoretical and practical, ten years ago. The outcome—transforming our ranch "operation" from the production of breeder calves to the cultivation of a well integrated multigenerational bison herd—altered our relationship to this land and to the buffalo. It also raised further questions about the nature, and culture—and business—of hunting.

Dancing bull. Photo by Doug Stange.

CHAPTER 8
The Business of Buffalo

🐃 The American bison has made a spectacular comeback, after facing near extinction at the close of the nineteenth century. However, the bison are back in radically different circumstances. These are not, by and large, wild, free-ranging herds. There are a few public herds—in Yellowstone National Park, in South Dakota's Custer State Park and Wind Cave National Park, in Montana's National Bison Range, and on public lands in Utah and Alaska—as well as herds being reestablished on Indian tribal lands. Altogether, these account for perhaps 15,000 bison. The rest of North America's roughly 350,000 bison are on private lands today, where they are, ironically, more likely to be classified as livestock than as large game. Viewed in this light, the return of the bison is arguably as much a matter of progressive ranching as of wildlife management.

We initially got into bison in the early 1990s, at a time when the market for buffalo was conspicuously more robust than that for cattle. With unstable cattle prices, growing health concerns about beef consumption, and a chronically anemic farm and ranch economy, many a ranch was then being saved—from receivership on one hand, subdivision on the other—by the switch to more profitable bison. What was good for business was also good for the environment. Bison being far more environmentally friendly than beef cattle or sheep, those ranchers who were helping bring back the bison were also helping to bring back the mixed-grass prairies of the High Plains and Southwest.

This return of the bison was not without some risk, however, to the former "monarchs of the plains." As more and more cattlemen became attracted to raising buffalo, there was, Doug and I quickly discovered, growing pressure within the bison industry to "cattle-ize" the North American herd, via branding, breeding for docility, dehorning, and grain-finishing in feedlots. The logic was essentially one of efficiency; what worked for one bovine species would work equally well for the other. Never mind that the feedlot system of corporate meat production was geared toward a volume of output the bison industry could never duplicate: the beef cattle slaughtered in one week in this country outnumber the entire North American bison herd. Never mind that precisely what attracted health-conscious consumers and gourmet chefs alike to bison meat was its leanness and low cholesterol: Americans would learn to prefer "well marbled" bison in the 1990s, just as they had bought into the marketing idea that fatter beef was better beef in the 1950s. And never mind that the drive to domesticate bison as exotic captivity-raised alternative livestock—akin to ostriches, emus, and pen-raised elk and deer—flew in the face not only of the animals' natural and cultural history, but of common sense as well: animal agriculture was animal agriculture, we heard time and again, and what was good enough for Dad was still damned well good enough.

From the outset, our sympathies ran with those who supported the idea of keeping bison as wild as possible, and feeding them on native grasses and grass hay. We had visited a number of bison ranches prior to building a herd of our own, including a major producer in western South Dakota who had converted his father's cattle finishing facilities—a system of high walled cramped corrals designed for minimal animal mobility, hence maximum weight gain—so that he could market his grain-finished buffalo directly to the processing facility then being built by the newly formed North American Bison Cooperative (NABC) in New Rockford, North Dakota. He bragged that his "pasture to paddock" approach was the same system Ted Turner was adopting, on his Flying D ranch in Montana. It neither looked nor felt like something we'd want to do, but we planned a smaller operation anyway, geared more toward selling weanling breeder stock than meat-on-the-hoof.

When we purchased our starter herd of twenty-five weanling heifer calves, then, we knew we were walking into an ideological minefield, but as academics we figured we could weather that readily enough. And as far as the market was concerned, how animals were raised ultimately mattered less than their bloodlines and overall condition. That was in 1993, when quality heifer calves were selling for $1,000 apiece. The following year we bought from a local producer our second twenty-five weanling heifers for $1,500 apiece, along with two breeding age bulls. In 1996, we had our first calf "crop," and were able to sell our weanling heifers for $2,000. A year later, having added another breeder bull to the mix, we achieved a 98 percent production rate from our fifty cows, and sold our weanling heifers for $2,200 apiece. In 1998, we invested in another breeder bull from a major producer in South Dakota, and our weanling heifers went for $2,400. Bull calves were generally about 50 percent of the "crop." Most of them would eventually go to slaughter after a year or so, although a few would mature as breeder bulls; as weanlings, they consistently sold in the $650 to $750 range.

In short, life was pretty good. Doug's income from the ranch was equaling mine from college teaching. Getting our bison operation up and running had involved some major investment: $62,500 for our cows, $20,000 for the breeding bulls, and another $25,000 for handling facilities. But with prices rising as they were, and our near-perfect annual production rate, we were beginning to make a substantial dent in the loans we had taken out up front. All of our sales were off-the-ranch "private treaty" sales, that is, we set the price and buyers came to us, to collect their calves. Our banker was happy, and so were we.

We were also growing nervous, however, about the fantastic rate at which bison sale prices were appreciating. We had seen something very like this before, in the llama world where certain key auctions— most notably the annual "Firecracker" and "Celebrity" sales—set the standard for prices across the board. Those same auctions were driven by breeders largely buying from one another, which had the predicable effect of artificially driving prices up. The most notorious case was of a big-wooled "celebrity" of a herd sire named Catman, that sold to a corporation of Montana investors for a cool $175,000 in 1989. We hadn't moved in those rarified circles, of course, having paid $4,500 for Silver Sage's Garth Brooks at the 1991 Firecracker sale. But in that economically inflated climate, all it took was one unpredictable development to bring prices crashing down across the board.

That development was an unexpected clean bill of health for Latin American llamas. Since 1930 the USDA had essentially banned the importation of llamas from South America, owing to concerns over hoof-and-mouth disease. In the early 1990s, several llama producing areas south of the border achieved disease free status, leading to the importation of fresh Latin American llama stock to this country. With these sexy new bloodlines from Peru, Chile, and Bolivia, and a growing glut on the market of less-than-perfect U.S.-bred llamas (some of them sired by the likes of Catman), auctions took on the aura more of a pyramid scheme than of bona fide alternative agribusiness. Apart from a few breeders shuttling their animals back and forth in a semblance of legitimate sales, the market completely imploded. We got out while the getting was possible, if not exactly good, selling our last few llamas for bargain rates, giving a couple away, and cutting our losses.

To be sure, the picture for the bison industry was fundamentally different, and theoretically much better. These animals, after all, have clear economic worth primarily as meat, with head, horns, and hide providing additional collateral uses. (When things were heading south in the llama world, producers bemoaned the fact that although llama meat is commonly consumed in the Andean region of South America, North Americans just could not be acclimated to that use for the petlike wooly wonders. A similar quandary faces horse breeders in this country today, in the face of massive horse overpopulation, and a collapsed auction market.) The smart money certainly seemed to be on bison—not only was Ted Turner a proponent, so too were investing firms like Goldman Sachs and Merrill Lynch, listed alongside Turner as members in good standing in the National Bison Association's directory. Indeed, thumbing through our first copy of the directory, we joked that there appeared to be as many bison producers in Manhattan as in Montana.

From the outset, Doug and I were avid supporters of the bison business. We were members of state, regional, and national bison associations, in which we participated actively. I did a workshop at one National Bison Association summer meeting, about constructive ways to deal with animal rights activists who had, at the time in the mid-1990s, sought to appropriate the buffalo as a potent symbol for getting their antimeat, anti-agriculture, antihunting messages across to the American public. Doug spoke at a winter meeting of the Montana

Buffalo Association, working from our experience of the llama debacle, and warning his fellow bison ranchers not to make the same mistakes as had the camelid crowd, propping up prices to create a bubble that was bound to burst, and in the process pricing all but the very wealthy out of the market. He also wrote a cover article for the *North American Bison Journal*, "So You Want to Raise Bison? Ten Tips for Newcomers," offering practical on-the-ground advice on how to break into bison ranching.

One of the points Doug made in that article had to do with what a congenial group bison ranchers were. "Bison producers," he wrote, "are invariably proud of their ranches, immensely enamored with their animals, and interested in questions as to how their animals behave and how their ranches function. They tend to exude a friendliness and optimism that comes with economic growth and promise." That was in October 1999, when life still looked good in the bison world. Prices for calves and yearlings had wobbled a bit, in what looked like a predictable market correction. But auction results remained overall encouraging, particularly at the bellwether sales at South Dakota's Custer State Park and the Gold Trophy sale in Denver. At the latter, a Grand Champion bull had sold a few months earlier for one hundred thousand dollars. Compared to cattlemen, bison ranchers had reason to be in a collective good mood, which they generally maintained unless, or until, someone raised the question of grass-fed versus grain-finished "product."

Larger producers, most of whom had transited over from cattle to bison or raised both species on their spreads, tended to favor grain-finishing. They also tended to be in key positions of power in the NBA. Smaller operators, many of whom like ourselves had no background in the cattle industry, were more likely to lean in the direction of grass-fed bison. One of them, Nebraska rancher T. R. Hughes, in 1999 founded the Great Plains Buffalo Association with a declared commitment to raising free-range bison. (We were charter members.) "We stand with the Native Americans and others on this issue," Hughes told a reporter for the business publication *Insight on the News*, allying the grass-fed producers with those Indian groups who were working to bring bison herds back to Native lands, under the umbrella of the South Dakota–based InterTribal Bison Council (ITBC). Fred DuBray, ITBC's founder, explained that group's point of view this way: "We want to restore bison as a wild animal, so they can maintain the integrity of who they are. Feeding them for the purpose of 'fattening them up,' then administering shots of worming medicine and such, kills the spiritual relationship with the animal, and you can't separate the spiritual aspect from the economic."

It wasn't exactly a replay of the Indian Wars, or indeed of the range wars of the nineteenth century that had pitted "sod-busting" homesteaders against don't-fence-me-in cattle barons. But there was something of an echo of both, however twisted, at work. I somewhat unwittingly entered the fray in 2001. On Valentine's Day that year, *The New York Times* food section published a terrific "Eating Well" article by their longtime food writer Marian Burros, titled "Buffalo Steak Frites with Bearnaise? Well, Yes." Therein, Burros remarked that she personally had replaced beef in her diet with bison, and had discovered that she was not alone: there was a growing demand for bison not only among consumers, but also among top chefs in New York. She interviewed several, who gave various reasons for their preference for bison meat, all of which would ring a bell with any proponent of grass-fed bison. One remarked on its similarity to "Argentine beef . . . more gamy, more tender." Another noted that "Ranchers raise buffalo like cows were raised thirty years ago. Buffalo travel a lot during the day and eat just the flower part of the grass, the part that grew the night before. They definitely have more flavor than beef and are sweeter." Yet another praised bison's "cleaner, lighter flavor." Burros went on to note that these chefs unanimously preferred grass-fed bison over grain-fed.

Doug and I were both excited by this article, and thought it deserved a wider readership within the bison industry. So I penned the following note:

> Greetings fellow and sister bison producers,
> This wonderful article, by *The New York Times* top food writer, appeared in last week's food section. The good news is that gourmet chefs are choosing bison over beef. PLEASE NOTE: Their main reasons for making this choice have to do with the superior quality of grass-fed, free range animals. What clearer argument against the "cattle-ization" of the bison industry can there be, than the fact that one of the major suppliers of bison meat to New York's high-end restaurants, D'Artagnan, buys their meat from Canada?
> The handwriting is on the wall, regarding the future of our industry. The question is, will we be smart enough to read it?
> All good wishes,
> *Doug and Mary Stange*
> CRAZY WOMAN BISON

I e-mailed this message, with a link to the article, to several state bison associations, as well as to a number of individual bison ranchers we knew. I received a few "thank you" replies, some merely polite, some genuinely supportive. I also received the following annoyed response, from the president of a bison association in a midwestern state where it is fair to say that corn is a major commodity:

> The [state association] has emphatically refrained from starting an internal war regarding the grass-fed/grain-fed issue. There are more important battles to be won in this fragile industry. . . . Many members of [our association] feed their buffalo grain on a regular basis. Not one of these people can be accused of ruining the industry. All are hardworking producers enjoying the benefits of bison. Therefore, because it is a free country, I choose to let them continue to do so.

> I will also wager the reason they are using Canadian meat is because of the fact that it is sold in the U.S. cheaper than the animals raised here in the U.S.

He probably didn't even bother to skim the *Times* article. He probably didn't feel he needed to, to form his opinion of it, or of us. A couple of years earlier, Doug had been at a roundtable session at the summer meeting of the National Bison Association, devoted to different feeding systems for buffalo. A crusty old-school Wyoming rancher was explaining the advantages of setting up a feedlot geared especially toward finishing bison on grain, and expounding on his success in that regard. He was casually challenged by a young man, from a Nebraska ranching family and apparently fresh out of the ag program at the university in Lincoln, who explained how on their place they were getting identical or better results by feeding their bison exclusively on native hard grasses. He could match the Wyoming rancher's results pound for pound. This reasonable challenge to conventional wisdom generated an apoplectic response. The old man's face puffed up and reddened. He rose out of his chair, jabbed his finger at the young man, and bellowed, spit flying: "You do things *your* way, and *I'll* do things *MY* way!"

Of course, when the going is getting tough, the tough can have a tendency to dig in their heels. And that was happening in the bison world by 2001, when things were beginning to feel, as my Midwestern antagonist had put it, "fragile" indeed.

BUFFALOED

The grass-fed/grain-fed debate within bison circles was, in turn, played out against the backdrop of two widely reported news stories, both of which captured national interest and to a great extent framed buffalo issues for the American public. The first was the controversy, begun in the late 1980s and to some extent still ongoing today, over the management of the Yellowstone bison herd. Bison can be carriers of a disease, brucellosis, which can cause abortions in cattle, and undulant fever in humans, should they come into contact with the fresh afterbirth of infected bison cows. The wild Yellowstone herd was known to harbor an undetermined number of infected animals. And the herd had grown too big for the Park to support year-round; annually, in winter, bison drifted out onto public and private lands within the larger Yellowstone ecosystem. Montana was certified a "brucellosis-free" state, which gave its stockmen a number of advantages when it came to marketing their cattle across state lines and internationally. Fearing loss of that status, cattle ranchers pressed for a reduction in the Yellowstone herd, to protect cattle grazing in summer on leased public land by keeping the bison in the Park year-round.

It was a bureaucratic boondoggle from the get-go. Agencies involved in setting policy included the National Park Service (the branch of the Department of the Interior which administers Yellowstone), the National Forest Service (the wing of the Department of Agriculture that has authority over most of the public land in the greater Yellowstone ecosystem), the Bureau of Land Management (another Interior division with jurisdiction over some of the public land), the U.S. Fish and Wildlife Service (because the Yellowstone bison are classified as wild game), the Montana Department of Fish, Wildlife, and Parks (for the same reason, and because it sets the rules for any "taking" of wild game in Montana), the Montana Board of Livestock (representing cattle concerns), and a number of special interest groups, including the Montana Cattlemen's Association, the Buffalo Field Campaign, and the ITBC.

Hunting was determined to be the best way to manage the herd, although the killing of 569 Yellowstone buffalo in 1988 amounted less to a hunt than to a cull—there was absolutely no sport involved—supervised by Montana fish and game officials. It attracted the attention of animal rights activists, who on skis and snowmobiles tried to haze the bison back into the park, and one of whom assaulted a shooter with his ski pole and smeared bison blood on the man's face. The national media had a field day with the story, fueled by press releases and video provided by antihunting animal rights groups like PETA, as well as from the Buffalo Field Campaign, which took a somewhat more ambivalent view of the role hunting might legitimately play in managing the herd.

Over the ensuing years, different strategies were attempted to control the Yellowstone herd, ranging from quarantining them and shooting only infected animals, to dispatching federal agents to kill wandering bison individuals on demand, to more and less successful variations on the state-regulated hunting theme. In March 1997, after a particularly large kill of eleven hundred bison by federal agents the preceding winter, the issue again made national news when, at a public information meeting in Gardiner, Montana, an antislaughter protester splattered Secretary of Agriculture Dan Glickman, Montana senators Max Baucus and Conrad Burns, and Governor Marc Racicot with a bucketful of rotten bison guts.

Meanwhile, although transmission of brucellosis from bison to cattle could be accomplished in controlled settings, there was no documented evidence that it had ever happened in the wild. Indeed, it was highly unlikely to, since transmission depends on cattle coming in contact with the fresh products of a bison birth, and by the time the Yellowstone bison are calving in spring, they are back within the confines of the Park. That the herd needed to be thinned for its own long-term health was unquestionably true, but the bison brucellosis "problem" was largely a cattlemen's association canard. Ironically, when Montana did lose its brucellosis-free classification in 2008, the cause was traced to infected elk migrating out of Yellowstone and coming into contact with cattle. The same thing had happened five years earlier in Wyoming.

An additional problem arose over the question of how best to deal with the meat and hides from "harvested" Yellowstone bison. The obvious, and ostensibly most politically correct, solution was to give the carcasses of culled animals to Native Americans who, it was assumed, owing both to widespread reservation poverty and to their historical relationship with the buffalo, would be more than happy to take over the responsibility for processing the animals for meat and ritual uses. Unfortunately, because the circumstances in which the Yellowstone bison were killed rendered them ritually unfit, the Indians wanted no part of them. The one solution that might have made practical sense—to allow Native hunters themselves to thin the Yellowstone herd and deal with the animals communally according to their own history and traditions—was never on the table.

By the end of the 1990s, even as the Yellowstone story continued to unfold, the bison industry itself was facing a national embarrassment in the press. It had to do with the NABC bison processing facility at New Rockford, North Dakota, which, by 1999, was processing about half the buffalo meat sold in the United States. That year, the USDA added bison to its subsidy programs and purchased from the NABC six million dollars worth of "trim," that is, the meat that is left over after cutting steaks, roasts, and other prime cuts. The ground trim was to be funneled through the federal Native American Feeding Program. The initial effect was to infuriate Native members of the ITBC, for two reasons. Not only had the tribal bison cooperative not been offered a chance to sell their own meat through this "bonus buy" arrangement, but the meat offered through the federal subsidy program was the fattiest and least desirable bison meat around. There was also some evidence that it was past its sell-by date: the New Rockford facility, in an effort to keep per-pound bison prices up, had stockpiled ground meat, at one point even refusing to sell in bulk to a willing French buyer if it meant lowering the price. The meat now being sold to the government and distributed on reservations as a commodity was two or three years old. That was bad enough, but there was worse to come.

An article originally published in the *Rapid City Journal*, and subsequently widely syndicated, claimed that the bonus buy had been engineered by Ted Turner, who held a 10 percent interest in the New Rockford co-op, and who would thereby profit from this government "handout." In point of fact, Turner's 10 percent interest meant little more than that he could bring proportionally more animals to slaughter there than other shareholders. He liked to describe himself as "just another banana in the bunch," and while this may have been stretching things a tad, at this time the co-op was seriously behind in making any payments at all to any of its 350 members, most of whom were small operators (we were not among them). The government payment went straight into the plant's operating costs. But the story nonetheless had legs and led to splashier treatments, like Lisa Anderson's "How Buffalo Ted Hunts Bison Bucks," in *Insight on the News*.

The following year, post 9/11, North Dakota senator Kent Conrad managed to work a $10 million bison subsidy into the economic stimulus package then making its way through Congress, and the "handout to billionaire Ted Turner" resurfaced in an exposé by Bill Hogan in *Mother Jones*: "Rushing to enlist in the war on terrorism, corporate lobbyists are doing their patriotic duty by seeking federal handouts for everything from bison meat to chauffeured limousines." The bison industry was well on its way to being identified as one of the suspect "special interests" catered to in the 2001 farm "bailout" bill, which included a total of $220 million in subsidies. Most of that money was targeted for the standard commodities (corn, soy, wheat, sugar, cotton), but some of it, like the $10 million allocated for bison meat, was diverted to such less obviously essential crops as watermelons, eggplant, cauliflower, and pumpkins. Senate Majority Leader Trent Lott nattered, "I don't see how spending money on watermelon and bison meat will help the economy to grow." Montana senator Max Baucus countered that smaller producers needed help, too. The bill failed.

The bison industry was by then reeling. Between 1998 and 2002, bison sale prices fell precipitously. Weanling heifer calves were off 85 percent, and yearlings down 89 percent. Spokespersons for the National Bison Association scrambled for explanations: It was a market adjustment. Farms prices go up and down, and we were in a down cycle. The bison industry was experiencing "growing pains." The economy was in a post-9/11 slump, with fewer people getting into alternative ranching and less credit available for newcomers interested in ranching or investing in bison. Consumers were avoiding high-end restaurants, and that helped account for the flagging sales of bison meat. And so on. Dave Carter, then newly installed as executive director of the NBA, saw marketing strategy as the essential problem: "We've been giving people so many messages that it's confusing. We've been telling them it's healthy, it's environmentally friendly, it's part of our Western heritage. The one thing we haven't been telling people is 'Buy it because it tastes good.'"

By 2000 marketing was perhaps the least of our worries. When prices had started to slide in 1999, we held back our calf crop and adopted a wait-and-see attitude. In 2000 we turned down a cash on the barrelhead offer of fourteen hundred dollars for our heifers, which in retrospect we came to regret. But we also resisted the temptation to increase our herd when prices fell even further, a temptation to which our neighbor—the one from whom we had bought our second twenty-five heifers and our first three bulls—succumbed, and it eventually drove him under financially.

There was no market for breeder calves, and we were not a large enough operation to switch solely to meat sales. We actually dodged a bullet in that regard; that was why we never joined the New Rockford co-op, from which to this day most members have extracted only a fraction of what they are owed. We hadn't gotten into the bison business to be meat producers, anyway. We knew we had to do something different. Some bison ranches, including Colorado's Blue Mountain Bison from whom we'd bought our first twenty-five calves, offered guided bison hunts as part of their overall operation. That idea had appealed to us from the beginning, and we'd kept it on the back burner. Now seemed like the right time. The first step was a drive to town, to sound out our banker as to how he felt about shooting some of his collateral. As long as a share of the proceeds went to service our loan, that turned out to be just fine with him.

CHANGING THE CRAZY WOMAN SCENE

The narrative above sketches out the economic reasons why Doug and I commenced our bison hunts in 2001. I hope, however, that it does not suggest that economics provided the only rationale. Indeed, as I wrote it, I found myself cringing—as I always do—at the use of terms like bison *industry*, and meat as *product*, and ranchers as *producers* or *operators*. These terms form a sort of verbal shorthand, and they are those most frequently used in agricultural circles. Yet they also distort our relationship to our animals in some fundamental, and sometimes entirely unconscious, ways. For all of our good intentions about keeping our bison as wild and free-ranging as possible, for example, we had nonetheless unwittingly bought into a key concept derived from cattle ranching: that the purpose of a herd of cows was to produce an annual *crop* of calves, analogous to the wheat and barley and canola harvested on neighboring fields. In our first few years raising buffalo, we might hold back at most two or three promising heifers to mature into producing cows, selling off all the rest, along with all our bull calves. This resulted in a herd that was homogeneous, but that also lacked the multigenerational structure that would be present in any truly wild herd.

For two years, aside from selling a few individual animals locally for meat, we had held onto our entire calf production. This had two consequences. The first we had anticipated: we would have to thin the herd. For the sake of our pastures' health, we have always run fewer stock than our ranch's "carrying capacity," as set by federal agencies. And we were heading into what portended to be a protracted drought cycle. Grass and hay were in short supply, so short in fact that in 2001, unbeknownst to me, Doug took the painful step of shooting a majority of our then unmarketable calves, to preserve the health of their mothers. Our herd was, nonetheless, growing to proportions that might prove unmanageable down the road.

The second consequence of holding onto our calves was unintended, but presented us with an opportunity to rethink the way we managed our bison. The herd was, ipso facto, evolving into a multigenerational bison herd, with mature adults, young adults, adolescents, and small fry. And as a group they began to function more as they would, were they left to their own devices.

We had, from the start, observed certain key behavioral traits in our bison. The top cows in the pecking order tend to be the decision makers for the entire herd. These herd leaders are not necessarily the biggest, but they are obviously the smartest cows. And they tend to hang out together. Now we began to notice other patterns of what can reasonably be called family ties on the one hand, and friendship on the other, among our females. We were still ear tagging our bison then, and readily observed how certain individuals affiliated with each other— yellow-tagged "Bette Davis" (because of her lovely eyes) and "Lucky" (her tag number was seven), for instance, were two lower-status cows who were invariably together. At the same time, it was not uncommon to see mother-daughter-baby triads, where the yearling heifer would perform baby-sitting duties from time to time. Bulls, meanwhile, had their own way of sorting things out in terms of power. Big mature bulls—the two or three we designated as our herd sires—tended to pick up protégés, two- or three-year-old young adult males who invariably were among the most promising prospects for future sires. Bison bulls can begin breeding at age two, but are only fully mature at around six, and before then they generally get to breed only if an older bull lets them. Younger or less well conformed bulls tended either to hang out with their mothers or pal around in groups of two or three or four, on the fringes of the herd.

Getting to know our herd's structure and behavior in this way allowed us to make what we felt to be more intelligent decisions, as time went on, as to how best to manage the Crazy Woman hunts. And the hunts themselves afforded us the chance to really let our bison be bison. Because we were not selling breeder stock, we no longer needed to work all the calves through the chutes, TB-testing each (and affixing a corresponding numbered metal ear clip), vaccinating heifers against brucellosis, and ear tagging them all for identification purposes. Over time, we have pretty much ceased ear tagging altogether, with the exceptions of cows and some bulls we want to mark as definitely off-limits to hunters. We have also found that, because we run our bison in large pastures and employ a vigorous program of rotational grazing, we do not need to worry about deworming them; parasites are largely a by-product of overcrowding. Ours is still a managed herd, to be sure, to the extent that they move within the fenced confines of our ranch and according to our grazing system. They welcome the occasional treat of feed cake, which is the way we move them from one pasture to another, and native hay when winter weather is especially harsh, or when calving time is near. Beyond that, they are born, they live out their lives, and they die on their home range, with minimal human interference.

The economic and practical circumstances that led us to focus our bison "operation" on hunting thus meshed well with the philosophical and ecological considerations that drew us in the direction of bison ranching in the first place. Countering the pressure to turn buffalo into exotic cattle required keeping the animals as wild as possible in a ranch setting. This meant letting them live and die in as natural a fashion as possible. Hunting, we reasoned, turned out to be one key way to accomplish this. And, given the stresses facing bison producers, it made good economic sense as well. It's a sad if simple fact that older or more obstreperous animals need to be removed from any herd. Bulls, especially, have a tendency to "just want to be buffalo" as they age; they can become unpredictable and irascible. One solution to the problem was to truck these animals to a slaughterhouse. Another solution, at once more lucrative for the rancher and more humane to the animals involved, would be to give them a death with dignity, on the grassland they've called home throughout their lives. If market hunting nearly eradicated the wild and free bison in the last century, communal and sport hunting might just help save them in the next. And, in the process, it might contribute to a return to our own human ecocultural roots.

Being hunters and hunting advocates ourselves, Doug and I realized from the outset that we would need to carefully distinguish our Crazy Woman bison hunts from some other hunting opportunities that had begun to spring up as times got tough in the bison world, and that could only go by the name of "canned hunts." These were no more genuine hunts than the Montana Fish, Wildlife, and Parks Department's initial "solution" to the problem of the Yellowstone bison, which had amounted to a hunter's being driven up to within a few yards of a designated bison and firing upon it when an accompanying game warden gave the signal to shoot. Canned hunts, whether of trophy elk or deer in chain-link fenced "preserves," or of ducks "released" from towers, or of bison confined in a corral or paddock, fall well outside anything that can claim to aspire to the ethic of fair chase. And so we gave considerable time and thought not only to the logistics of our hunts, but also to how we would package them, which meant, as well, to what kinds of hunters we wanted to bring to our ranch. We developed a statement of our bison hunting theory and practice, which we initially distributed as a brochure and eventually posted to our Web site:

The Crazy Woman Bison Ranch Experience
TEN THINGS THAT DISTINGUISH CRAZY WOMAN BISON HUNTS FROM OTHER BUFFALO HUNTING OPPORTUNITIES

ONE. Some ranches offer "hunts" held in corrals or pens or paddocks. We differ with those bison producers, as to the ethics of such "canned hunts." Our animals live out their entire lives in large pastures on our 4,400 acre ranch. We aim to give hunters a bona fide hunt in the field. We will not arrange a corral shoot, and we turn away anyone who asks for one.

TWO. Bison ranches that are geared primarily toward meat production frequently cull their poorer specimens to use as hunt animals. But hunting is our Number One priority. Aside from a very small number of exceptional bulls and heifers we hold back for replacement breeding purposes, we view our entire herd's annual production as hunting stock. And we will not let a hunter shoot an animal we wouldn't take ourselves.

THREE. Many bison ranches ear tag the animals they offer for hunts. Some say this aids in tracking wounded bison. Others are virtual hunt-by-numbers operations. Whatever the stated reason, we find hunting ear tagged bison aesthetically distasteful. The animals we designate for hunting are not ear tagged.

FOUR. Unlike those bison hunting operations that require you to take an animal within a short time-frame (e.g., ninety minutes) in order to accommodate as many hunters a day as they can, Crazy Woman gives any hunting party of up to three hunters an entire day to complete their kills.

We do not schedule more than one party per day, unless we have their prior permission. We never schedule more than three hunters in a day.

FIVE. Some bison hunts require additional payment for the meat. Others limit the amount of meat hunters can take home with them. At Crazy Woman, every hunt price includes the head, the hide, and *all* the great meat. In addition, our enlightened state of Montana lacks the general sales tax hunters in most other states must pay.

SIX. There are bison ranches offering hunts in parts of the country in which bison are not native and do not thrive. Not only is the ambiance wrong, these bison are frequently underweight and lack proper conformation. The Crazy Woman Bison Ranch, with its High Plains location, is at the epicenter of the traditional bison range. Our animals flourish on the same hard-grass prairie that their ancestors did thousands of years ago. And our hunters walk the same ground as the original bison hunters of North America.

SEVEN. Most bison ranches that offer hunts do it more or less as an afterthought and/or a secondary source of income. We at Crazy Woman see hunting as a primary way to expand and maintain the bison's ecological niche on the Great Plains. Because we care about the land as much as we do the buffalo, we reinvest a significant portion of the income we derive from bison hunts in a wide variety of wildlife habitat improvement projects on the ranch.

EIGHT. Many ranches offering bison hunts treat buffalo as if they were cattle. They incorporate aspects of the cattle industry that environmentalists and hunter-naturalists are finding increasingly distasteful: de-horning, branding, antibiotics, growth enhancers, feed lots, artificial weaning, and so on. At Crazy Woman Ranch, we don't employ any of these methods of the meat industry. We simply don't.

NINE. Many bison ranches feed buffalo as if they were cattle. They give them various supplements they don't need and "finish" them on heavy doses of grain. The Crazy Woman bison has been fed on our grass and our grass hay since birth, has never received any feed supplements other than minerals, salt, and limited amounts of grain-based feed cake, and has never been inoculated with antibiotics, hormones or insecticides. The meat from our animals is totally natural.

TEN. Unlike the many bison hunt operations that focus their advertising and publicity on expensive trophy bulls, we feel our main constituency is the sportsman and sportswoman who wants an affordable, enjoyable hunt in beautiful, western scenic surroundings. We therefore offer a range of hunts for yearling bulls and heifers, young mature bulls and heifers, and only a limited number of trophy-size mature bulls—all at the most reasonable prices around.

THAT'S THE CRAZY WOMAN BISON EXPERIENCE. WE WOULD LOVE TO SHARE IT WITH YOU.

That was the easy part. We still had to learn the business of buffalo hunting.

HUNTING THE CRAZY WOMAN

You think that cats are all natural hunters, but it isn't really true. We have a barn cat, she has a litter or two every year, and it's fascinating to watch how she figures out which kittens to spend time with, training them to be mousers. She shows them how it's done—I swear she even sets up hunting trials for them, using dead mice as props. And you can see that some of the babies couldn't care less about hunting, they would rather just wrestle with each other or snooze in the sun, while others . . . well, like some of us human beings, they just thrive on it . . .

Our first bison hunting season commenced in the fall of 2001 when I was home on sabbatical leave. Our very first hunter was a woman named Deanne. She and her husband Geoff were Michigan farmers who annually traveled west for elk hunting in Montana. They thought it might be fun to add a bison to that year's hunt. A few hours after an exciting stalk and her efficient kill of a yearling heifer, Deanne looked as sleek and satisfied as the well fed barn cat whose hunting she described as she sat at our kitchen table, basking in both the sunlight filtering through the bay window and the afterglow of a successful hunt. We were feeling equally pleased and mellow. Up until then, the only guiding Doug or I had done had been with friends visiting our place to hunt antelope or deer. Even on those more casual occasions we had remarked how the pressure mounts, when one is trying to facilitate another hunter's success. Now the guiding was part of a business transaction: money was involved, as was the shooting of one of our herd animals. Expectations were high, on both sides. Our customers wanted a quality hunting experience, and we wanted them to effect a quick, humane kill. With Deanne, we were certainly off to a good start.

We were also lucky. It had been a clear, windless morning. The herd was calm, lazily meandering along the forest edge, unaware of our presence as Doug and Deanne worked their way uphill to crest a slight ridge overlooking the bison, Geoff with his camera and I with binoculars hanging back a few yards. When she first saw them, Deanne registered what we would come to recognize as a pretty typical, *WOW* reaction— "buck fever" pales in comparison to the pulse-racing eye-blinking gasp commonly induced in first-time buffalo hunters by their initial sighting of a bison herd in its natural setting. But Deanne settled down quickly, calmed her breathing and, when Doug helped her isolate a yearling that presented a good shot, expertly placed her bullet behind its ear. The heifer staggered a bit, then fell. The sound of the shot set the herd in motion but, as almost invariably happens, a few bison circled back to the downed heifer, nudging her, trying to nose her back up, so she could run along with them. After a

few minutes, as their efforts to stir their now lifeless little sister failed, they lost interest, and trotted off to rejoin the herd. We skidded down the hillside to Deanne's bison, shared a joyous round of smiles and hugs and photographs, and then Doug brought the tractor down to retrieve the carcass which

Our Crazy Woman Ranch logo.

Geoff and Deanne intended to field dress and quarter on their own. That turned out to be a somewhat more daunting task than they had anticipated, and at lunchtime we offered them sandwiches and a chance to come in for a while from the late-October chill. It was then, over a mug of hot tea, that Deanne reflected on feline and human variations on the hunting instinct.

Not all of our hunts have gone off so happily, or flawlessly. One learns by doing, and over time and after dealing with different hunting situations and with varying degrees of hunter ability, we developed a set of ground rules for Crazy Woman hunts. I say "we," although the work has mainly been Doug's, as have the sometime headaches. He is the "master of the hunt" on this ranch. I do what I can, as I can, to support the hunting venture, but given my academic schedule my participation has of necessity been more episodic. He nonetheless counts upon my input and collaboration, and whether I'm fielding phone inquiries or assisting him with a party of hunters, it is important that he and I are on the same page.

First off, then, we require our hunters to sight in their rifles before going afield. This is customary practice for most hunt operations, and it's generally a good idea anyway for any guns that have travelled, particularly via air, with the potential that their scopes might have been knocked out of alignment in baggage handling. Sighting-in serves other functions as well. It gives us the opportunity to observe a hunter's gun handling, as well as any shooting problems he or she may have. And it provides a nice warm-up, to release some of the nervous energy hunters tend to bring to what, for many of them, is the hunt of a lifetime. Most of our hunters arrive well prepared, with properly sighted-in guns and some prior practice on the shooting range, and things go fine. When their shooting looks less than ideal, Doug knows to be prepared to shoot backup if necessary. If it looks absolutely atrocious—and this has, to date, only happened once, when after successive attempts with a properly sighted-in rifle a hunter failed to hit the paper target—Doug is equally prepared to refund a shooter's money on the spot and send him on his way. He also informs hunters that they have up to three shots to kill their bison, after which he will exercise the prerogative to provide back-up.

Field experience with hunters also led to other ground rules. Bison, even relatively small ones, can be difficult to kill: a perfectly adequate rifle for deer is not enough gun for the job. So we require .30 caliber or larger, and Doug consults with hunters in advance about the best bullet type and weight for their particular rifle. We do not allow handguns in any circumstances. Nor do we admit archery hunters. This is as much an aesthetic as a practical matter: Doug and I are both rifle hunters because we both prefer the instantly lethal force of a well-placed bullet to a slower death by blood loss. Besides, only the most expert of archers could hope to down a buffalo with a single arrow. Before the advent of firearms even Native Americans, skilled as they were in archery, knew better than to trust their arrows to bring down this largest of North American prey animals. They employed buffalo "jumps" (more precisely, stampeding a herd over a cliff to its collective demise) to effect their bison kills.

We tailor the rigor of a hunt to our hunters' ages and physical ability. Ideally, hunters stalk their bison on foot, with one or the other of us as a guide. Sometimes a hunter is not up to that, either because of age (we have had hunters who were well into their eighties), or due to physical limitations ranging from bona fide disabilities to the condition of being overweight and out of shape that afflicts too many adult Americans these days. In these cases—or, more rarely, when weather conditions or the herd's collective temperament dictate a more prudent approach—we will position hunters in the bed of a pickup and attempt to get them to within reasonable shooting range of the herd. We call this hunting "safari style," and there is some merit to the analogy.

There are several skinners in the area who contract with our hunters independently to field-dress for them, and two of them—Don and Rick—do really excellent work. While some of our hunters, like Geoff and Deanne, prefer to do their own field-dressing, we strongly encourage them to avail themselves of one of our skinners' services. Buffalo—as Deanne and Geoff readily admitted, after spending several hours wrestling with hers—make elk look easy to work with. It's well worth the relatively modest additional cost to have a professional do the job, particularly if—as is the case with many of our hunters—one plans to tan the hide.

Originally, we offered hunts from mid-October through February, hoping on the one hand to accommodate fall hunters and on the other to ensure top quality hair on hides for those who were looking for a bison robe. Over time, and as we built a clientele of satisfied returning customers, we determined we could shorten our season. It now runs from November first through mid-January. The animals' coats are in optimal condition then, but more importantly the shorter season—even if it may at times involve more concentrated hunting pressure—ultimately minimizes stress on the herd. Our bison, particularly the cows who begin calving in late April or early May, are happier and healthier.

JOYS AND JERKS

One final ground rule should perhaps go without saying. Hunters are paying guests of ours. That is, they are paying a very reasonable price for the privilege of hunting our bison herd, on our private land. We therefore expect them to respect our land, and our animals, and to heed our directions at every phase of the hunt. Given the vagaries of human nature, it's probably not surprising that this rule has from time to time been honored more in the breach than in the observance.

There were, for example, the group of a dozen hunters who descended on our place in December 2003. I am embarrassed to say they were from my home state, New Jersey, and were frankly the kind of guys that make New Jersey a good place to be *from*, if you get my drift. Doug had scheduled their three-day hunt during the week before Christmas, so that I would be home to help out. They would try to shoot four bison a day, more than our usual limit, but this was a big group. They didn't want to spring the extra bucks for a skinner; one of their number, a fellow I'll call Vince, would do that job for each of them. They turned out to be a motley crew distinguished primarily by the fact that they mostly couldn't stand one another. Why, aside from sharing gas and motel costs, they had determined to trek cross country and spend concentrated time together is anybody's guess. The nearest they came to camaraderie was in engaging in conversational blood sport at one another's expense.

Take, for example, one afternoon of this three-day hunt: We are hunting "safari style," and I am in the back of our Toyota pickup with three Great White Hunters. My job is to make sure only one man shoots at one buffalo at a time—not to mention making sure he shoots the right animal. We drive within range of the herd. I am working with (I'll call him) Al. We isolate a young cow for him. He shoots. She reacts to the shot, but doesn't fall. "Shoot her again," I tell him. He hesitates, says he thinks she might yet go down. "Please," I say more firmly. "Shoot her again. She might just as likely take off and get lost in the herd, and then we've got a problem on our hands." He pulls a sour face, sighs heavily, shoulders his rifle, and shoots again. This time she collapses, more squarely hit.

The next hunter up I'll call Dennis. He turns out to be either a better or a luckier marksman than Al, effecting a nice single-shot kill of the heifer I point out to him. His immediate reaction? He turns to Al and sneers, "*Schoolteacher* made you shoot twice." George, the third hunter in the truck, thinks this is hilarious. Al looks like he would like to strangle me. "My first shot was the kill-shot anyway," he barks, then glares my way, snarling, "I didn't need the second one!"

We turn to the task of finding a cow for George. By now the herd is understandably getting pretty restless, and the only shots that present themselves are longer than Doug or I would like, upward of two hundred yards. No problem for him, George says, he's used to long-range western hunting. Doug—sensing that I am having a rough time with these guys—has alighted from the cab of the truck to provide *me* with some backup. He and I agree on which animal is George's: a young cow standing well away from the rest of the herd. We point her out, assuring that George has a good solid rest for his gun, and tell him to shoot. "Not big enough," George replies. "What about that one in front of her?" She's a nice cow, but if she has a tag in her right ear—indicating she's a keeper for us—we cannot see it because she's facing left in profile. With the herd becoming antsy and our mutual desire growing to get these guys their bison so they can be on their way, Doug and I give reluctantly him the nod.

George shoots, and hits her badly, in the haunch. We've no humane option but to instruct him to shoot her again. She is now on the run; he hits her in the belly, she slows a bit, and he shoots her once more. The cow staggers a few more yards, coughing up saliva and blood, then finally goes down on her knees and rolls over onto her side. She is still. Doug and I tell George to wait behind and we run toward her, to discover that she is in fact one of our favorite young cows—a member of a group of four nice yearling heifers we had last year nicknamed the Spice Girls and added to our breeding herd. The mishap is our fault, to the extent that we could not see the yellow tag in her ear. She is also still breathing. Doug puts a bullet where he needs to. By the time we get back to the truck, Vince has arrived to begin field-dressing the three downed bison, and Dennis and Al are both regaling him with the florid details of George's bad shooting. When Vince dresses out our yellow-tagged Spice Girl, we discover she was carrying a fetus.

Those turned out to be three very long days. Vince himself expertly shot a very nice bison, which he then refused to skin out as he had all the others. "I want to take it home skin on, so my wife can see it," he said. "She hunts too, and she'll be real excited." Doug tried to explain to Vince that with the hide on and the corresponding inability to cool the carcass down properly, the meat would be worthless by the time Vince got back to New Jersey. The hide itself wouldn't even be fit for tanning by then. Vince's cohunters suggested maybe Doug had a point, and a photo or two of Vince with his bison might be sufficient, but they couldn't sway him. There was obviously something of a macho display thing going on here: Vince insisted on positioning his buffalo on the flatbed they were pulling so that it was something like the figurehead on a ship's prow. Visually striking to be sure, but also ideally poised to collect road spray, salt, and sand on the way back. I suppose you could argue that he had paid his money and could do what he pleased with the bison he had shot. But we knew it to be a tragic waste in all respects, not least among them reverence for the animal herself.

Doug likes to say that every time a new hunter drives down our road, he wonders whether the person will be a Joy or a Jerk. At this point, by the time they've finished up the paperwork (balance of payment, receipt, liability release) and sighted-in the hunter's gun, he usually already has his answer. The Jerks won't be coming back. Among their number are the guys from Jersey, who did seek a return hunt the following year. ("Sorry, we're all full up!") And a Californian who showed up for his late November hunt wearing a Hawaiian shirt and tennis shoes, wielding an elephant gun with which the best he could manage was wounding a heifer in the cheek—after blithely ignoring Doug's instructions about where to aim—which angered her so that she charged the hunter and Doug, who had to scramble back to the pickup, diving into the cab just as she crashed headlong into the front bumper. And a local hunter, the relative of a friend of ours, who passed up on several good opportunities to shoot a rogue bull we needed to thin from the herd because he wasn't close enough—"close enough" apparently amounting in this shooter's lexicon to point-blank range— and said he'd be back for another try the next day. Doug wound up shooting the bull himself and sending the man's money back.

Jerks, for the most part, do not follow the rules—either of responsible hunting in general, or hunting our ranch in particular. But, in the aggregate, they are—blessedly—far from typical. Most of the well over two hundred hunts we have hosted in the last nine years have, by comparison, been positive, indeed rewarding experiences for us as well as for our hunters. We have by now established a clientele made up almost exclusively of returning hunters and people referred by them. Word of mouth is much more reliable than advertising. The Jerks are fewer and farther between. We are getting to the point where some of our hunters almost feel like family.

They come, and come back, for various reasons: the quality of the meat, certainly, and of the prairie hunting experience. Some are matter-of-fact meat hunters who don't even care to take their hides home with them. Others are looking for a trophy in addition to a freezer full of burger, roasts, and steaks. For many, the mystique of shooting America's largest big game animal holds sway, although it can take various forms. One hunter, Darrell, who has hunted in Africa, ranks the bison he has shot here with the greater kudu and Cape buffalo he took over there, and includes their photos in his trophy album. Steve, a Minnesotan of somewhat more modest means, had Doug photograph him with his yearling bull, wearing a Viking helmet and holding aloft a spear: it made a great Christmas card for him, he said. A number of our hunters have come armed with Sharps .45/70 rifles, seeking the perfect quarry for that original buffalo gun. It's fair to say that for many of our hunters, although they might not articulate it this way, hunting the Crazy Woman serves what Aldo Leopold dubbed the "split-rail value" of hunting: a way of reconnecting not only with the past, but with a more genuine relationship between human and nonhuman nature. It's a way of coming home to one's more primal self, rooted in a deeper and older experience of being human in this world.

Surely, for the sake of affording that experience to fellow and sister hunters, it's worth putting up with the occasional Jerk. I don't want to veer too sharply in the direction of philosophizing about our hunts, because this is a business after all. But its real rewards are, ultimately, less about money than about shared moments. These often have to do with deeply personal concerns our hunters bring to our ranch— concerns to which they may or may not give voice, but which etch into these hunts an added poignancy. Bison hunts are often family affairs of one sort or another, as when a California mother gives a hunt to her teenage son, or a Connecticut father to his fifteen-year-old daughter— the latter having won a bull hunt we had donated to a charity shoot benefiting breast cancer research. Sons who were initiated into big game hunting by their dads a generation or two ago return the favor by bringing their fathers here for the hunt of a lifetime. Husbands and wives hunt together, not infrequently using the occasion to celebrate anniversaries or birthdays or the winter holiday season.

Some of our hunters have battled with cancer or other major illnesses. Most have been survivors who had thought they might never hunt large game again. But at least one was in the terminal phase of throat cancer, and he and the hunting buddies who came with him, his brother among them, knew this would be his last hunting trip. We have also had some hunters with physical disabilities we could work around (we inform hunters in advance if we feel we cannot accommodate them). More than a few of our hunters have been "disabled" merely by advancing age, like one octogenarian, a lifelong big game hunter who remained a dead-on rifleman, and who quipped when Doug asked him whether he foresaw another big game hunt in the offing, "Let me put it this way. At my age, I don't even buy green bananas anymore!"

One of my favorite hunters was a man named Tim. He was a master stonecutter, who had for many years worked at a Minnesota monument works, carving statues of war heroes for city parks and headstones for cemeteries. Now in his mideighties and "semiretired" for several years, Tim was finally thinking it was about time for him to take some real time off. His boss, Ron, who owned the company and who had hunted our place more than once, gave him a bull hunt as a retirement gift. A man soft-spoken to the point of taciturnity, Tim reminded me somewhat of my late father—the sort of man to whom the hackneyed phrase "older gentleman" really properly applies. He arrived one cold November morning in high spirits, eager to succeed on this very special hunt, and like most of our hunters a bit trepidatious. A young co-worker of his, who had served as his cross-country driver, stayed back at the house and we set off on Tim's hunt. It was to be a modified stalk on foot. Tim was not exactly frail, but not precisely spry either. The years had taken their toll as, apparently, had a brush with serious illness of some sort.

As we were getting our gear together for the stalk, Tim, fishing around in his pocket, dropped something shiny on the snowy ground. Doug picked it up to hand back to him. It was a set of keys, the charm on the key ring being a highly polished large-caliber spent rifle cartridge, engraved with initials and a date. "Very nice key ring," Doug said as he handed it to him. Tim took it with a wistful smile. "That was from my last elk hunt, couple of years ago," he explained. "I was having some, uh, health problems, and my son and I figured it'd be my last big game hunt. When I shot my bull, he retrieved the cartridge, had it made into this ring, and surprised me with it that Christmas. A memento of a lifetime of hunting, you might say." He shrugged a little, and flipped the keepsake back into his pocket.

Tim's stalk and subsequent kill went beautifully. We didn't have to travel very far to find the herd, and his bull obligingly moved to a position where Tim could have a good, clear shot. The bipod he'd brought as a rifle rest didn't work so well, as his arthritic body refused to conform comfortably to a prone shooting position. But he managed to steady himself against an old fence post, and dispatched his bull with one expertly placed shot. As he and Doug walked the hundred or so yards to his bison, I fished around in the snow to find the ejected shell, which I pocketed.

Doug had to walk the mile or so back to the house to get the tractor. He suggested Tim and I could wait for him in our pickup, which wasn't too far away. I was happy enough to keep Tim company, although he being an archetypically Minnesotan man of few words, I wasn't certain how we'd while away the next half hour. "Uh," Tim ventured shyly, "I brought along one of these danged disposable cameras. Don't suppose you'd be willing to take a picture or two, of me and my buffalo?" I was more than happy to, and not a little relieved to have something to do to fill the time. All we needed to do was stretch a couple of photographs into several minutes.

That turned out not to be a problem. "OK," he said handing the camera to me, and slinging his rifle strap over his shoulder. "First, let's go back to where I shot from, so you can get me in shooting position." Agreed. We discussed the best camera angle, evaluated the near-noonday light, deliberated the best background. *Click. Click.* I snapped a couple of good photos, from different angles, of Tim taking aim.

"OK, now I've just shot him," he said as he lowered his rifle and looked ahead intently.

Click.

"OK, now I'm walking toward my bull. You might want to shoot me from behind, like this is exactly the way it happened."

Click.

"OK, now I'm coming up on him closer, really getting my first good look at the size of him. Here, you might want to come around over here, capture the look of surprise on my face."

Click.

"OK, now a couple of candid shots of me looking at him, admiring his horns, his coat, you know . . ."

Click. Click.

"OK, now maybe something a little more formal? Me posing with my bull and my gun?"

But of course! *Click. Click. Click.* Maybe a couple of close-ups, too? *Click. Click.*

It was the most delightful impromptu photo op I've ever participated in, with Tim seemingly more animated with every snap of the shutter.

We were still at it when Doug returned with the tractor, and with our friend Maggie in tow. She was visiting us for deer hunting and had volunteered to help with field-dressing Tim's bull, since this was one of the rare occasions when none of our usual skinners were available. Tim was intending to have the hide made into a buffalo robe, which meant taking painstaking care in the skinning. It was a formidable task for nonprofessionals like the three of us, methodically working our way inch by inch to remove the hide from the bison which was suspended, upside down, from the raised tractor loader. About an hour into it I made the unfortunate—and totally unintended, if anatomically accurate—remark that we were, at least, now over the hump. Tim, along with his younger coworker who had now joined us, found it all quite amusing. For the older man, this hunt had obviously been an exhilarating experience.

It was quite late in the day by the time Tim and his driver were fixing to get on the road back to Minnesota. As we were saying our good-byes in the oncoming twilight, I remembered the rifle shell in my pocket. My eyes met Doug's, who nodded and smiled when he saw what I had in my hand.

"For a key ring for your son," I said as I handed the cartridge to Tim. "A memento."

Tim gruffly choked back a tear. Then he softened. "Thanks," he said. "Thanks for everything."

And then they were on their way.

Sighting in rifles. Photo by Doug Stange.

CHAPTER 9
The First, and Last, Annual
Buffalo Gals Hunt

🐾 It was Doug's idea, and it seemed like an excellent one at the time. Our bison hunting operation was up and running, and—the occasional Jerk notwithstanding—it was exceeding our expectations both in terms of our own and our hunters' satisfaction. Over the course of several years devoted to researching and writing about women, guns, and hunting, I had achieved a modest reputation within hunting and shooting circles. I had also discovered how few and far between were the opportunities for reasonably priced all-women hunts for large game. Aside from the National Rifle Association's "Women on Target" program, and a few very high-end hunts sponsored by Safari Club, there wasn't much out there for women seeking a female-friendly group hunt. As most of our bison hunters were shooting yearling heifers and bulls, we had a surplus of two-to-three-year-old bulls. These are young mature bulls, at the ideal age both for meat and mounting. Why not advertise a "Buffalo Gals" hunt, Doug suggested, featuring not only a discounted price for these bulls, but also guiding services and gourmet game dinners by noted author Mary Stange? I wasn't sure the latter constituted much drawing power, but I did think it would be fun to share hunting on the Crazy Woman Ranch with a group of like-minded women.

We worked out the logistics. The first big question related to guiding. Each of us, we reckoned, could handle two hunters over the course of a three-day weekend hunt. Our good friend Maggie, whom I had originally met at a "Becoming an Outdoors-Woman" workshop in Texas, was a wildlife educator by profession and had worked for several years in South Dakota's Custer State Park, where there is a large, free-ranging bison herd, so she had experience working with bison. She was happy to sign on as a third guide. That meant we could handle a total of six hunters.

Our house is too small for us to offer lodging, but we would be able to arrange for accommodations at the Guest House, a small but quite welcoming motel in town. The ladies—as female hunters are invariably called, for some reason—would be on their own for breakfast, after which each day they would meet up with our skinner Don, who would escort them out to the ranch for a day's hunting, capped off by drinks and dinner before they headed back to town. As with our other hunters, we would arrange for transport of their meat to the processor in Baker. And we would take the extra step of helping them salt down their hides for shipping to the tanner. Once hunters had bagged their bison, if they acquired the proper tags from Montana Fish, Wildlife, and Parks, they would be free to hunt turkey or whitetail does, both of which would be in season on the hunt's projected dates, the weekend before Thanksgiving in November 2002.

It was a nice package, modeled more or less on the format most of the "Women on Target" hunts adhered to. In fact, we pitched the idea to the NRA women's program. Their response was surprisingly cool. Women, the NRA informed us, would not be interested in hunting animals like buffalo; they just didn't see any market for it. That was actually all right with me: I had been on one of the NRA's "Women on Target" hunts (a pheasant shoot in upstate New York) and wasn't crazy about the amount of propagandizing on NRA's behalf that affair had entailed. We advertised in two publications, one oriented toward women and hunting, and the other a national gun magazine. The hunt was fully booked within a week of our ads' appearing.

Our six hunters looked to be an interesting and diverse group. They included (these are all pseudonyms): Kelsey, a Wyoming cattle rancher and black powder enthusiast, who also participated in Indian War reenactments; Margo, an attorney in private practice in Minnesota, who with her husband had hunted on virtually every continent; Charlotte, a dentist in Indiana, who loved both rifle hunting and shotgunning, but was particularly keen on the crossbow; Trudy, a former Marine and avowed gun nut, who now worked as a security guard for some government agency in Washington, DC; and Betsy and Sarah, both of whom worked as regional directors in midwestern states for the National Wild Turkey Federation, and both of whom were also shooting black-powder rifles. I had actually met these two at a Turkey Federation event the year before, and also knew Charlotte slightly from that NRA-sponsored pheasant shoot.

All six women looked to be serious hunters and experienced shooters. Charlotte and Trudy had the feel about them of being a bit more "high maintenance," and so Doug agreed he would guide them. I knew the two Turkey Federation gals were the kind of down-home, no-nonsense types that would mesh well with Maggie's personality. That left me with Kelsey and Margo, who in their phone calls and e-mails came off as easily the two most accomplished and level-headed women in the bunch. Since I was doing double-duty as cook and bottle washer, not to mention "celebrity author," I was more than happy with the luck of the draw when it came to my shooters' competence.

The weekend before the Buffalo Gals Hunt I flew home to grocery shop for the event and spent two days engaged in advance preparation for those promised "gourmet game dinners," which I envisioned as upscale camp cuisine. Venison Bourguignon, a pheasant variation on coq au vin, a blanquette of antelope, a bison-based moussaka: these went into the freezer, along with the bison taco meat and bison barbeque that, with Don's great bison summer sausage, would work for lunches. I had already stockpiled zucchini nut bread from that summer's garden, and Maggie volunteered to provide some desserts. In the "potent potable" department we decided we would stick to beer and wine, in addition to a variety of juices and soft drinks, all in ample supply. Some good cheeses and crackers for hors d'oeuvres, artisanal breads and salad makings, and other last-minute items could be procured when I arrived back home the following week, on the eve of the hunt.

A few days before the hunt, I e-mailed our lady hunters with a weather update and all the requisite reminders about the gear they would need. I verified their arrival plans: the Turkey Federation gals were driving in, as was the Wyoming rancher Kelsey. The other three were flying, all arriving at different times and all renting their own vehicles. They had directions to Ekalaka, and from there to the ranch. As they were all staying at the Guest House, I encouraged them to carpool out to our place—this was for the sake not only of leaving a lighter carbon footprint, but also to provide as little disruption as possible of the ranch routine, bison being particularly alive to changes, like unfamiliar SUVs, in their environment.

The hunt schedule was as follows:

- Friday evening: dinner and socializing, orientation to the ranch and details of the hunt.
- Saturday: sighting-in rifles and a first round of hunting, lunch, then hunting 'til dusk, then dinner.
- Sunday: hunting morning and afternoon, lunch and dinner as the day before.
- Monday: same as Sunday, with evening good-byes and departure.

We were all set, assuming everything went according to plan.

Of course, everything didn't. To begin with, my Friday flight into Rapid City was delayed. Maggie, who lived there, was to pick me up, and was also in touch with the other incoming hunters. One of them, Trudy the ex-Marine, was nervous about driving remote country roads in the dark, and wanted to drive back to Montana in tandem with us, which amounted to a longer delay, as her flight came in even later than mine. By late afternoon, it was clear that by the time we would actually be able to get on the road, we wouldn't make it back to the ranch until after nine o'clock. I called Doug with that news, and we figured that, all things considered (including the facts that he had no idea how to put the finishing touches on the venison Bourguignon and I was just now shopping for some necessary comestibles to complete the meal), he should contact the other women and suggest they stay in town for dinner. An unfortunate beginning, but we would all be fresher in the morning that way, anyway.

So, grocery shopping accomplished, Maggie and I hit the road for the ranch, with Trudy following in her rented Jeep. "Amazing weather we've been having," Maggie enthused. "Can you believe how balmy it is for this time of year?" I remarked that that might change in a day or two, judging by the forecast. "Oh, dear," she replied. "I just realized, I forgot to bring a winter coat!" Not to worry, I responded, we could if necessary come up with something for her. Good friends reconnecting, we chatted amiably and the country miles passed on the gravel highway northward, Trudy's headlights always a precise two car lengths behind us. When we were finally back on pavement, and arrived at the cutoff road that afforded a shorter route to our place, Maggie pulled over and I hopped out to give Trudy directions to town. "Just stay on this road another fifteen or so miles," I told her, "turn left at the blinking light and then right, and you're on Main Street . . . the Guest House is on your right."

Trudy, wide-eyed, gasped, "You're not going to escort me to town?!" I explained that doing that would take us a needless twenty miles out of our way.

"But what if I get lost? What do you mean, 'fifteen *or so*' miles? What if I miss my turn?" she whined. It took some doing, but after two or three repetitions of the salient facts that: a) as long as she remained on this paved road, clearly marked County Road #323, she was on the right road; b) Highway 323 ends in Ekalaka; and c) the blinking light in question is the only traffic light within a forty mile radius—Trudy finally gritted her teeth, gazed ahead with a look of steely, if annoyed, determination, and gunned off into the darkness. By the time she was checking into the Guest House, Maggie and I were pulling in at the ranch. We stowed the groceries, worked out hunt logistics with Doug over wine and cheese, and then retired relatively early. This was exciting! It would, we three agreed, be great fun.

BUFFALO GALS HUNT, DAY I

Saturday

The motorcade arrived promptly on schedule, at 8 a.m. Heedless of my recommendation regarding carpooling, every one of our hunters insisted on driving out on her own: that meant five vehicles (the Turkey Federation gals were traveling together) in addition to Don's big Dodge truck. We aren't exactly set up for valet parking, but we managed to squeeze them all into the limited space available in the circular drive in front of the house. There followed a good deal of milling around, hand shaking, introductions, and the general jollity tinged with awkwardness that seems to invariably accompany the start of a group hunt. Moving inside, there was the usual business of collecting and writing receipts for the balances owed by each hunter (we require a 50 percent deposit, with the balance payable upon arrival), signing liability releases (legally probably not worth the paper they are written on, but psychologically quite effective), and finally Doug's well honed presentation about where to aim for an effective bison kill (facilitated by X-marks-the-spot illustrations provided us by a veterinarian who had hunted with us the year before—pictures we use to this day).

The next order of business was the sighting-in of rifles. It was a bright, near-windless morning, and as the women took their turns at the shooting table—or, in the case of Betsy and Sarah, with their black powder guns, using their preferred shooting sticks—everything went pretty smoothly. Only one shooter experienced some difficulty: Margo, one of my hunters. She shot completely off the paper at first, then hit wide of the bull's-eye. "I'm flinching," she said. "I don't know why I'm nervous . . ." We all tried to reassure her, and one of the other hunters, Charlotte, volunteered to shoot a group of three with Margo's rifle. After all, the problem might well be with her gun, not her shooting. Charlotte shot a good, tight group, an inch or so high of the bull's-eye: just about right. Margo tried her gun again, with better results this time. All was well; this had been just a bit of performance anxiety. I have been there myself.

By now it was midmorning. We had time for a round of hunting before lunch. Our bison herd was split into two groups. The larger of the two, which we had designated the southern herd and was comprised of around eighty buffalo, was customarily up on the top of the divide in a 120-acre hayfield, from which they could freely filter down, through a gate, into the pine forest and thence into a large pasture. The smaller northern herd of about sixty animals was in an area of the ranch we call the "tri-corners," because it is where three tributaries of Spring Creek converge, threading their way through a series of buttes and rolling hills. The situations of both herds provided good opportunities for stalking. Our strategy—and it was the one we intended to follow, in one way or another, until all six women shot their bulls—was that I would take my two hunters up to the top of the divide, and Doug would take his two back to the tri-corners. Maggie and her hunters, meanwhile, would be stationed in between, in a position where they could glass the area and pick up on either of the two herds which could migrate their way, prompted by our presence and, hopefully, by some successful shooting. Meanwhile, Don and his friend Tom, who was assisting him, would wait for a signal from one of us that we had a bison down. Our three parties set out, agreeing to rendezvous back at the house for lunch around one o'clock.

I drove Kelsey and Margo up to the edge of the woods and cautioned them, as we got out of the truck, that they may need to be ready to shoot fairly quickly, depending on where the bison were. Who, I asked, wanted to shoot first? "Oh," Margo chirped, "I'm happy to wait to put mine on the ground. You go first, Kelsey." Kelsey, one of the most even-keeled personalities I had ever encountered, said that was fine with her. We eased our way through the trees and, sure enough (thanks less to my superb guiding skills than to plain good luck), as we emerged at the forest edge, there was the herd, lazily grazing. Margo hung back, and I shinnied closer to the bison with Kelsey. I pointed out a nice bull to her, a clear, open shot of perhaps 150 yards. She was shooting a hefty Sharps .45/70, and perfectly placed her shot. Her bull fell immediately, but he still quivered a bit; he was fatally hit, but not quite dead yet. She stood, walked closer to him, and fired again—point-blank to the base of his skull—to finish him off.

"You didn't need to do that," I told her.

"I know," she said. "I just don't like to see 'em suffer."

After a few minutes devoted to congratulations, admiring comments, and the obligatory photo session, Don and Tom arrived to begin the work of gutting and skinning. We went back to the house to lunch, and to discover that Kelsey's was the first bull down. Bragging rights, not to mention downright gloating, seem to figure largely in most hunting camps, and this one proved no exception. After some quick sandwiches, our three parties regrouped—this time Maggie taking her hunters up to the divide, and I and my two hiking back to a spot where, with luck, she might haze the southern herd our way. That strategy ultimately failed, and Kelsey, Margo, and I spent an hour or so semireclining on a south-facing embankment in the waning afternoon sunlight, killing time by exchanging hunting stories—most of them about Margo's exploits hunting caribou in Alaska, elk in Colorado, polar bears in the Arctic, and the likes of eland and Cape buffalo in South Africa.

At dusk, we all converged back at the house. No more bison had been taken. That was okay; we were off to a great start. I broke out some cheese and crackers, directed the ladies to help themselves to beer and wine we had in a cooler, and set about getting dinner together. As I have mentioned, our house is small, actually more of a cabin, with the living room and kitchen/dining area occupying two halves of the open main floor. Our hunters settled in the living room, sharing jokes and hunting stories. It became clear pretty quickly that there were two alpha females, and one wannabe, in this pack of huntresses. Charlotte and Trudy gave no quarter in the one-upsmanship department, whether it be the far-fetched hunting yarn on the one hand, or the raunchy joke on the other. Margo, if less flamboyant, was still no slouch herself when it came to tales of past adventures. She had come armed with photo albums of her and her husband's global hunts, by way of illustration. When dinner was served, buffet style, the ladies filled their plates, refilled their glasses, and returned to the living room for only somewhat quieter dinner conversation. At one point Betsy called out, "Gee, Mary, you'll have to find some time to sit down with us." There were a couple of random nods, of the "yeah, whatever" sort, and then the ladies were back in their own world. Dinner completed, and food duly complimented, the group mobilized to retreat en masse to town. On their way out the door, as I was gathering up the assorted dishes, glasses, utensils, and trash they had left strewn about living room and kitchen, Sarah asked perfunctorily, "Oh, would you like some help with the dishes?" No, I smiled, waving them off, and Maggie quickly added, "We'll take care of them—you gals just run along. Drive safely!"

I was beginning to think I might not be cut out for the hospitality industry. But hey, they were paying customers, or "clients" as Maggie referred to them, and they seemed to be enjoying themselves. I could deal with a little "good ol' girl" behavior. I could also switch, tomorrow evening, from china to paper plates.

THE HUNT, DAY 2

Sunday

The caravan of trucks and SUVs was somewhat late in arriving, the ladies having partied hearty at the Old Stand Bar in town 'til closing time. Overnight, the sky had cleared, and the temperature had dropped sharply. Now, thick clouds were rolling in and a strong wind was gusting out of the north. The weather would make for a much rougher day's hunting than the sunny midfifties of the day before. For the first round of hunting we decided to repeat the previous day's strategy. Kelsey had traded her rifle for a camcorder to record Margo's hunt with me. Alphas Charlotte and Trudy, both a tad on the bloodshot side, nonetheless were anxious to "throw some lead" at a couple of bulls. Sarah and Betsy, who looked somewhat better rested than the others, were eager and upbeat.

When Kelsey, Margo, and I reached the top of the divide, the bison were nowhere to be seen. I did note, rather wistfully, the presence out in the field of an impressive whitetail buck I had nicknamed "Mr. Punctuality" for his habit of being the last deer off the hayfield and into the shelter of the forest each morning. But as I was guiding this morning, it would be bad form to say to my hunters, "Uh, please excuse me while I try to take the excellent shot that deer is offering me." I could only hope he'd still be around in another day or two.

The three of us walked along the forest edge, just inside the trees, and before long we came upon the southern herd. They were spread out nicely, contentedly grazing, and there was a good young bull standing in the open, close enough—in fact, really close, no more than fifty yards away—that the wind ought not to be a problem. "There's your bull," I said to Margo. Meanwhile, Kelsey had her camcorder trained on the animal. "Great shooting distance!" she whispered. Margo got into a comfortable shooting position and, after what seemed like an awfully long time during which the bull stood stock-still, fired. The bull had had his head down grazing. He now looked up quizzically in our direction, and then ambled off with the other buffalo, the herd having been set in motion by the rifle blast.

"Wind must've blown my bullet off target," Margo sighed. I wasn't so certain; it really was a ridiculously easy shot. She might not have put him down with one bullet, but it seemed impossible she could have missed such a big target entirely.

"Well," I told her, "he didn't react to your shot, but I want to be certain he wasn't hit. We've got to make sure there isn't any blood trail." I walked out onto the windswept field to where the bull had been standing and began quartering back and forth to be satisfied there was no evidence of a successful hit. Kelsey joined me while Margo hung back, leaning on a fence post, by turns fiddling with her gun, repositioning her hat, refreshing her lipstick, staring off into space. Meanwhile, having heard the shot and assuming we had an animal down, Don and Tom had driven up to the field. I told them it looked like Margo's shot had missed. They said they'd wait while we tried to track down the herd again.

We walked the forest edge the length of the hayfield, about a half mile, and finally encountered the herd again. They were now bunched up near the fence bounding our neighbor's property—not ideal, but not impossible either, should a bull wander free of the now slightly more edgily milling group. I carefully glassed the herd and was satisfied that all the bulls looked fine. "All right," I told Margo, "this may be a more challenging shot. They are more wary now. We'll just sit here, let them settle down, and see whether a shootable bull works his way free of the herd." Kelsey nodded, and we three hunkered down on the now-frozen ground.

Snow flurries were beginning to swirl in the wind. I had loaned coatless Maggie the only hunting parka of mine that would fit her, which also happened to be my warmest. I had a very warm down jacket but, not wanting to depart from hunting attire, had opted instead for an old hunting coat that was less well insulated. Neither the first nor the last time I've been done in by considerations of style: I noticed I was shivering.

The bison were arrayed on a gradual slope we were facing, and eventually they began to spread out somewhat. They were still closer to the boundary fence than I would have liked, but our herd had never run through a fence, and I reckoned it would take more than a rifle blast or two to trigger that sort of disaster. In time, a nice bull came practically clear of the others.

"There," I gestured, "there's a cow with her calf. Near the fence. See her? To the left, slightly downhill from her, there is a good bull for you."

"To the left," Margo whispered back. "Now, is that our left, or the cow's left?"

"Our left. See the cow and calf, look down hill to the left, maybe ten yards, there's a bull. There's another cow behind him right now, but if she moves, you have a shot at him." I turned back to Kelsey, who was sitting somewhat behind us, and had her camcorder trained on the bull. "You see him, right?" She nodded, "Yep, just down and to the left of the cow and calf."

I turned back to Margo. "I'd make that about a hundred and fifty yard shot. Are you OK with that?"

"Oh, yes," she nodded. I suggested she carefully work her way a few yards to the barbed-wire fence that bounded the hayfield where, should the opportunity arise, she could use the fence post to steady her rifle. Where we were nestled, between the woods and the hillside, the wind was not such a factor, and she appeared to have a pretty rock-solid rest. We waited. In a few moments, the herd rearranged itself in such a way that Margo's bull was now in the clear. I verified with her: "You see, now, that cow that was behind him has moved away. The other cow and calf are where they were, uphill from him to the right. See, he just looked back at them. Now he's looking in our direction . . ." I glanced back at Kelsey, who briefly looked away from her camcorder, smiled and nodded. I focused my binoculars on the bull, and told Margo to shoot whenever she was ready.

BANG! The bull, apparently not hit but perhaps startled by the sound of a bullet whizzing past him, whirled away to the right. But lowering my binoculars, I saw that another buffalo, a younger yearling bull a good twenty yards farther up the hillside in the midst of several other animals, was reacting as if he may have just been gutshot, and a cow nearby him appeared to have blood running down the side of her head.

"Did I get him?" Margo asked. Kelsey and I looked at each other in stunned disbelief. No, I told her, but one, perhaps two, animals looked to be wounded, I wasn't sure how seriously. The herd had by this time vacated the area. I saw Don's truck heading our way, and ran to meet it. "Sorry," I said, "another false alarm. But I think we have a wounded bison, maybe two, running with the herd." Don and Tom had driven past the herd and hadn't noticed any wounded animals—but then, they hadn't been on the lookout for wounded bison, either, and the herd had been running fast. "Actually," he said, "I just got a call from Doug. The Tooth Fairy got her bull, so we're going on down to field-dress that one."

The Tooth Fairy?

"What's-her-name. The dentist."

"Well," I told him, "things are getting out of hand up here. I need Doug to help me sort things out here." Don said he'd send him on up. Meanwhile I rang up Maggie on her cell—she and her two hunters had been stationed, as the day before, waiting for the bison herd to filter down off the divide—to let her know that, until we figured out what had happened to one or more wounded buffalo, the southern herd was going to have to be confined to the hayfield. I said it was awfully cold up here, and we'd appreciate a thermos of hot tea or something. Then I walked the half-mile back to Margo and Kelsey—at least the walk was a way to try to warm up a bit—to tell them we simply needed to wait it out until Doug was able to come up to assess the situation.

"Oh, that's all right," Margo said offhandedly. "I can always shoot another one tomorrow." I pretended not to have heard that.

Kelsey took me aside and said, "I think she must feel really bad about this." I asked Kelsey whether she had rewound her tape of

Margo's misplaced shot. "Yeah," she winced. She didn't need to say anything more.

For the next forty-five minutes, the three of us milled about on the top of the divide, trying to fend off frostbite, waiting for Doug and Maggie to show up, barely speaking. Maggie arrived, finally, explaining that after sitting in her truck for so long waiting for some action, she and her hunters felt chilly and she'd made them tea first, which they sipped while they warmed up by the wood stove, before driving up to the divide. I wished she hadn't told me that. I had long since lost feeling in my hands and face, and was having trouble forming a coherent sentence. It occurred to Sarah, probably accurately, that I might be verging on going hypothermic. They loaded me into Maggie's heated truck cab and Betsy thrust a couple of hand-warmers into my gloves. "The tea?" I asked, through chattering teeth. "Oh, shoot!" Maggie exclaimed. "We must have left the thermos on the kitchen table!"

Another fifteen minutes or so in the blast of the truck's heater and I was more or less thawed by the time Doug arrived. I asked what had taken so long, and he said he'd explain later: it had been a long morning.

It was about to get longer.

He and I watched Kelsey's videotape of Margo's shot. It was as I had seen, and recounted, it. We weighed our alternatives. With all the shooting, and the human and truck traffic in the hayfield, the bison were becoming ever more restive. Doug didn't think it would do any good in the long run to confine them to the top of the divide, and if we could work them through the gate that gave them access to the forest, we might be able to spot any wounded buffalo. Once we had the herd taken care of, we'd figure out what to do about certain human animals we were having a difficult time managing.

Maggie had been waiting in her truck, with all four lady hunters, as Doug and I were conferring. I jogged back and told her what we intended to do. "The buffs are on the nervous side right now," I said. "We do not want to stress them any more than they already are. They're used to Doug and me. We'll get them through the gate, since that's where they clearly want to go at this point. You just stay back here, until the bison are all through the gate, and we'll give you the all clear." Maggie nodded, and I climbed through the fence and began to slowly walk its length toward the now-open gate. Meanwhile, driving our truck, Doug was slowly leading the bison toward the gate. This was a maneuver we had used often: the buffalo knew what he was suggesting they do, and since that squared with their own desire to get off the field, they were in a mood to oblige. My presence, walking parallel to the truck on the offside of the fence, was a simple reminder for them that the fence was there. We took our time, and were making nice progress; the herd was moving fairly calmly, we had another fifty yards or so to go, and they would be through the gate. Doug eased the pickup ahead and positioned it near the gate, angled in such a way as to encourage the herd through the gate, rather than either past it or back out onto the field. We were almost there.

All of a sudden Maggie's truck came roaring up along the fence line, behind the herd. Doug jumped out of his truck, and I wheeled around, both of us simultaneously waving our arms and shouting, "No! Maggie, *NO!*" But it was too late. The bison, suddenly squeezed between her oncoming truck and Doug's parked by the gate, made a fairly quick group decision not to wait until they got to the gate, and exploded through the fence and down into the woods. I ran, stumbling helter-skelter, to get out of the way, and caught up with Doug. Hugging, we both groaned. "Jesus," he moaned, "they just learned a very bad trick they likely won't forget any time soon." By now Maggie had alighted from her truck. Why, we yelled, had she come rushing up that way, when we had told her to stay put?

"I had to," she said urgently. "Mary, you have no idea how much danger you were in!" I replied that I sure as hell could have been in danger, had the bison decided to breach the fence a few yards nearer to me than they had. But up until she forced the issue, things had been going smoothly. Up until a few moments ago, they had always respected this fence, constructed as it was of five barbed wires, and an additional electrified smooth wire. With several metal fence posts bent clear to the ground and busted wire strewn all over the place, that respect was now clearly a thing of the past.

We drove the three miles back to the house for a late lunch. On the way down, Doug told me about his morning. He, Trudy, and Charlotte had been stalking on foot, working their way along a meandering creek bottom. Doug stumbled upon an ancient elk antler, partially sticking out of the ground. Elk pretty much disappeared from this area a long time ago; they are only now being reintroduced, so this was a rather special find. He pointed it out to the alphas. "*WOW! I want it!*" Charlotte—the Tooth Fairy—fairly screamed, grabbing a downed tree branch and picking frantically at the ground. After several minutes of vigorous tugging and grunting, she managed to pry the antler free. "This'll look great on the wall in my waiting room," she exulted, brandishing her trophy, "a real conversation piece." Doug was speechless: too polite as well as too downright thunderstruck to point out that she was scavenging our land.

They resumed the stalk, and shortly thereafter Charlotte effected an efficient, one-shot kill of a very nice bull. Trudy was now, predictably, seething with jealousy, since the morning had been all about Charlotte. "They've eaten already," Doug said as we arrived at the house, "so I'll take Trudy out now. Maybe we'll get lucky. Then we'll figure out what to do about our other hunters." Charlotte, who had helped herself to a beer (not, apparently, her first of the day), said she'd love to go along as "moral support." Doug agreed, just so long as she left her rifle behind.

As he would later tell me, it turned out to be a shorter but nonetheless dramatic hunt. They caught up with the northern herd after a short stalk. A shootable bull had obligingly separated himself from the others and Doug moved Trudy into position for her shot. She hit the bull badly, in the haunch. Doug raised his rifle, to put the scope on the bull. "NO!" the ex-Marine shrieked, lofting her rifle above her head with both arms, commando-style, and running toward the now slightly wobbly bison. "This is my bull! *MY bull!*" She dropped to the ground and shot. And shot again. And again. And—if Doug remembered correctly—again. It was, he said, difficult to watch the bull slowly crumple to the ground, but she finally managed to dispatch him. Congratulating her warmly, Charlotte could not help but note that, nice as he was, he was somewhat smaller than hers. Perhaps so, Lady Rambo replied, but he had a finer trophy head for mounting.

Meanwhile, back at the ranch house, the rest of us were warming up with the help of warmed-over bison barbecue and hot tea and coffee. "So what exactly happened up there?" one or another of the hunters asked. "Well, some mistakes were made, and now we have a bison herd with a very bad attitude," I replied—I will admit, angrily. "It is going to take that southern herd a while to calm down. We won't be able to hunt them again any time soon." I gave Maggie a perhaps more level look, at that point, than I should have. She focused on her sandwich.

After lunch, I suggested Maggie go back out with her hunters, on the off chance that Doug could persuade the northern herd in their direction. That left me with Margo—who was getting rather weepy—and Kelsey, who was trying to make the best of an awkward social moment. We made small talk, centering mostly on Margo's intense dislike of children and her devotion to her King Charles spaniel, as I puttered around the kitchen cleaning up lunch things and getting some other things in order for dinner. Eventually, on some pretense or another, I excused myself and walked up the road to where I knew Maggie and her hunters were stationed. I felt awful for Sarah and Betsy; in a day and a half of supposed hunting, the only real glimpse they had had of either bison herd was of the blowout on top of the divide. They had been in a holding pattern, and had been remarkably patient, all things considered. I told them that we would still work to get them their bulls, but that I also understood that their work schedule precluded extending their stay. We wanted them to have a quality hunting experience, and would work to make that happen, if not on this trip, then—guaranteed—sometime later in the season, or next year. I think they appreciated the sentiment, but it was clear they were both frustrated.

By the time I got back to the house Doug had returned, with the news that Trudy had her bull. There was still perhaps an hour of light left, and he had a good fix on where the northern herd was. He suggested that he and I take Sarah and Betsy out and try to get a bull for at least one of them. Since they were shooting muzzle-loaders, they would need to get somewhat closer to their prey than rifle shooters. "The herd's a little skittish at this point," Doug said. "If it's OK with you, Maggie, Mary will ride 'shotgun' in the back of the truck with Betsy and Sarah. We'll hunt 'safari style.'" Maggie said she had no problem with that, Betsy and Sarah agreed, and we took off in the now waning light.

The northern herd was right where Doug expected them to be, and as we drove toward them, Doug called back that Betsy or Sarah should be ready to shoot. He stopped the truck, they loaded their guns, and we readily isolated a bull. I was coaching Betsy, who already had her gun shouldered. "Go ahead," I told her, but just as she was about to squeeze the trigger, Sarah blasted and down went the bull. Betsy and I exchanged a rather dashed look—and I realized that she and Sarah had apparently not sorted out who was going to shoot first. Ah, well, at least one more bull was on the ground, and it was a good clean kill.

Betsy was as gracious as could reasonably be expected. We drove back to the house and Don, who had already put in a long day, ventured out to field-dress Sarah's bull by the glow of his truck's headlights.

Maggie, who knows her way around our kitchen, had laid out an assortment of nibbles, and by the time we returned the other ladies were already well into cocktail hour. Margo's palpable nonsuccess weighed heavily on the conversation, enhanced by her intermittent outbursts of tears. In contrast to the previous evening's levity, the living room conversation revolved around her ever more earnest rationalizations about what had, and had not, happened on the divide. It had become increasingly clear that our hunters were distinguished not simply by alpha- vs. beta-female standing in the pack, but also by more—or less, depending on how one looks at it—subtle class distinctions. Kelsey, Sarah, and Betsy were working women, by no means financially hard up, but hardly affluent, either. Charlotte, Trudy, and Margo had bucks, and the attitude of entitlement that went with more serious money. In this scheme of things, Margo risked figuring as an embarrassing loser. Meanwhile poor Betsy, who had her own "issues" to sort out with Sarah, sat sullenly silent.

The alphas' joking turned to sniping, and Margo's rationalization to recrimination, with dinner still a good half-hour to readiness by my reckoning. Charlotte suggested the lady hunters caucus on the front porch. They presently came back inside and announced that they had decided to go to town for dinner. "We can see that Mary's upset," Trudy declared, by way of explanation. "Fine," I said, laying down the chef's knife I was using to chop vegetables for salad and trying not to imagine other more creative uses for it. I was definitely not cut out for the hospitality trade, that was for sure. As the ladies left, several of them grabbing from the cooler a brew or two for the road, Trudy and Charlotte called back: "We'll be back here before sunup, for turkey hunting!"

Doug, Maggie, and I each had a good stiff drink, then ate in exhausted silence. Maggie then retreated to the guest bedroom downstairs, to call her fiancé and report on the day's doings. A few minutes later she blazed back upstairs to announce that she was furious with me.

"How dare you?" she shouted. I acknowledged that I had maybe been a bit harsh over lunch—but that she really *had* screwed up, and ought to have known better than to charge the bison herd as she had, up there on the divide. Doug was taking this in, over his after-dinner tea, with the kind of bemused detachment men get at these moments. "But," she countered, "it would have been one thing to talk to me about this in private. You criticized me in front of . . . in front of *clients!*" Unfortunately, given the way the day had gone, this phrasing stuck me as nonsensical, and Doug as funny. For the next several minutes, Maggie and I engaged in a good old-fashioned hissy-fit: two women who were the best of friends, crying and screaming their heads off at each other. Doug tried his best to referee. We eventually settled down enough to agree that tomorrow was another day, and we all turned in early.

"Wow," Doug mumbled as we were cuddled together and drifting off to sleep, "it sure doesn't get any better than this, does it, Mare?"

THE HUNT, DAY 3

Monday

By early morning Maggie and I were, naturally, back on speaking terms. Doug was intent on devising strategy for the day. Fortunately we wouldn't have to worry about the two alphas, who should by now be settled in for a morning of trying to call in turkeys somewhere up in the woods. Betsy was a capable shooter, we were sure. We were equally certain that Margo was not—and I was, quite frankly, beginning to wonder about her mental stability. Doug said he would take her out, alone, and get her a bull if he had to shoot it himself, which seemed not unlikely at this point. Then we would provide Betsy with a good hunt and, with any luck, we'd have all our hunters on their way well before dark.

After yesterday's shooting gallery atop the divide, the southern herd would be left alone. At first light, Doug went out to fire up the tractor and take a load of hay back to the northern herd, to settle them down for today's shooting. He was still out, and Maggie and I were peacefully savoring a second mug of tea, when the first wave of ladies arrived from town: a delegation comprised of Margo, Trudy, and Charlotte, who had assumed the role of spokeswoman. I met them on the front porch. "I thought you two were turkey hunting," I said, smiling, to the pretty obviously hung-over Tooth Fairy and Lady Rambo.

"We have more important things to do," Charlotte declared, her tone imperious. "We had a group meeting last night and, frankly, Mary, we don't feel you have done an adequate job of guiding. Margo has no faith in you. *I* shall guide Margo myself, today."

I heard a sharp intake of breath coming from the living room and knew Maggie was stifling a laugh.

"Uh, no," I replied cordially, "actually, Doug is going to take Margo out himself this morning."

"Then I'll go with them and act as her spotter."

I told her that was up to Doug, but I doubted he would go for the idea—as indeed, when he presently returned, he did not. Charlotte and Trudy therefore decided that they had other more important things to do, namely driving in tandem back to Rapid City for their evening flights out (and, no doubt, to get there in time for happy hour beforehand). By now the other hunters had arrived. Kelsey was also figuring on hitting the road for home, and the two Turkey Federation ladies pitched in and helped Maggie and me get their trucks loaded with their bison hides and heads. They were on the road by ten, about the time Don was arriving: we'd told him to sleep in for a change.

Meanwhile Doug dealt with Margo. "Here's what we'll do," he had told her. "You can stay in the cab of the truck and, when we isolate a bull for you, shoot from there. I will shoot back-up, if there is *any* uncertainty about your shot placement. All you have to be sure of is that you mark which animal you have hit, and keep your eye on him, to give me a chance to get out of the truck and into shooting position. If you draw first blood, I'll do the rest."

"Right," Margo had said. "I understand."

They drove back to the northern herd which, unruffled by the familiar pickup, continued munching hay: not the way we would prefer to set things up, to be sure, but this was a last resort as far as Doug was concerned. Firing a rifle in their midst would, of course, get them moving, so—as he pointed out a good bull to her, at nearly point-blank range—Doug reiterated his injunction that she be sure to mark her bull. Margo fired, and Doug saw it was a solid, if not immediately lethal, hit. He jumped out of the driver's seat, slid his .30/06 from the gun rack, and ran around to the passenger side of the truck, where Margo was now standing, and looking confusedly at the herd. "Which one is it?" he asked.

"I . . . don't . . . know," she said vaguely. "I couldn't keep track. They all look alike to me. I know I hit it, though." Within moments, the bison were in retreat, a badly wounded bull among them.

Having heard a single shot, back at the house we were all ready for some celebration when Doug and Margo returned. And Betsy was eager, finally, for her turn to shoot a buffalo. When Doug pulled the truck up, it was clear before a word was said that we had had a change of plans.

Knowing buffalo, Maggie and Don immediately comprehended, in ways our lady hunters did not, how difficult and potentially disheartening a search for a wounded bison could prove to be in terrain like ours. In the dynamic structure of a bison herd, a wounded animal will be helped along—sometimes literally held up, pressed between them, by two healthy animals—unless, or until, it becomes clear to the herd that the wounded member is becoming a liability. Depending upon how badly hurt the bull was, he might still be moving with the herd. But he would eventually either be gored to death by other bulls or forced from the herd to wander off and die alone. In the former two cases, we might well find him by tracking the herd. In the latter case, there was a good chance we might not.

Doug and Don, both of whom are crack shots, focused on the herd itself, hoping to isolate the wounded bull and finish him off. No luck there. The rest of us fanned out from the herd, along a ridge above where they had migrated, glassing the area and being on the lookout for any sign of a wounded or freshly dead animal: not merely movement, or a dark profile on the ground, but also looking skyward to the behavior of scavenging birds like crows, magpies, and vultures. We spent the bulk of the day, late into the afternoon, so engaged, with no luck.

The temperature began to drop precipitously, and a light snow was falling. And Betsy, who was being an exceedingly good sport about it, still had nothing to show for now three frustrating days. While the rest of us continued to search for Margo's bull, Doug took her back to the creek bottom to which he believed the northern herd had retreated. He explained that at this point the truck would spook them, and Betsy said she really preferred a stalk on foot anyway. They carefully worked their way along the creek and after a while found the herd and, finally, a shootable bull for Betsy. Doug told her to fire when ready. She managed a less than perfect hit. She attempted to load another round, but her muzzle-loader jammed in the cold. Wrestling with her gun and with tears welling in her eyes, Betsy let out a yelp. Doug offered her his rifle. She took it, and dropped her bull with one bullet.

Amen.

Betsy and Sarah would return early the next morning, to retrieve their hides and trophy heads and get on the road. Margo had to head straight for the airport in the morning. We assured her we would keep looking for her bull. And we had to be frank with her: If we found him, at this point the meat would likely be beyond salvaging. But we would still have the hide and head for her. She said she understood and would keep in touch.

And so ended the first—and last—annual Buffalo Gals Hunt on the Crazy Woman Ranch.

AFTER THE HUNT

Maggie, by prearrangement, was staying on with us for a couple more days, for deer hunting. In the course of our hunting we all kept a watchful eye for any sign of Margo's bull, and we made a point of traversing every draw in which he might have lain down to die, every ravine into which he might have tumbled. At night, we listened for coyotes. To no avail. As impossible as it may seem that an animal weighing in at around fifteen hundred pounds could just vanish, this is country vast enough for a big animal to disappear into it. Margo's bull was out there somewhere. But we could not, and would not, find him.

Maggie went home to Rapid City the day before Thanksgiving. Doug and I spent a blissfully relaxing holiday, with deer hunting in the morning and football and a leisurely feast of wild turkey and sundry trimmings stretching into evening. That night we got a phone call from a reasonably distraught Kelsey. What, Doug asked, was the matter?

"I can't find my scrotum!" she replied. "I mean of course, my bull's scrotum. I was wondering whether you maybe found it lying on the ground where my truck was parked or something?" Kelsey was an Indian War reenactor, and she had been intending to make her bull's scrotum into a black powder pouch. Doug explained that we had not stumbled upon anything that looked like her bull's privates, but offered that he believed a hunter we had coming to shoot a bull in a week or so might well be willing to donate his bull's scrotum to her quest for verisimilitude. Would that work? "Oh yes," she said, "that would be great." These little things can mean a lot.

The day after Thanksgiving we realized, after one more morning's failed search for Margo's bull, that one or the other of us would have to take on the less pleasant task of calling her with the unhappy news of our failure to locate him. "It'll be easier coming from you, Mare," Doug ventured, "you know, woman to woman." I wasn't so sure about that, but I agreed to make the call. Her husband answered, tersely, and handed the phone over to Margo. I explained, as tactfully as I could, that after several days of searching we were very sorry, but we had at this point to give her bull up for lost.

"Well, then," she said icily, "I want my money back."

I reminded her that, both in our promotional literature and in the contract she signed, we had been quite specific in offering no guarantee of hunter success. Up until that time our hunters had, in fact, enjoyed a 100 percent success rate. But, as she herself had discovered, things can go seriously wrong on any hunt. We had provided her with three excellent opportunities to shoot a bison bull. She had paid for a guided bison hunt, and that is what she had gotten. Biting my lip, I refrained from reminding her of the extent of bison carnage she had left in her wake: one mortally wounded for certain, two others we still weren't sure about.

Her rejoinder—"Then I think you are a total fraud"—nearly knocked me speechless. I realized I was talking to an attorney. She commenced babbling about how if we did not make things right, actions would be taken against us that would expose us public scrutiny, we would definitely regret this, there were damages to consider, this amounted to false advertising . . . Interrupting her I said, "I think this conversation is over, Margo. Happy Thanksgiving." And I hung up the phone.

Doug, who had overheard my half of our brief interchange said, "Well, that's great, you just hung up on a lawyer."

"She called us a fraud," I said. "I called her bluff."

Doug checked his account book. "Well, at least she paid the balance in cash," he noted, "so she can't stop payment on a check. We may need that dough for a lawyer, ourselves."

We didn't hear anything more from Margo. We did get a very nice thank-you gift package from Betsy and Sarah at Christmastime. And we also received an e-mail from Kelsey to let us know that the scrotum we had sent her arrived in great condition, and saying how much she and her family were enjoying the bison meat. She added, in a postscript, that she was glad Margo had dropped the idea of legal action against us; she, Kelsey, had tried to persuade her against it. Reading between the lines, we gathered that Margo had attempted to rally the other five hunters to sign on to some sort of lawsuit. Kelsey, of course, was in possession of Exhibit A for our side of the story: Thank heaven for that videotape.

We never heard anything more from Lady Rambo or the Tooth Fairy. However, a couple of years later, a female outdoor writer I know contacted me to let me know she had offered to review my latest book, an anthology of women's writing about hunting, for the NRA's (now defunct) *Woman's Outlook* magazine. The editor declined the review, commenting that she had heard "very unsavory things" about me. Knowing that Trudy and Charlotte both moved within NRA circles, I presume one or the other of them to have been the source.

Doug and I remained puzzled over the mystery of Margo's shooting. After all, she had brought for show-and-tell all those albums of photos of exotic hunts for wild big game, with the stories—plenty featuring one-shot kills—to go along with them. These must have been, we concluded, classic instances of "guide shots," and we subsequently polled a few professional hunting guides about how they handle chronically, perhaps pathologically, inept shooters. They acknowledged that they do train themselves to get off a killing shot a split-second after the client shoots. It's an especially useful skill for those outfitters that do make guarantees. As one guide we spoke to put it, "There was this one woman who couldn't hit the side of a barn, and she *kept coming back*. I was never going to get rid of her, if I didn't shoot her a moose myself." Such hunters are not necessarily female, of course. But, male or female, they are surely ultimately ill served by their guides: Margo had been led to believe she was a much better markswoman than, for whatever reasons (and I believe they were fairly complex), she was. "Guide shots," while they perhaps feel necessary in some outfitting situations, obviously don't do game animals any favors, either, when one takes into account the corresponding wounding rate.

We never located the remains of Margo's bull. In the eight years since, we have on occasion had to track down other wounded bison and have located all but one of them. As to the bison on Kelsey's video, the ones wounded up on the divide: Not too long after the Buffalo Gals Hunt, we noticed a cow was missing a horn. This was, no doubt, the one that had had blood running down her face that morning. Margo apparently shot her horn off. That bullet must have then continued its trajectory, or else ricocheted, to hit the yearling bull we had seen react to the shot. He survived, as far as we knew, and was most likely the three-year-old bull in which Don discovered the evidence of an old healed over bullet wound in the belly when he field-dressed him a couple of years later. These animals are tough. That does not, needless to say, make their wounds any less painful, or regrettable.

The Buffalo Gals left their traces in other ways. We were turning up beer cans and wine bottles all over the place—in the tractor loader, tossed in the beds of our pickups, under the porch steps, stuck in hay bales—long after their departure. Their memory lingered longer in town where, by all accounts, they were the life of the whoopin'-n-hollerin' party in the Old Stand every night. They made a similarly memorable impression over breakfast at the Wagon Wheel. "A couple of those gals, they really knew how to fill out those camo pants, and sashay across the room for the coffeepot," as one local recollected. "Although, how you can shoot a gun with fingernails like that, I'll never know!"

POSTSCRIPT

This has not been an easy story for me to tell. In part because it was not an easy story to live, nor has it been particularly fun to remember now. But it is especially difficult for me, as a feminist and as a staunch advocate of women's and girls' hunting and shooting, to retrace those events, to try to put them into a meaningful narrative. It feels, on some level, as if I am "dissing my sisters." Worse, it feels as if I am giving ammunition to those antifeminists on the one hand and to those antihunting feminists on the other, who are ever eager to say, "See! You women hunters just want to be like men, to claim your right to be as boorish as Bubba!"

Which, of course, does appear to be true, for some women. A friend of mine, Montana nature writer Susan Ewing, coined the term "Bubbettes" for the Good Old Girls among us. That was several years ago, in response to a question I had put to her, in connection with a magazine article I was working on, the subject of which was the question, "Do women make better hunters than men?" It was, of course, a teaser question, yet it pointed to some potentially significant differences, I thought, between what women and men bring to the experience of hunting. Women, after all, aren't burdened with all the macho baggage men tend to carry into hunting camp; we have no masculinity to prove. And, because so many female hunters took up hunting as adults, with fully formed ethical perspectives already in place, it seemed to me there might just be an argument that we approach hunting with somewhat more maturity than men do. Part of that maturity, I thought, might display itself in more mutuality, and less competitiveness, among women hunters. Outdoor editor Diana Berger Rupp verified that hunch of mine: her "overall experience," she told me, was that "women aren't particularly competitive with each other about hunting, not in the way men are. Every women-only hunt I've been on, there has been absolutely no resentment about someone else filling a tag when others don't. I think," she concluded, "that attitude carries over; there are still few enough of us [women hunters] that we welcome newcomers and want everyone to be successful."

I had then just recently attended my first all-woman hunt, an archery deer hunt ("Bows and Does") in Alabama. It had made quite an impression on me, and had pretty much borne out Diana's experience. As I summed it up, in the January–February 2000 issue of *Bugle*, the magazine of the Rocky Mountain Elk Foundation:

> I have a lot of memories from that weekend. It was not only my first all-woman hunt, it was my first bowhunting experience, my first time in a tree stand, my first southern hunt, my first (and I hope my last) encounter with chiggers. But the memory that really stands out—the defines the hunt for me—is of the last evening, when Pat, a postmaster from the Midwest, arrived back at the lodge late for dinner with news of her 4 x 4 buck. A hush fell over the 30 or so female hunters in the room, followed by a thunder of applause, followed by demands for the story, the whole story, several times, the telling which was punctuated by hoots and hollers, laughter, cheers and more applause.
>
> I had never experienced a group of people so genuinely thrilled about someone else's good fortune. . . . We were happy not just that she had done it, but that she had done it so well. By the fourth or fifth time she recounted the kill, we were all glowing with shared excitement and pride. I could not help but wonder whether the same thing would happen in an all-male hunting camp.

That hunt had occurred three years before the Buffalo Gals Hunt. And I confess, in retrospect, it was clear that I had set myself up, in terms of expectations about the latter. Hoist with the petard of my own feminist stereotypes, I had assumed that if we brought together a group of female hunters, they would rise to the occasion, bonding in a network of sisterly support.

Of course, I knew better, or I ought to have. I have, over the years, been at my share of women's studies faculty meetings and conferences, in which the process of achieving "consensus" was positively coercive— more than one arm has been twisted, and dissenting voice stilled, in the name of a "feminist collective." Early in my tenure as a women's studies administrator (as director of Skidmore's program), I read an article penned by three major voices in second-wave feminist scholarship and published by a major feminist press. The thrust of their argument was that, in the name of the feminist cause, we must take care not to "air our dirty laundry in public" (yes, they did resort to that cliché). Difference, disagreement, the various ways in which women in real life fall short of, or diverge from, the way they are supposed to shape themselves in theory: these were topics that should, they argued, be off the table for feminist analysis, or criticism. Their argument struck me then, and still does, as at best disingenuous, at worst intellectually dishonest.

Could a half dozen women from disparate backgrounds, mostly strangers to one another, have come together for a warmly satisfying, truly collaborative bison hunt? Of course it could happen; I had seen it happen, in a much larger group, in Alabama. In part we had simply been victims of the luck of the draw; the first six women who signed on for the Buffalo Gals Hunt—and we subsequently had had to turn some others away—turned out to be an unfortunate mix. The chemistry was bad. Doug and I certainly wished it had been otherwise. If only one could hand select one's hunters, this business would be a lot easier.

Interestingly enough, our first-ever bison hunter, Deanne—whom we surely would have handpicked for any hunt—had returned with her husband Geoff for a second buffalo hunt the Saturday after the Buffalo Gals event. They asked how it had gone. "Well," we hedged, ruefully, "it had its ups and downs." Geoff said he actually had offered to give Deanne a place in that hunt as an anniversary gift. She had declined—she said she had a hunch a bunch of women might not mesh so well, and preferred hunting on her own. Turns out, in this case anyway, her hunch was right.

Aerial view (from Erland's plane) of Spring Creek during the 1988 drought. Photo by Doug Stange.

CHAPTER 10
A Nice Place to Visit

🐚 There are two sorts of people, Doug and I have long agreed: those who say, "The door is always open, drop in anytime," and actually mean it; and those who don't so readily cotton to unanticipated visitors. We both happen to be of the latter sort, placing a premium on our privacy and our personal "space." This is doubtless one of the shared traits that not only brought us together as a couple, but led us to settle in this remote corner of Montana. Nonetheless—and surprisingly for people who live as far off the beaten path as we do—Doug and I have become relatively accustomed to being dropped in on, in ways and with effects that city folk just don't get the opportunity to experience.

There are those visitors who quite literally drop in, as happened on our very first morning here. It was around 7 a.m. on a sunny Sunday morning in late July, and we had spent the previous day driving in tandem across the state in blistering heat. Our dog, Jorinda, was out on the porch and we were still in bed. We awoke to Jo's barking, and to some sort of motor noise. Doug scrambled amidst our as yet unpacked luggage to find a fresh T-shirt and some jeans, and ran outside. A moment later, he was back.

"An airplane just landed, up in the hayfield," he said, referring to a raised, reasonably flat area immediately southeast of the house. He went back outside. I quickly dressed, and by the time I made it outside, Doug was strolling back down our road with the plane's pilot, Erland, a rancher from across the Chalk Buttes who also has some land adjacent to our place. He'd been flying over to check on his cattle, saw our vehicles parked outside the house, and figured he'd just touch down to say "Welcome to the country." In weeks and months to come, he and his wife Thea Lou would prove invaluable resources, helping us to get to know the neighborhood and the facts of life around here.

One of those facts, surely, is that no self-respecting rancher is still in bed at seven o'clock, even if it is a Sunday morning. Another is that if folks just show up on your place, it's probably because they have—or they think they have—a good excuse for being there. A day or two after Erland's visit from above, we looked up and saw, in that same hayfield, a horseman looming on the horizon. Doug jumped in the pickup and drove up to meet him. He introduced himself as a good old friend of Bud, from whom we had purchased the place, and said he'd ridden down the road which he claimed was an established public right-of-way (it isn't), to check on whether the pumps on several stock wells needed to be turned off (they didn't). A few weeks later, I encountered this same fellow peering into our mailbox. That fall, Doug discovered he had helped himself to the use of some corrals up on the divide, to sort his freshly weaned calves while their mothers took advantage of some free grazing. "Bud always lets me use 'em," he explained. To Doug's rejoinder that Bud no longer owned the place, he angrily mumbled something about being neighborly, and how folks like us didn't understand how things work in the country.

We came to grasp pretty quickly at least one aspect of how things worked around here: that ownership of a fairly sizable piece of property seemed to carry with it the assumption, especially among some townsfolk, that big land might as well be public land. Within short order after our arrival here, we were informed by various friendly folks that Bud and Betty: "always gave us permission to come out to cut firewood up in the woods" . . . "let us get our Christmas tree here every year" . . . "always allowed us to come out to pick chokecherries—wild plums —juneberries—red currants—wildflowers—(you-name-it)" . . . "never minded our taking a shortcut across the place" . . . "always welcomed us to bring the kids out to look for Indian artifacts" . . .

We had no idea Bud and Betty had been so generous. Neither, I'm sure, had they. We reckoned that, in part because of this area's homesteading history and the fact that virtually everybody seems to be related to everybody else, by blood or marriage or both, it may be only natural so see the landscape as the expanded backyard of a very extended family. But we also knew full well that we were being taken for a ride, as a couple of citified greenhorns who probably believed every sappy thing they'd ever heard or read about the down-home generosity of rural folks. We cultivated the delicate art of polite refusal.

There have been times when it hasn't been so easy to be polite. One afternoon a few summers after we moved in here we were returning from a long hot day's worth of running assorted errands in town and up in Baker. As we approached the house, looking forward to some cool drinks and a refreshing salad from the garden, we saw a young man semireclining in one of our lawn chairs on the porch. He stood up, took a leisurely stretch, and jogged down the steps and across the lawn to meet our truck. We recognized him as Greg, the Fish, Wildlife, and Parks biologist then assigned to this area, with whom we'd had some conversations about a potential wildlife habitat restoration project.

"Hey, guys!" he waved, "'bout time you two got back here. Did you know your door is locked? I've been tryin' to figure out which window would be the easiest to break into, to get at the phone." Greg explained he had been stranded here for some hours, after getting his truck hopelessly mired in mud trying to cross the creek over on the "Little Joe Place"—that is, on the western section of our ranch, a thousand-plus acres of grassland with some rough breaks and sandstone buttes, most of which constitutes our BLM grazing allotment. (When we came here, we asked locals why it was called the Little Joe Place. "Because Big Joe had a place farther up the Powderville Road," was their thoroughly reasonable response.)

Now, this was a late-August day in a drought year. It would not be an exaggeration to say that the creek crossing in question was the only patch of green grass on the entire Little Joe Place. Wouldn't that have indicated to a biologist—especially one familiar with this ecology—that there might be water there, and hence mud, and that maybe it would therefore be a bad idea to try to drive across there? "Nope, didn't think of that," Greg laughed. "So you'll need to pull me out."

Doug asked if he needed the tractor, or would our 6-cylinder Toyota T-100 have enough muscle? Greg assured him the truck should be fine, so we drove him the couple of miles back to retrieve his "outfit," as they tend to refer to trucks around here. Greg's outfit turned out to be a big Dodge Ram, mired up past its hubs in gumbo goo. It needed to be freed from the muck and pulled thirty or so yards up a twenty-foot rise. Doug whistled in thinly veiled annoyance. We drove back to get the tractor, then in tandem back once again to Greg's truck. On the way I asked Greg what he happened to be doing on the Little Joe Place anyway. Was he by chance taking a look at the plans for the fence project we were hoping to negotiate with fish and game? "Nah," he said, "I'd been at Gib and Verna's place with some papers they needed to sign, and was just cutting across your place, taking a shortcut to the Powderville Road." Great. By now late-day shadows were lengthening; it was getting past suppertime.

As Doug and Greg messed with tow chains and such, I walked along the edge of the creek embankment and noticed, looking down on Greg's truck, that its bed held an old wooden wagon wheel—a particularly nice one at that, completely intact with both its metal hub and rim. It was the sort of thing a big-city landscaper would pay good money for, as a garden "accent piece." But out here, for us such artifacts are rare finds of a different sort, sketching as they do the material outlines of pioneer history. We have always been delighted to stumble upon such things, and equally happy to leave them in place. It's one small contribution we can make to keeping what materially remains of the frontier narrative intact.

So, as I was nervously watching Doug's repeated efforts to free Greg's monster truck from the creek—he nearly tipped the fifty-horsepower Kubota over on more than one attempt—I found myself growing increasingly irked about that misplaced wheel.

A gritty, sweaty, white-knuckle hour or so passed, and Doug finally managed to extricate Greg's rig, just as the sun was setting. I strolled over to the tractor. "Uh," I began to ask, "did you happen to notice . . ."

"Yes, I did," Doug grimaced. He walked over toward Greg, who was swinging open the door to the driver's seat of his truck. "Thanks much, appreciate it," Greg grinned, folding his lanky frame into the cab.

"Nice wagon wheel you've got there," Doug gestured toward the truck bed. "You find it around here?"

"Oh, well, it wasn't on your deeded land, if that's what you mean. I picked it up on BLM land, over there," he said, pointing toward no place in particular.

"Well," Doug continued amiably, "if it had been on our land, you'd have been taking it from us, I guess. But it being on public land, weren't you sort of taking it from everybody? I mean, it's exciting to come across these things. They have value as historical artifacts. The fact that a wagon wheel is on public land doesn't make it free for the taking. You're depriving other people of the potential experience of coming across it, imagining the history behind it, making up stories about it."

Greg, who clearly couldn't care less about historical preservation, let alone lectures from erstwhile academics, took a halfhearted stab at looking sheepish.

"Now, I can't tell you what to do, but I know you're a good Lutheran, with a well developed conscience . . ." Doug—who was old enough to be Greg's father—was laying it on pretty thick at this point. "I believe that, if you reflect on it for a few moments, you'll agree the right thing to do would be to take that wheel back to wherever it was you found it, and leave it there."

"Yes, you're right, of course, I guess I wasn't thinking." Greg's demeanor was that of a middle schooler called in to the principal's office.

"Well," Doug said. "I'm sure you'll do the right thing. Drive carefully now." Greg gunned his engine, and was on his way.

Doug shook his head. "What an idiot," he sighed.

We were neither of us surprised, several months later, when we went to a housewarming at the new log home Greg and his wife had built down in Broadus and noticed morning glories twining around the wagon wheel that served as the focal point of their garden fence.

THE SCENIC ROUTE

It must be stressed that our little corner of this big state is not on the way to anywhere—one must go considerably out of one's way to get here. Up until the last few years, when funding finally was secured to put blacktop down on County Highway 323 heading southward toward the Wyoming border, Ekalaka's unofficial town motto was "Ekalaka: Where the paved road ends." The Main Street Market in town sells T-shirts depicting a desolate stretch of road with a mileage sign reading, "End of the World: 10 miles. Ekalaka, Montana: 20 miles."

Nonetheless, people do manage to find their way here, some more intentionally than others. Some are tourists. This area is not exactly a vacation destination, but it is close enough to the Black Hills to make for a day-trip to the Medicine Rocks, maybe, or Miles City. Each August we catch some overflow from the huge motorcycle rally in Sturgis, South Dakota, and on some days there are more Harleys than hay trucks on Carter County's back roads. The area is popular in the fall with deer and pronghorn hunters, most of them from the upper Midwest. It is also a draw for certain academic researchers: archaeologists and paleontologists searching for human artifacts and fossils, Western historians and Indian Wars history buffs intent on doing oral histories, and a couple of New Jersey university professors of geography and land-use planning whose ideas raised quite a ruckus in these parts a few years ago, about whom more, in a while.

Just about everyone who wanders our way seems to come equipped both with some well developed ideas about what they will find out here in the Wild West, and with a camera to record those findings. We try not to disappoint. And, especially when we're dealing with those urbanites whose threshold for "adventure" is relatively low, we generally manage to satisfy without half trying. For example, some years ago friends of ours from Alexandria, Virginia, arrived in Rapid City late in the day and without their luggage. Their airline agreed to have the bags delivered to Ekalaka the next day. Early that Sunday afternoon, we received a phone call from the person making the delivery; he was in Alzada and would be in town in about an hour. We agreed to meet him for the baggage transfer at the Wagon Wheel Café and headed for town. When we got there and turned onto Main Street, Dede and Bernie couldn't believe what they were seeing: "WOW!" they both exclaimed. "This looks just like western towns in the movies!" They were especially taken by the one-room town hall, which houses the office of the chief of police (who also happens to be the entire police department). On its door was posted a sign: "Out of town. Back next Wednesday." Bernie began madly snapping photos.

We proceeded to the Wagon Wheel, and as we were strolling up to its entrance, a sedan with South Dakota plates pulled up. Dede nudged her husband as the driver emerged. "Maybe you should put the camera away," she murmured. "We, uh, wouldn't want him to take offense or anything." Not that the man wasn't a walking photo op. Bikers in Sturgis for the rally often take on part-time jobs to scare up some cash; this one had apparently contracted with the airline to deliver waylaid luggage. He was an ideal specimen of his type: Burly, with slightly graying hair pulled back in a ponytail, mirror-lens aviator sunglasses, black Harley Davidson t-shirt with black studded leather pants and boots, silver earrings and several silver and turquoise finger rings, most of them variations on the skull-and-crossbones motif, tattoos covering both arms and—a là *Night of the Hunter*, speaking of things straight out of the movies—"LOVE" tattooed across the fingers of one hand and "HATE" on those of the other. He must have pulled baby-sitting duty that afternoon, because there was a small child of indeterminate gender sitting in the car's passenger seat. He greeted us genially, with a vaguely menacing gap-toothed smile, and hefted the bags from the trunk. After a few pleasantries about the weather—"Hot enough for ya?"—and words of thanks, Bernie realized he should fish out his wallet and give the man a tip. I'm not sure what denomination of bill he pulled out, but after a surreptitious but steely look from his wife, he pulled out another and handed them to the man. He took the money with a gracious bow, strode into the Wagon Wheel and out again, a minute later, with an ice cream cone for the child, and was gone. "I wish I had a picture of that guy," Bernie sighed.

Later on in their visit we encountered a recently killed rattlesnake on the Alzada road, and Bernie insisted that we stop for photos. Dede and I waited in the truck while he and Doug spent about a half-hour trying artfully to rearrange the snake into something like a coil, using a rock to prop up its head, as if it were poised to strike. Some while later Doug read that a rattler, if disturbed, can strike via pure reflex for a considerable period of time after its death. The men were lucky. And, in the end, the snake pictures were the only ones they took on the entire trip that didn't turn out—a fact to which our East Coast friends attributed a significance that escaped us.

Friends and tourists aren't the only ones roving this terrain with cameras in hand. Even the Jehovah's Witnesses missionaries are shutterbugs, as we discovered one Saturday morning when a van with California license plates drove up to our gate and a half-dozen men, women, and children dressed in their best go-to-meeting clothes emerged and began taking pictures of the Chalk Buttes, our house, our tractors and trucks and so on. I was not at my best, having the day before badly sprained my ankle. I'd been icing it down on the living-room couch—still in my bathrobe at midmorning—when they arrived. Seeing these strange Californians wandering around our yard with cameras and camcorder rolling, I hobbled out the front door, wincing in pain and shouting "What the hell do you people think you are doing?

Who are you, anyway?" They surely had me pegged as a godless floozy who spent the day lounging on the couch, cursing in her pajamas and munching on bonbons. Doug arrived back from whatever chore he had been doing. They introduced themselves as Jehovah's Witnesses, offering him issues of the *Watchtower*, which he declined, explaining we were Lutherans.

The camcorder continued to roll. Doug asked them about that, and the man running it objected—rather testily, we both thought—that they were simply admiring the view. (Of our *tractors?*) Things got a bit sticky when a woman shepherding two small children asked to come inside to use the bathroom—it was beginning to feel less like they were proselytizing than casing the joint. It is not as if there is a toll-free number one can call to verify that the people at your door claiming to be missionaries are legit. When, at our moment's hesitation to let her in, the woman began ranting about human decency and proper hygiene, we figured it looked as if she wasn't any happier with this situation than we were. We obliged, re: lavatory privileges. Then they asked if they could have some cool glasses of water. Sure, I said, handing them some paper cups and pointing them to the garden hose.

They eventually left, heading down the Chalk Buttes Road to Gib and Verna's. They were not at home, but a foreign exchange student from Macedonia who was staying with them—a young man with only a modicum of English at his disposal—was there. He later reported that these crazy people drove up, thrust some reading material into his hands, took a bunch of pictures and video, piled back into their van, and drove away. Some odd American custom, no doubt. We subsequently put it together that the photos were probably a way of documenting, for whomever it was they reported back to, that they actually had made it all the way to the far-flung, and very out of the way, domiciles to which they had been assigned.

Of course, it is not as if we are lacking in wonderful photo opportunities here. In the lingo of urban planning and landscape design, the Chalk Buttes and their environs present a magnificent "viewshed." And the views are nowhere better than from several vantage points on our place, beginning with our own front yard. If it's scenery you are looking for, especially scenery with the aura of the pioneer West— two-track roads, broken-down remnants of homesteads, rough country crisscrossed by antique barbed-wire fences, wildlife in abundance and buffalo on the open range—we've got it all. That may be the reason we've been approached, on several occasions over the years, by documentary filmmakers looking either for a backdrop or for a piece of a story on which they are working.

Some of these inquiries have led nowhere because the projects themselves, worthy as they may have been (and two were very worthwhile projects on women and hunting), never got off the ground; for every film documentary that gets made, dozens more die for lack of funding. Some requests have been downright bizarre, as when a producer working on a film about the Yellowstone bison called Doug about the possibility of filming footage of *our* bison, if possible walking down a paved highway, as if they were the Yellowstone herd in winter. Not possible, Doug replied. A Montana-based film crew working on a documentary about human/bison interactions over time and space filmed a hunt here this past fall, and as I write that film remains in production for Montana Public Television. But surely the most interesting documentary experience we have had to date involved a two-person crew who had to cross the Atlantic to get here.

THE FRENCH CONNECTION

It began innocently enough, with an e-mail from a French documentary film producer—I'll call her Sophie—who said she was working on a film about women and hunting. She had read my book, *Woman the Hunter*, and wondered whether we might set up a phone date to discuss her project, and perhaps to involve me in some way in the documentary which, she explained, she was producing for France's equivalent of American cable television's Outdoor Life Channel. Over the years I have often been interviewed about women's hunting and have consulted on several kindred projects, so I was happy to oblige. She assured me she was fluent in English—a good thing, as my college French is on the rusty side.

A few days later, at our agreed-upon time, she rang me up from Paris and we immediately hit it off as congenially as two strangers can manage to do, via long distance. Her project sounded both fascinating and ambitious: Sophie would interview women hunters, and film them actually hunting, on two continents. She had, so far, lined up a pheasant shoot in Scotland and deer hunting in northern Italy. Since an African safari was somewhat beyond the limits of her production budget, she was arranging to film a women's hunt on an exotic game ranch in Texas. And, as our conversation developed, she wondered about the possibility of filming one or more women hunting a buffalo on our ranch, along with interviewing me about women's hunting in various cultures and time periods.

The memory of the Buffalo Gals' Hunt was then still sufficiently raw and I told her a group hunt for women was not on the horizon. But I checked with Doug to see whether we had any other female hunters signed up for that upcoming season. It turned out we did, and the hunter in question was an ideal subject, from Sophie's point of view: a young college senior I'll call Beth who, having grown up in a hunting family, was planning a career as a wildlife biologist. Her hunt—an early graduation gift from her parents—was scheduled for her spring break from Montana State University, which happened to coincide with mine from Skidmore. So the timing was perfect for me, as it was for Sophie, whose Texas hunt was scheduled for the following week in mid-March. The scenario we agreed upon was that I would guide Beth on foot, Sophie and her cameraman following at a discreet distance, aiming for as naturalistic a hunt as possible. Once Beth shot her bison and filmed some interview footage, we'd return home for lunch, then spend some time in the afternoon doing "talking-head" footage of me on women and hunting, and of Doug, on buffalo hunting more generally.

The appointed day dawned cold, wet, and windy, after several days worth of sporadic rain and snow showers. Early March tends to be one of the least congenial times of year in southeastern Montana, with winter typically doing its best to fend off spring, and this year proved no exception. Still, there promised to be a few breaks of weak sunshine amidst mottled cloud cover. By midmorning, the weather could be predictably "bracing," and by no means unpleasant for anyone properly outfitted.

Don, our skinner for the day, had met up with Beth and her father in Baker, and they drove down to Ekalaka in tandem. There, they rendezvoused with Sophie and her cinematographer, whom I'll call Alphonse. They had flown into Billings from Paris two days earlier, and driven to Ekalaka in a rental car, fortunately (at our strong suggestion) a 4-wheel drive SUV. Sophie was petite, vivacious, a nonstop talker, winsomely attractive, and seriously underdressed for the weather. Alphonse was tall and lean, intense in a craggy sort of way, a man of few words at all and fewer still in English, and outfitted in the kind of multipocketed bush jacket professional photographers universally seem to favor. They both exuded a nervous energy, no doubt partly attributable to jet lag and, in Alphonse's case, to the fact that he was the pair's designated driver and clearly not used to the kind of road conditions Big Sky Country presented: their rented Subaru was encrusted with ice and mud.

The bison herd was in the tri-corners pasture northwest of the house. Once the usual preliminaries were taken care of, Beth and I set out on foot, closely trailed by Alphonse and Sophie, with Doug following behind and out of camera range.

"You won't even know we are there," Sophie had assured me in advance, about the filming. "You and Beth will simply go about your hunting, and we will follow at a discrete distance to record it." And if I bought that, I thought, she had a tower in Paris she would like to sell me. I had had enough on-camera experience by then to know that this hunt would be, to some extent necessarily, something of a simulation of a bison hunt. I had, nonetheless, no idea precisely how "directed" our activities would be in the next couple of hours.

Time and again, to Sophie's refrain, "Just go about your hunting. Walk! Talk! Act naturally! Pretend we are not here!" Alphonse would provide the chorus: "*Mais non! Non! Non!*" The light wasn't right, or the background. Or the frame had no "meaning." Or he had some problem with his camera, and needed something redone. Could we perhaps retrace our steps? No, not there, because we'd already made footprints in the snow. Perhaps walk up that hill over there instead?

Sophie, wielding the mic, had recurring concerns about sound quality:

"That was a wonderful impromptu exchange you and Beth had just now, about how nice it was to be out hunting on spring break. Could you perhaps repeat it, just as spontaneously but a little louder?"

Or: "*Et, Marie!* Could you perhaps narrate what you and Beth are doing, as you are doing it? And Beth, can you say something very informal about the feelings you are feeling now?"

With Alphonse's punctuation:

"*Non. Non. Non!*"

At regular intervals the two would pause to confer, chattering in a rapid-fire slangy Parisian patois of which I could make no sense whatsoever. I had the sense that, even had I kept it up better, my four years of French would have been to no avail. Sophie and Alphonse may as well have landed from another planet.

Beth was coping in reasonably good humor, all things considered. For their part, the bison were in a less than cooperative mood. The herd had been hunted relatively hard that year, and by the time of this unusual late-season hunt, all it took was the echo of a rifle being sighted-in to convince them to forego their customary midmorning rest period, and keep them on the move. Alphonse had no trouble getting shots of buffalo migrating over the next rise and out of sight, as happened time after time.

As morning stretched toward noon, the herd finally settled down to grazing in a place where we could sneak up a ridge to get within reasonable shooting range, with care and with permission from Alphonse—the sun had broken through the clouds, and the flare on his lens was giving him fits. He wanted to be able to film a fairly long shot, with both Beth and her target buffalo in the frame. It took a bit of doing, but we managed to get into position without spooking the herd. I pointed out a yearling bull to Beth, and she raised her rifle to shoot. She eased off the safety.

"Ah, non, attendez!"

Beth sighed, clicked on the safety, and lowered her gun. Alphonse was having some sort of trouble, but he got it sorted out fairly quickly, and apologetically gave us a thumbs-up. Beth raised her gun again, steadied herself, released the safety, and fired. It was a good, fatal hit. Alphonse seemed pretty pleased with his shooting, too. There followed the filming of some more mundane "talking head" footage, and then we left Beth, who was finally able to exhale and enjoy her success, to her dad and their own photo op with her bull.

Back at the house, we sat down to a simple lunch of bison sloppy joes and salad. I hadn't had time to make dessert, so I opened a couple of bags of Pepperidge Farm cookies. Sophie, who proved to have a truly prodigious appetite for her petite size, praised the meal—"Real food! So good! And so healthy!," and she found the cookies absolutely scrumptious—"You buy these in the grocery store? *Incroyable!* We don't have anything like this in France." That seemed hard to swallow (no pun intended), but the pair had for a couple of days been eating road food, which in Montana can be pretty grim. Alphonse ate his meal quietly, then adjourned outdoors to the porch to fiddle with camera, lenses, and lights for the afternoon shoot, and smoke several Gauloises.

I retreated to freshen my eye makeup and try to do something with a bad case of "hat hair" before the afternoon shoot. Meanwhile, Alphonse orchestrated a major rearrangement of our living room to accommodate his camera tripod, assorted lights, and reflectors. After

Alphonse and Sophie, staging the shot. Photo by Doug Stange.

deliberating various camera angles and backdrops, removing a print he didn't care for from the wall, experimenting with the drapes open and drawn and redistributing throw pillows, he got around to inserting me into the scene, which meant redoing pretty much everything else. I had experienced this sort of activity before with documentary videographers who, as a group, seem to have been pack rats in a former life.

We eventually got down to doing Sophie's interview with me. It went as these sessions usually do. The goal is to create convincing enough sound bites, which carefully edited and strung together will give the impression that a probing conversation took place. Almost invariably, the best of said sound-bites require two or three takes, and the trick is to make take number three look and sound as off-the-cuff as the original comment had been. After about an hour or so of make-believe dialogue, Sophie thought she had what she needed from me. She and Alphonse proceeded to do a rather more informal session with Doug, out on the front steps, and then they gathered their things, to get on the road before dusk.

As they were loading up their gear, Sophie bubbled about what a wonderful day it had been: They had gotten some terrific footage, she was certain, and they had had a truly great time and so appreciated our opening our home to their project. Indeed—and we should understand that she was a private person and would not usually even think of saying such a thing—anytime we were in Paris, we should count on staying with her. We must plan to come for a visit: her fiancé was an outdoorsman, and would just love to meet us. She couldn't explain it, but she felt a special bond with us; we were her kind of people. It was rather charming, in a goofy francophone sort of way. She was thrilled when I gave her the rest of the bag of Milanos to munch on the road back to Billings, and we hugged, and waved them on their way.

I never heard from Sophie again. We never received the videotape she had promised. We tried on successive occasions to track down programming information about that French TV station, to no avail. My several e-mails to Sophie went unanswered. Maybe they really had landed from another planet, after all. They came, they filmed, they disappeared.

MOVING PICTURES

It isn't surprising that people wielding cameras are drawn to this part of the world, with its stunning "viewsheds." In popular imagination, this is what the West is all about: views, vistas, panoramas, expansive terrain, big nature. Of course, it is people with cameras who have, quite literally, framed our ideas about the western landscape, and its meaning. This is a central point in Jane Tompkins's *West of Everything: The Inner Life of Westerns*. We all learn, if not to experience the West then at least to see it, through the movies. As she astutely observes:

> Big sky country is a psychological and spiritual place known by definite physical markers. It is the American West, and not just any part of that but the West of the desert, of mountains and prairies, the West of Arizona, Utah, Nevada, New Mexico, Texas, Colorado, Montana, Wyoming, the Dakotas, and some parts of California.

In childhood, given those summers I spent in Ventura County, I pretty much refined it all down to California, with a nod (in the abstract) to Texas. I remember as an adolescent, having grown up on *Hopalong Cassidy* and *The Lone Ranger* and *Bonanza*, being shocked to the point of disbelief to discover that Dodge City was in Kansas. *Kansas?* Kansas was for Dorothy and Toto, it was corn country. Marshal Dillon, Doc,

Chester, and Miss Kitty lived out West! A few years later, I was equally dumbfounded to learn that Annie Oakley, whom I had adored as played on television by Gail Davis, was born and raised in Ohio. "The Maid of the Western Plains" was a stage character, the creation of Buffalo Bill Cody; before there were movies, there were Wild West shows.

The television Annie's ranch was located in the town of Diablo, state or territory unspecified. But its geography was that of the mythic West, as it had by the 1950s been defined by a generation of filmmakers. Tompkins fittingly illustrates the lay of that land, via the opening shots of several classic westerns:

> Desert, with butte, two riders galloping toward camera.
> *Stagecoach* (1939)
> Cattle on a trail, flat country.
> *Texas* (1941)
> Landscape with butte, a wagon train, cattle.
> *My Darling Clementine* (1946)
> Desert, with wagon train, flat country, a few hills.
> *Red River* (1948)
> Flat foreground, river, large mesa on the opposite shore.
> *Rio Grande* (1950)
> Desert landscape framed by the doorway of a house. Song:
> "What makes a man to wander, what makes a man to roam,
> What makes a man to wander, and turn his back on home?"
> *The Searchers* (1956)
> Blank horizon, prairie, sky.
> *Gunfight at the OK Corral* (1957)
> Flat desert, lone tree.
> *Lonely Are the Brave* (1962)
> Total blank, misty.
> *High Plains Drifter* (1973)

To the extent that people figure in these cinematic landscapes at all, it is as if in miniature. The sky is so big, the country so vast, that human beings—who occupy so much space in their hustling, bustling Eastern cities—are reduced to mere supporting players in a drama in which earth and sky play the starring roles.

And yet, inhospitable as this country so clearly is to human settlement, the western script calls for shopkeepers and cowhands, gunslingers and lawmen, schoolmarms and dance-hall girls to come and populate the place. We know that, whatever hardships they may encounter on film, they ultimately must have endured because towns like Ekalaka are here today, to continue telling the rugged tale and looking like something straight out of the movies. When *Brokeback Mountain* came out in 2005, friends and colleagues of mine in New York were all curious as to how "authentic" it was. I could tell them, truly, that Ang Lee's film was a dead-on depiction of what life is like in the Rocky Mountain West. I'm sure they mostly thought I was referring to camping and horseback riding against the backdrop of breathtaking scenery (which in this case actually happened to be in Alberta). But what I really had in mind was the film's relentlessly spare portrayal of small-town life: the hard-edged people, their prejudices, the hand-to-mouth quality of so much of existence in a rural Wyoming not too different from eastern Montana, the meanness—the "What makes you think you deserve nice things?" aura—of it all.

Long before *Brokeback Mountain*, another classic western, George Stevens' 1953 masterpiece *Shane*, drew a picture of a West similarly beautiful and brutal. Set in Wyoming with the Grand Tetons as background, the film, which A. B. Guthrie Jr. adapted from the novel by Jack Schaefer, loosely derives its plot from the Johnson County War of 1882. Although *Shane* is set in the Jackson Hole area, the historical scene of what became the archetypal "range war" of the late nineteenth

Riding the open range, with our friend Maggie. Photo by Doug Stange.

century was actually farther east, in the Powder River basin. It was a clash between organized cattle interests on the one hand and homesteaders on the other, over how best to manage public land. The large-scale cattlemen, many of them transplanted from European aristocracy, relied upon open rangeland to run their cows. Homesteaders were for the most part farmers, or involved at best in limited cattle or sheep ranching. They cleared grassland. They built fences. They got in the way of the cattle barons' open range.

The outlines of the conflict have been trivialized in ditties like "Don't Fence Me In," and the musical *Oklahoma*'s rousing chorus to "The Farmer and the Cowman Should Be Friends":

> Territory folks should stick together, territory folks should all be pals.
> Cowboys dance with the farmers' daughters, farmers dance with the ranchers' gals!

The reality was far more complicated than anything that could be resolved by a barn dance. Following blizzards in winter and summer drought, the Wyoming cattle barons had suffered heavy stock losses. Rather than attributing them to the weather, they blamed the small ranchers who were intruding on their rangeland. Hired guns, ostensibly "guardsmen" brought up to Wyoming from Texas, invaded Johnson County supplied with a veritable hit list of seventy homesteaders, to round up and eliminate them as cattle rustlers (which, to be fair, some of them probably were). A goodly amount of blood was shed on both sides and a lot of ammunition spent before, at the request of the governor of Wyoming, President Benjamin Harrison called out the Sixth Cavalry to subdue the "insurrectionist" homesteaders who had banded together to protect their claims. The Texas thugs surrendered themselves to Army custody, were granted bail, and promptly flew the scene. Those homesteaders arrested and held for trial were eventually released as well, when material witnesses failed to appear and the cost of lodging them as prisoners grew prohibitive. It was not the prettiest moment in Western history.

Shane supplies a more satisfying metaphorical treatment, a starkly rendered morality tale in which, while the story has its share of moral ambiguity, the black and white hats are neatly distinguished. Clearly taking up the cause of the homesteaders, the screenplay provides the rationale for their self-defense. At a climactic moment in the drama, with the Tetons looming in the deep background, many miles of wind-whipped, dead-flat, sage-studded prairie away, the homesteader Joe Starrett, played by Van Heflin, declares—with a sweeping gesture toward that same desolate prairie—"*This valley is farm country!*"

We believe him. His wife and son believe him. Shane (Alan Ladd, in his signature performance) so deeply believes him that he is willing to return to his forsaken gunfighter ways, to kill so that Joe and his neighbors will be able to save their family homesteads. It is a profoundly moving story. We are all right there with young Joey Starrett (Brandon DeWilde) in the end, as he calls out into the gathering prairie darkness, after his wounded hero: "Don't go, Shane! Shane, come back!" It is powerful. It is real. It is nearly Shakespearean in its tragic undertow.

It is, however, not very good history. And it is a lousy model for range management. That is where those two New Jersey professors I mentioned earlier enter the picture.

THE BIG OPEN

In 1987 Frank Popper, a professor of land-use planning at Rutgers University, and his wife Deborah, a geographer then completing her doctoral dissertation, also at Rutgers, coauthored an article that appeared in *Planning* magazine. Titled "The Great Plains: From Dust to Dust," it was a thought experiment of sorts which, the couple later claimed, they expected would attract little if any attention beyond the urban planning crowd that read that particular journal. As things turned out, they could not have been more wrong. The subtitle of the article was "A daring proposal for dealing with an inevitable disaster," and when word got around of the nature of their proposal—the deprivatization of the Great Plains and the establishment of a "Buffalo Commons" under the direction of a massive government agency—a considerable amount of hell broke loose throughout the Plains. The Poppers' article, as *Billings Gazette* writer Lorna Thackeray recollected years later, "made them almost as popular on the Plains as an invasion of Mormon crickets."

Taking into account the Great Plains region's history of boom and bust cycles, and the current rate of depopulation ("out-migration") with an aging resident rural population, the Poppers' thesis was simple, and starkly stated:

> [O]ver the next generation the Plains will, as a result of the largest, longest-running agricultural and environmental miscalculation in American history, become almost totally depopulated. At that

point, a new use for the region will emerge, one that is in fact so old that it predates the American presence. We are suggesting that the region be returned to its original pre-white state, that it be, in effect, deprivatized.

Their suggestion was received in these parts with about the same level of antipathy as had been New Jersey Senator Bill Bradley's initiative, a few years earlier, to return the Black Hills of South Dakota and surrounding federal lands to the Sioux. What did these New Jersey types know about the facts of life out here, anyway, and what business was it of theirs how High Plains folks managed their land?

It was a reasonable enough question. In the Poppers' characterization, quality of life in the Great Plains—short- and mixed-grass prairie that encompasses portions of ten states stretching from Montana and the Dakotas southward to Texas, and accounting for one-fifth of the total land area of the United States—could be summed up fairly succinctly:

- "The Plains are endlessly windswept and nearly treeless; the climate is semi-arid . . . The country is rolling in parts in the north, dead flat in the south. It is lightly populated. A dusty town with a single gas station, store, and house is sometimes 50 unpaved miles from its nearest neighbor, another three-building settlement amidst the sagebrush."
- As to climate: "The Great Plains are America's Steppes. They have the nation's hottest summers and coldest winters, greatest temperature swings, worst hail and locusts and range fires, fiercest droughts and blizzards, and therefore its shortest growing season. The Plains are the land of the Big Sky and the Dust Bowl, one-room schoolhouses and settler homesteads, straight-line interstates and custom combines, prairie dogs and antelope and buffalo."
- The Poppers do add, in a slight nod to aesthetic appeal, that "the oceans-of-grass vistas of the Plains offer enormous horizons, billowy clouds, and somber-serene beauty."

Now, as critics quickly and rightly pointed out, while all the above statements may be true of one or another High Plains location, at one time or another, they constitute in the aggregate an egregious oversimplification of a varied and diverse ecology.

Nonetheless, the Poppers did offer a powerful analysis of the impact, on both people and land, of successive cycles of boom and bust over the past century. And, based upon the region's history, the picture they painted of what lay ahead was both realistic and dire: "Soil erosion is approaching Dust Bowl rates. Water shortages loom . . . Important long-term climatic and technological trends do not look favorable. Government seems unable to react constructively to these trends, much less to anticipate them." If the farm crisis of the 1980s was bad for farmers in the Corn Belt, it was worse for farmers and ranchers here who "have always operated under conditions that their counterparts elsewhere would have found intolerable, and now they are worse." As to the prospect of High Plains farmers and ranchers solving their problems by selling out to the highest bidder, "The brute fact is that most Plains land is simply not competitive with land elsewhere. The only people who want it are already on it, and most of them are increasingly unable to make a living from it."

When it came to plotting the future of what they called "the Plains ordeal" and "the curse of the shortgrass immensity," the Poppers cited various proposals that had been put forth to restore the Plains to their prehomesteading, open-grassland state. Among them was the suggestion by University of Oklahoma geographer and MacArthur fellow Bret Wallach that the U.S. Forest Service enter into contracts with individual ranchers and farmers, to pay them the full value of whatever they would cultivate over the ensuing fifteen years, providing they didn't actually cultivate it. Instead, following Forest Service guidelines, they would reestablish native shortgrasses. At the end of the fifteen-year contract, the Forest Service would buy out the ranchers, allowing each to keep a forty-acre homestead. A similar plan would transfer the oversight of these lands to the Bureau of Land Management, toward a massive expansion of national grasslands.

Robert Scott, of the Institute of the Rockies in Missoula, Montana, ventured a more audacious plan: to turn over about fifteen thousand square miles of eastern Montana—about a tenth of the state's total land area—to the development of "an East African–style game preserve" called the Big Open. With state and federal assistance, fences would be torn down, domestic livestock eliminated and replaced by game animals: Scott estimated the land could support seventy-five thousand bison, forty thousand elk, and forty thousand antelope. This plan, arguably, would turn now-struggling ranches into lucrative hunting operations, creating at least a thousand new jobs in service sectors from outfitters to innkeepers to taxidermists.

The Poppers acknowledged that plans such as these were probably too expensive to carry out. They also noted—with no apparent sign of irony—that such revisions of the region's land-use could "provoke great resistance from the landowners because they would constrain their property rights." Their modest alternative proposal? The federal government should step in and take back the land that had been privatized during the homesteading era. Given the way out-migration, weather patterns, and farm prices were all trending, the government would probably even be able to acquire the majority of these farm and ranch properties "under distress-sale circumstances." Of course, there were social and economic consequences to consider:

> It will be up to the federal government to ease the social transition of the economic refugees who are being forced off the land. For they will feel aggrieved and impoverished, penalized for staying too long in a place they loved and pursuing occupations the nation supposedly respected but evidently did not. The government will have to invent a 1990s version of the 1930s Resettlement Administration, a social work-finance-technical assistance agency that will find ways and places for the former Plains residents to get back on their feet.

Once the "refugees" were out of the way and their homes, animals, outbuildings, and fences removed, the land could revert to its pristine wilderness state: "a vast land mass, largely empty and unexploited." As wildlife populations flourished and the buffalo were reestablished, it could make a great tourist attraction, sort of an American Serengeti.

Well. It turns out folks in the boondocks do pay some attention to thought currents emanating from back East. The potential refugees in question didn't think much of the Buffalo Commons idea. Newspaper editors railed against "New Jersey ethnocentrism" (the Aberdeen, South Dakota, *American News*); they complained, "The Poppers cannot comprehend what we love about this wide-open and windy space, and you can't explain it to them" (Mandan, North Dakota, *News*). Striking a common theme, a journalist in Wichita, Kansas, suggested, "Let's turn New Jersey into a Dumping Commons, the permanent home of anything America wants rid of . . . nuclear waste, garbage, Jimmy Hoffa's body."

In the years following the publication of the *Planning* article, Frank and Deborah Popper toured the High Plains, gathering fresh insights and preaching to the mostly-unwilling-to-be-converted.

Reading somewhat between the lines of journalist Anne Matthews' fascinating chronicle of that time, *Where the Buffalo Roam*, it becomes clear that, whenever the Poppers came to town, there was a certain degree of failure to communicate on both sides of the ideological divide. Much of it was rooted in social stereotypes: Frank and Deborah were readily typecast as East Coast academics who didn't have a clue about how real people lived, which placed them at the intersection of locally prevailing currents of anti-urbanism and anti-intellectualism. But, for their part, they seemed more than happy to play the part of effete intellectuals. A photo in Matthews' book shows them in professional attire—he in suit and tie, she in dress, stockings, and heels—sitting on top of a big round hay bale in the middle of a farmer's field, staring fixedly into the camera lens. What were they hoping to convey in this image? A gentle sense of self-parody, perhaps? If so, they failed: the photo looks, if anything, like two brokers who have just come to take possession of the place. There is something vaguely imperialistic about the image, albeit in a daffily out of place sort of way.

The dynamic that developed between the Poppers and their real live demographic data-set is perfectly illustrated by a showdown that occurred in Billings on a wintry March day in the late 1980s. They had come to Rocky Mountain College to speak at a forum sponsored by, of all things, the Harvard Club of Montana.

The Poppers started things off with their usual recitation of bleak facts about the "Plains ordeal": population loss, resource depletion, failing agricultural economy. It was all there, in the numbers. In a patchwork of 110 Plains counties, accounting for 139,000 square miles of semiarid short-grass prairie, population was down a third since 1920, and the decline was continuing apace. Many of these counties, with six or fewer persons per square mile, were reverting to "frontier" status and indeed, statistically, some of them were already there, with two or fewer persons per square mile. The farm and ranch economy was in trouble, water becoming ever more scarce, the topsoil nearly depleted. The numbers didn't lie, and it was time for Plains residents to face the facts.

The first few questions from the audience were guarded, but constructive. What, one audience member asked, about pooling resources, say in a cooperative, like Land O'Lakes and Sunkist and Ocean Spray—how about a "meat-and-wheat" co-op to save the Plains economy? Nope, Frank responded, won't work here. A discussion of interest rates and the insensitivity of "big out-of-state banks" darkened the collective mood. And then the topic turned to Native Americans: "The Native Americans often see the Buffalo Commons as a metaphor for a giant white agricultural pullback," Frank offered, perhaps too jauntily, and things turned ugly in the auditorium. Accusations flew: "We don't have tenure in *our* business," an eastern Montana farmer yelled. A representative from BLM expressed concern about the Poppers' "policy agendas": Were they aiming for eastern control of the Plains? Were they socialists? Maybe even Communists? There were cries from the audience: "Go back to New Jersey!" . . . "You're covering up a federal land grab!" . . . "Why do you want to control us?"

Deborah snapped back: "This recurring talk of plots and secret agendas offends me. We threw out an idea, backed it up, and you refuse to talk about it. Those kinds of questions show a real unwillingness to deal with what you plan to do after you have no topsoil and no water and no towns." So there. It was pretty much downhill from that point on.

Both Doug and I have personally encountered the Poppers. He met them both at a National Bison Association conference at which they were speaking, sometime in the early 1990s; Frank told him about how they fell in love with Ekalaka when they happened to visit during the annual "Days of '85" celebration. I met Frank a few years later at a conference at the Center for Great Plains Studies in Nebraska; he complimented a paper I had read on the restoration of the bison to the Plains and shared with me some of his and Deborah's then current work in progress. Doug and I both found the Poppers charming, and not at all incendiary. Of course, we are both academics, too, and so we know (all right, we *are*) the type. Yet I cannot help but think that, had we been in that audience at Rocky Mountain College, and had we known then what we subsequently learned about the pressures facing High Plains ranchers, we might well have been among the chorus telling Frank and Deborah to get the hell back to New Jersey because they didn't know what they were talking about.

But interestingly, and not at all surprisingly because they really are good scholar-researchers, the Poppers came to understand that fact themselves. Over the years they have considerably reframed their ideas about the Buffalo Commons, taking into account not only the cost (both human and economic) and complexity of their proposal, but also the necessity for compromise and cooperation. In 2001 Deborah Popper told a writer for *High Country News*, "We've learned over the years to be more sensitive and to write more carefully, avoiding words like 'empty' and trying to qualify it when we say, 'Your ancestors made mistakes.' Now we say they were responding to the incentives of their time and doing the best they could." Condescending, yes, but an important concession nonetheless. In 2007, she told the *Bismarck Tribune* that when she now rereads that original 1987 paper, she is struck by its sweeping language: "It was much more powerful than I would write it now."

And the subsequent twenty years have borne out that it was also not quite accurate, despite all of Deborah's numbers crunching. A generation later, while population loss, climate concerns, and economic woes remain a fact of life throughout the Plains, folks are still here, sticking it out. And some of those folks—Doug and I among them—think there may yet be hope for some variation on the Buffalo Commons theme to emerge after all. It's a matter of a way of living, yes. But it fundamentally comes down to a way of seeing: a way of imagining the West that gets us beyond the movies.

And here the Poppers are very helpful. In an article published in 2006, titled "The Buffalo Commons: Its Antecedents and Their Implications," they offer a far more refined take than their original article afforded. They write that as "a combination of literary metaphor, public-policy proposal, futurist prediction and ecological restoration project, the Buffalo Commons foresees a Plains whose land uses fall between cultivation on the one hand and wilderness on the other." They envision more bison and fewer cattle, more environmental protection and less extraction, more ecotourism and less conventional development. In another article from 2006, "The Onset of the Buffalo Commons," they acknowledge that the Buffalo Commons idea is itself part of a larger picture:

> Quite separately, our work on the Buffalo Commons has coincided with numbers of important shifts: from a paradigm of mastery of nature to one of cooperation based on ecology; from hierarchical thinking to more systems thinking that relies on a wider range of inputs; from regulatory approaches to public-private partnerships and more grassroots participation.

In that same article, they admit that their earlier vision was "somewhat fantastical," but they suggest—rightly—that it also generated an important, and ultimately constructive, conversation:

. . . wide-open spaces no longer fenced, replanted grasses, and free movement of all native species. One could imagine safaris following large, free-ranging herds of bison and pronghorn. Buffalo were central to this image of the regional future.

Many people in the region rejected the vision, deriding the notion of the return of buffalo as impractical. . . . The image of a Buffalo Commons took hold nonetheless. It worked as a way of getting discussions started on alternative ways of inhabiting the rural Great Plains. Just as a poetic metaphor can stimulate imagination, so too can a regional one.

After twenty-plus years of developing and promoting their idea of the Buffalo Commons, it's perhaps only natural that Frank and Deborah Popper have from time to time been hoist with the petard of their own metaphor. In the summer of 2000, the people of Gwinner, North Dakota (population 717), invited them to town for their centennial celebration. They were treated first with a performance of a play written by a local schoolteacher: *Professor Prank's Proposal, or Don't Let the Doctor Buffalo You*, the plot of which concerned a New Jersey professor who came to town, drugged the locals, and then snookered them out of their land for his buffalo herd. "We just poke fun," the playwright told *High Country News.* "Out here, we never trust folks from out East." Frank Popper's critical response to the performance? "It struck me as a nice instance of the grassroots cultural penetration of the Buffalo Commons idea." As honored guests, the Poppers also rode down Main Street in the centennial parade. Their conveyance for this festive occasion was a manure spreader.

You've got to give them credit.

Of course one person's metaphor may be another person's kitsch (which may have been what saw them through that particular parade ride). But what if the whole Buffalo Commons idea itself took a turn in that direction, becoming but the latest iteration of the perennial western script? The Poppers are aware of the danger of "unhappy outcomes . . . that would offer debased versions of the Buffalo Commons—the region as a Disneyfied 19th-century theme park, say, or as a vast source of agribusiness fast-food McBuffalo Burgers." Even were ecotourism to take a more friendly route, as James Sprecht, a professor of agronomy at the University of Nebraska–Lincoln, pointed out to Frank Popper when he was speaking there: "You can only have so many Westins and so many tourists looking at so many bison." Popper's response, reportedly, was to shrug his shoulders and remark, "Plan A has not worked. It's time to look at Plan B."

But those of us who live here, who have roots here—whether twenty years shallow like ours, or several generations deep like most of our neighbors of homesteader stock, not to mention Native Americans—cannot so readily shrug off questions such as these. Eastern Montana is a nice place to visit, metaphorically. It's the stuff good ideas, and great movies, are made of. But what is at stake in living here in the twenty-first century?

Bison in snow. Photo by Doug Stange.

CHAPTER 11

Next Year Country

🕉 A few axioms of ranch life:

- Whether measured in minutes, hours, or days, every task takes three times longer to complete than you thought it would, could, or should.
- The farther away from the house a ranch chore is, the higher the likelihood that you left an essential tool for it back at the house.
- When stringing wire for a fence, the more careful you are to keep the wires distinct, the more certain they are to become tangled.
- Every job requires one more pair of hands than are available to do it.
- Equipment always breaks down at the least opportune moment.
- The odds that inclement weather will make roads difficult or impassable increase in direct proportion to your need to be on the road for an important appointment, to catch a plane, or to tow a horse trailer.
- If you are missing a kitchen implement—a turkey baster, say, or a meat mallet, or a mortar and pestle—nine times out of ten, your husband appropriated it for some odd job for which it turned out to be just the ideal thing.

- Ten times out of ten, he neglected to mention this to you. In the case of the turkey baster, he will remember on Thanksgiving morning.
- Your medicine cabinet is better stocked with veterinary supplies than with products that might cure or ease what ails you.
- Your horses are invariably more up-to-date on their tetanus shots than you are.
- At certain times of year—spring especially—everything needs to be done at once.
- There is no such thing as a day off.
- There really is no such thing as a vacation.
- If you think you should have your head examined for ever having gotten into ranching in the first place, you are probably correct.
- On good days—when the weather is fine, the animals are content, the machinery is running properly, and the cable news offers up the usual blend of pop-cultural inanity and urban insanity—there is no place else you can imagine you would rather be.

Toward the end of the summer of 2008, Doug and I were seriously considering putting the ranch on the market and moving on. We had been here twenty years, and had essentially completed the habitat restoration we had come to feel was our duty to this land: we would leave it in far better condition than we had found it in. We were making progress, albeit slowly, working with an environmental organization on establishing a conservation easement on the place, to protect it in perpetuity. We had had our share of varied experiences ranching, but the quotidian grind was wearing, as were the months of separation we annually had to endure. Retirement was still some years down the road for me; Doug was technically already retired although, he being a full-time rancher, it wasn't as if one would notice it. Relocating to a smaller and more manageable place, closer in to a cultural center and an airport, looked ever more appealing to us both. I was home on a year-long sabbatical leave, so it seemed a propitious time for some major decision-making.

Then in mid-September the banking crisis hit, and by year's end the national economy had imploded. The farm and ranch economy stood to weather that storm better than most sectors. The land holds its value, or so they say. But we realized that until financial markets stabilized and the economy improved, we had little alternative but to ride out the recession, to weather the storm as best we could. Which, in ranching terms, is nothing new.

HEAVY WEATHER

I knew that eventually I would have to say something more extensively about the weather.

There are a number of familiar western-themed clichés I swore I would avoid at all cost in writing this book: snow-covered hills that look as if they were dusted with powdered sugar; the call of a rooster pheasant, sounding like a gate creaking on a rusty hinge; majestic mountains; the wind, whispering in the pines; an old barn, its roof as swaybacked as the old horse in the paddock; an ocean of grasses, like waves lapping in the wind; the sun setting over miles of purple sage . . . those sorts of things.

There are also more Montana-specific clichés, such as "Don't like the weather? Wait five minutes." Or, "In Montana we only have two seasons: nine months of winter, and three months of friends and relatives." A cliché by another name is, of course, a truism. And it is no accident that these particular two have to do with the weather. Indeed, the weather itself is something of a cliché on the High Plains. It's the first thing folks take note of in the morning, the first thing they talk about when they bump into each other on the street. It's about the only thing strangers have to talk about in informal situations where they are thrown together.

Not surprisingly, then, the weather also becomes a major factor— in some instances, amounting almost to a character in its own right— in reflective writing about the western experience. So, for instance, Kathleen Norris punctuates her *Dakota: A Spiritual Geography* with "Weather Reports." And Linda Hasselstrom's diary of ranch life, *Windbreak: A Woman Rancher on the Northern Plains*, follows the course of a calendar year, from early fall to late summer, recording the high and low temperatures and precipitation for each daily entry.

Early on, when I was mulling the structure of this book, I seriously considered a similar, seasonal approach. After all, pinning meditations on time and place to the passage of the seasons has worked for American writers from Henry David Thoreau's *Walden* to Annie Dillard's *Pilgrim at Tinker Creek*. But that seemed too constraining, somehow. Books— even very good ones—that rely on seasonal change to supply their narrative rhythms are, on some level, predictable. So, to be fair, is the weather in places like Thoreau's Massachusetts or Dillard's Virginia. In such generally temperate climes, the weather can function for the most part as a leitmotif, by turns underscoring the story and providing an occasional counterpoint to it. But in this part of the world, predictability is frequently beside the point. And the weather, just as frequently, *is* the story.

Take, for example, the first weekend of spring 2009. Friday, March 20, the spring equinox, dawned sunny and unseasonably warm: a welcome relief from the long stretch of winter that had preceded it. We took advantage of the lovely day to head over to Miles City to do some shopping. On the drive back, the brilliant sun warming the cab of the pickup, we remarked that it looked like we were in for an early spring, which felt much deserved after the last few months. That promise of spring was sustained over the weekend, with unusually warm temperatures on Saturday and Sunday. We spent those days mostly doing the kinds of outside work that feel pleasant after a long winter. Doug worked on repairing some fence and clearing dead brush from the shelterbelts. I cleaned up the flower beds and hung laundry outside to dry. We replenished our dwindling firewood supply. The grass was beginning to green up. Peepers were singing in the creek. Meadowlarks, having returned to the prairie ahead of schedule, were trilling in the sagebrush. We broke out the charcoal, and I barbecued chicken for supper one evening, and we grilled bison T-bones the next. Sunday was shirtsleeve weather, balmy enough to work up a sweat stacking wood. Our backyard thermometer recorded an afternoon high of eighty-one degrees.

All this while, according to the National Weather Service report out of Billings, we were under a "Blizzard Watch" for Monday afternoon through all day Tuesday. The "Watch" was elevated to a "Warning" at sunset on Sunday, about the time Doug was pulling the steaks off the grill.

Weather forecasters in this part of the country are for the most part accurate, and not given to exaggeration. There is a progressive hierarchy of impending inclemency, which everyone around here learns to read like a meteorological tarot deck: Winter Weather Advisory (could get nasty), Winter Storm Watch (might be pretty bad, if it doesn't track north or south of here and miss us), Winter Storm Warning (not going to miss us, and will probably be a snow-maker), Blizzard Watch (get ready for major snowfall and whiteout conditions), and Blizzard Warning (we'll be snowbound for the foreseeable future, let's just hope the power doesn't go out and the roof stays put). The last of these is seldom issued, and certainly not when the skies are clear and the thermometer is topping seventy degrees. This obviously made for a certain degree of cognitive dissonance.

But given the weather over the past few months, the forecast made a weird sort of sense. I had, Doug and I ruefully joked, picked a hell of a year for my sabbatical leave at home. It had been a rough winter, and one characterized by extremes. First, there was the mud. Ample November rains, alternating with early wet snows, had so saturated the ground that, as the subsoil began to freeze, there was no place for the moisture to go. Every day, as the morning temperature warmed above freezing, any exposed earth—be it a road, a corral, or a game trail— became a sodden morass of gumbo. It was nearly impossible to drive in the stuff, let alone try to walk in it. Outdoor activities pretty much had to be accomplished by 10 a.m., unless one wanted to risk an adventure like going kerplotz trying to sneak up a muddy embankment, shotgun in hand, to surprise into flight some geese rafting on a reservoir. (I speak from gloopy experience.)

Around the first of December temperatures plummeted, and it began to snow. Not a lot at any one time: we were in the realm of the Winter Weather Advisory for the most part, the sort of weather that would bring, say, Baltimore to a standstill, but doesn't even precipitate school closures or basketball game cancellations in eastern Montana. But as Christmas approached, it became unrelentingly, and increasingly, colder, with daytime highs barely ever breaking ten degrees and nighttime lows in the minus double digits. The snow began to accumulate; take an inch of snowfall one day, two or three the next, throw in some blowing and drifting and a few more inches, and pretty soon you've got enough to warrant hitching up the snowplow to the tractor. We were getting pretty well snowed in by a week before Christmas, when we ignored a Blizzard Watch to venture out a mile or so from the house to cut a juniper for our Christmas tree.

Christmas itself was to become a moveable feast. Longtime friends of ours, Sharon and Ron, were flying out from Cape Cod to join us for the holiday. They were scheduled to arrive in Rapid City on December 22. By that time, we were looking at several inches of snow on the ground and temperatures so frigid that Doug was unable to start the tractor to plow our way out to the county road, diesel engines being temperamental in such cold weather. Our friends good-naturedly endured a two-day layover in South Dakota, and we were finally able to get the tractor going and get over there to pick them up on the afternoon of Christmas Eve . . . just as everything was closing for the holiday. I had the mother of all shopping lists, having been unable to get any advance shopping accomplished. I made a quick stop for liquor, beer, and wine. Then, as we entered the Walmart Superstore, the lone grocery story still open, a voice was announcing that the store would close in seven minutes. (A Walmart *closing* at 6 p.m. on Christmas Eve? Only in South Dakota.) "What do you need? We'll get this done!" Sharon gamely offered, and I immediately morphed into something like a field marshal, ordering Ron, Doug, and Sharon down different aisles, and rushing around myself in frantic pursuit of sundry makings for Christmas dinner and more. Of course the store took a bit longer than seven minutes to close, but we were just about the last shoppers out. On the four-hour drive back to the ranch, we agreed to put Christmas on a one-day delay: tomorrow would be our Christmas Eve, St. Stephen's Day our Christmas. We were all adults, after all.

The day after Christmas (that is, our Christmas) we were under a Winter Storm Warning. It was a Friday, which is a mail delivery day, and we were expecting some last-minute Christmas gifts in the day's mail. So Doug and I drove up to the mailbox in what our Massachusetts friends aptly called "wicked" storm conditions, happily discovered that Santa had indeed arrived in the person of Stacey our rural mail carrier, grabbed the goods, and made our way back down to the house in the now near-blinding snow as the two-track was becoming just barely passable. The afternoon was given over to gifting and, eventually, to a leisurely meal of which wild turkey was the main event. It turned out to be a lovely holiday.

It snowed off and on the entire time Ron and Sharon were here, so by the time we had to get them back to the airport the day before New Year's Eve, it took Doug a good deal of creative snow removal with our big tractor to blast us out of here in my Toyota 4Runner, using the back route out of our place because the hill up to the divide and the Chalk Buttes Road was now too drifted in to negotiate. We got to Rapid City late in the day, quickly said our farewells,—"Maybe we'll do Christmas in July next year?" Sharon ventured, only half-kidding—picked up some necessary groceries, and drove back to Montana in the densest fog either of us had ever seen: more than a hundred solid miles of it. It lifted providentially just as we reached our turnoff across a neighbor's property, the last four miles in to our place.

It was nearly midnight. I was driving, and as we pulled into the home stretch I suggested Doug leave the tractor at the road where he had parked it until morning, when we could retrieve it in daylight. After all, the wind was calm and the sky was now clear. It would take the tractor motor twenty or more minutes to warm up in the cold; why take the time now, when we were both so very tired? We still had the afternoon's plowed track to follow back home. He wasn't crazy about the idea, but acquiesced. I subsequently managed to get the 4Runner hopelessly lodged in a snowdrift about a quarter-mile from our house. Some of our groceries were perishable, so that meant walking back to the house, starting up the smaller tractor, giving it the twenty or so minutes needed to warm up sufficiently to move, and driving back to fetch them. I am fortunate that my husband has a forgiving nature, although it took me a while to live that evening down.

Late January brought a change in the weather in the form of a series of midwinter thaws, followed by refreezing. The snow successively settled, melted, and congealed once again, a process repeated over the course of a few weeks, until there was a several inch thick glaze of ice on virtually every surface. After my fourth or fifth bone-jangling spill, and Doug's running commentary on the increasingly impressive pattern of bruises that now embossed my posterior ("Quite an interesting rose tattoo you've got there, lady!"), I became positively paranoid about attempting to walk on the stuff. Our horses seemed to feel pretty much the same way about getting around on a virtual skating rink. Such conditions are especially dangerous for deer, who tend to suffer pelvic fractures slipping on the ice; they ceased frequenting our hay bales, and disappeared into the comparative safety of the still snowy woods.

Whenever fresh snow fell on top of the ice, it became more treacherous still. You could see by their tracks that wild turkeys were skidding their way around. So too were our small flock of resident pheasants, four roosters we'd come to recognize as distinct individuals and a hen, who periodically visited our bird feeder to pick up sunflower seeds and cracked corn the chickadees and finches knocked to the ground. As the lone hen was obviously key to the future survival of our fledgling pheasant population, her well-being was a matter of some concern for us. She walked with a pronounced limp, and mostly hopped around on one leg. It looked as if she had somehow injured her foot, or perhaps it had gotten frostbitten. She was a feisty little gal, though, willing even to take on turkeys that tried to muscle the pheasants away from the feeder. I began to note her preferred pathways over snow and ice, and regularly tossed some seed and corn for her into denser brush than turkeys customarily ventured into. We made sure the big birds had their share of eats as well. We were all in this winter together.

February brought more snow, more ice, eventually more mud. The year's shortest month felt like its longest. March came in (pardon the cliché) like the proverbial lion, with a protracted stormy period of wet snow and freezing rain. But then, slowly, winter's grip seemingly began to unclench. A few days' worth of moderating temperatures set the snow and ice to melting, filling creeks and reservoirs, some of the latter to overflowing. Even on chilly days, the sun exerted a warmth on exposed skin that it had lacked in January. And of course the days themselves were perceptibly growing longer now. Life was getting easier. The hen pheasant, whom I'd christened Henrietta, seemed somewhat less gimpy.

By the time the first weekend of spring rolled around, we had been pretty much ranchbound, and mostly housebound, for months. In the twelve weeks since Christmas, we had made it off the place perhaps a half a dozen times, for essential shopping and business in town. And so, not surprisingly, that spring equinox shopping trip to Miles City and the accompanying onset of springlike weather felt positively liberating. Given the Blizzard Warning, there was one cloud on my horizon: I had a rather important meeting scheduled with a publisher in New York City, ten days hence. To play things safe, Doug and I decided to drive up to the Chalk Buttes Road in tandem so I could leave my 4Runner parked up there in the event that we were socked in for the rest of the week. That turned out to be a wise move, although it took us two tries. Sunday afternoon, the road up the divide was too muddy for us to make it up the hill. Monday morning, the balmy temperature having dropped below freezing overnight to firm up the road and with a light snowfall commencing, we made it up the hill. By the time we returned, the wind was picking up and the snow intensifying.

We had reasonably stormy conditions all day Monday, with about eight inches of snow on the ground by nightfall; it looked like we were destined to get the twelve to eighteen inches of snow predicted for our area. We were nonetheless unprepared for what we saw at first light the next morning: three feet of snow on the ground, with drifts upward of ten feet. It was heavy, dense, moisture-laden snow, hard packed by the wind, the kind I imagine the Eskimos must have a special name for—it would translate "the-snow-that's-good-for-cutting-into-blocks-for-building-igloos." Doug and I managed to dig our way around the front yard, although the snow cover was so deep that it actually felt more like tunneling through the white stuff. Snow was still falling, and the temperature hovered in the single digits; it would be impossible to fire up the tractor for a while, but the horses needed to be fed. Doug rummaged in the basement for his old pair of snowshoes and managed to perform essential chores. Later in the day, after the snow tapered off and things warmed up somewhat, he was able to drive our big tractor around in such a way as to make a few pathways with its big tires (the snow was literally too deep to plow); this allowed us to get water to the horses and hay to our now quite pregnant bison. For the next several days, our lives were basically taken up with navigating our way through waist-high lanes of packed snow, dealing with matters of basic survival.

Then, on Saturday, the second blizzard hit. This one, too, was predicted, the first time in anyone's memory that there had been two blizzards in Carter County within a period of six days. This second storm slammed into the area with cyclonic force: one moment around dusk on Saturday the wind was fairly light and a few flakes were flurrying about, the next a steady fifty-mile-an-hour wind was blowing in out of the east, with horizontally blowing snow so thick we couldn't see the rail fence a few yards in front of the house. I had been at the stove cooking supper. "Look at that!" I tried to draw Doug's attention to what was happening outside. "I'd rather not," he muttered, drawing the curtains and slipping a DVD into the player to compensate for the TV satellite signal we had just lost. He had a point. We were safe and warm, and thanks to our Miles City trip a week earlier, reasonably well provisioned for the next week to ten days, anyway. The wind rattled the windows all night long. By morning we had a fresh new layer of about ten inches of snow. You know you've been through a rough period of weather when you remark, as Doug did, "Well, that blizzard wasn't so bad!" We were, of course, quite hopelessly snowbound.

To the thrumming notes that pass for its climatological theme music, the Weather Channel dubbed it all "Spring Fury," and dispatched one of their stalwart meteorologists to Rapid City to provide storm updates. The Black Hills actually made out pretty well, compared to our neck of the woods, but the weatherman couldn't have made it here had he wanted to. The southeastern corner of Montana was ground zero of the first blizzard. Every road in Carter County was closed, some for days. Motorists (none of them from around here, the sheriff assured the *Billings Gazette*) and a few long-haul truckers who ignored the storm warning had been stranded on local highways for as long as thirty hours, until help could get to them, some of it in the form of Montana National Guard helicopters. Folks were just starting to dig themselves out when the second storm hit, although at least this time people had more sense than to venture out onto the roads. My planned trip to the Big Apple had to be scratched—a conference call was the next best thing since, defying credibility, a third storm was heading in our direction, scheduled to arrive the day I was supposed to depart. This one merited a mere Winter Storm Warning, and deposited a few more fluffy inches of snow on March 30.

INTREPID HIPPIES, REDUX

You know you have been through a *really* rough period of weather when you see an upside to additional snow: this stuff was the right consistency for snowmobiling. The snow from the first blizzard was too dense and heavy, from the second too granular. I wonder whether Eskimos have words for these as well? "The-snows-that-clog-the-snow-machines" perhaps? It had been years since our Intrepid Hippie phase, but Doug and I were getting desperate for a break from the ranch routine. We had two weeks' worth of mail in the mailbox. We were also running dangerously low on some essentials: diesel fuel, milk, orange juice, and vodka, in roughly that order of priority. On Thursday, April 2 we saw a one-day window of opportunity to make a break for it. We hitched up a makeshift trailer to the little Bravo and rode in tandem the five miles up to the road where the 4Runner was parked. When we got to town, the first thing we discovered was that everybody else in Carter County was as cranky, as sick and tired of, and as depressed by, the weather as we were. We also learned, to no small amusement on our part, that by virtue of our simple appearance on Main Street, we were a beacon of hope for better things to come: "If the Stanges were able to get into town, things can't be all that bad!"

Another week passed, during which time things began to warm up, and the snow slowly to compact. The thawing was, blessedly, gradual—otherwise, we would have been looking at a serious flooding problem. We kept reminding ourselves that, come summer, we would be look-ing back with genuine gratitude on all this moisture; it promised to be a glorious grass year, with no shortage of hay for next winter. But for now we were looking ahead, toward an Easter Sunday with no ham, no Easter eggs, no spring vegetables, no strawberries, no chocolate, no wine. Snowmobiling out was now out of the question, as broad swaths of exposed land had emerged from snow cover, even as other stretches remained buried in slushy drifts still too dense for a truck to negotiate. So on Good Friday we drove the tractor up to the 4Runner, ran over to Miles City for food and other supplies, and we then made our way back down to the house at twilight, the tractor loader filled with our purchases.

We were now set for another couple of weeks of seriously incapacitating mud conditions before we needed to get out again, by which time—late in April—spring was somewhat uncertainly arriving. Aside from hitherto deeply drifted areas, the snow was mostly gone once again, except for a depressing overnight three inches that, just for a change of pace, had *not* been predicted, and only lasted a day. The grass began seriously greening to the collective delight of hay weary bison and horses, and the temperatures began warming a bit more assuredly. The crocuses had evidently been foiled by the deep snow, but tulips were coming up now, and trees were beginning to bud. And Henrietta, who had been absent from the bird feeder ever since the first blizzard and who I had presumed hadn't made it through, was back, and nearly fully recovered from her winter injury. It is amazing how mood lifting the reappearance of a pheasant with a limp can be.

Nonetheless, the weather was grinding us down. Doug had taken to joking about the fortuitous planning of my sabbatical leave, how we had agreed it was good for me to be home at a stressful time like this: "At least we have each other, to yell at!" We were nonetheless better off than some of our neighbors, for whom the late-season storms had potentially dire financial implications. One of them remarked, "Well, we're doing okay so far; only one of us is crying at any given time."

"We're getting too old for this, Mare," Doug declared, not for the first time, on the morning of that unanticipated April snowfall.

"Why," I asked, "do we keep on doing it then? Why put up with this?"

"Well," Doug smiled wistfully, "things always start looking better when the calves begin to arrive." He was, of course, right about that. Our bison calves generally begin to hit the ground in mid-April, with most of them being born in May. That's late for calving in cattle country, where ranchers like to breed their cows back to the bulls in early June, aiming for calf crops in February and March—this makes for a longer summer before weaning, and better overall weight gain for calves going to market in the fall. It's possible to thus regulate calving because the reintroduction of bulls to the herd is what prompts domesticated beef cows to go into estrus. Bison, by contrast, retain their wild rutting season. Bulls can remain with the herd year-round, but they don't become interested in breeding and the cows don't "cycle" until late August and September, hence their customarily later birthing times. This means—not surprisingly, since they've been here for millennia— that bison are far better adapted to the vagaries of High Plains weather than their domesticated European bovine cousins. It also means that, although bad weather can still be rough on a bison herd, a "stockman's advisory" doesn't carry the same force of potentially impending disaster for bison ranchers as it can for cattlemen.

As people began once again to get out and about, and with them word of how things were in various parts of the county, it became clear to us that we were among the lucky ones. The blizzards had hit at the tail end of calving season, and just as lambing was commencing. Livestock officials in Carter County, and in Powder River County immediately west of here, reported thousands of animals lost, most of them babies but a fair number of them adults. Calves tend to suffocate in the snow and freeze to death. Cows more typically become disoriented and wander onto frozen creeks and water holes, where the ice gives way and they drown or die of hypothermia. Some animals—sheep, especially—simply become hopelessly trapped in deep drifts. After a winter like we had just suffered, some of their corpses wouldn't be discovered until late spring. And many calves that survived the storms would subsequently succumb to "scours" (a severe form of diarrhea) or pneumonia or diphtheria.

Cattlemen and sheepherders conducted the requisite body counts for "loss reports" to the Farm Services Agency, which would reimburse insured operators up to 75 percent of the estimated worth of lost stock. But as the loss is figured in terms of fair market value at the time of the animal's death, a payment for a newborn calf that might eventually have sold for six hundred dollars would be more like one hundred dollars. To ranchers, like many in Carter County who had lost sixty or eighty calves, and who generally operate on a razor-thin profit margin, that was an awful bite. The director of Carter County's Farm Services Agency estimated cumulative losses in the range of $1.5 million.

Some supplemental feeding helps our calves weather the storm. Photo by Doug Stange.

The governor sought federal disaster designation for southeastern Montana to facilitate low-interest operating loans for ranchers suddenly suffering such sharp shortfall in annual income. Nonetheless, it was taken for granted that the winter of 2008–2009 would put some folks out of business. The prevailing mood in the county ranged from dark to disconsolate, especially as word got around in late April that the *Farmer's Almanac* predicted that a killer of a snowstorm—the worst of the year—would hit the area early in May. This rumor turned out to be an urban (more appropriately in this context, a rural) legend, as a quick check of the *Farmer's Almanac*'s Web site would have borne out for anyone who bothered to look. It was nevertheless hard to shake a sense of foreboding whenever grey clouds amassed on the horizon, which seemed to be practically every day.

Doug and I had never experienced anything like this winter. We wondered whether our neighbors had, and asked around. The general consensus was that you had to look back to the late 1970s for a comparably severe stretch of weather, although some older Carter Countyites insisted that it used to be this way every year . . . of course, they would add with a wink, that was back when they had to walk ten miles each way to a rural one-room school, and each way that walk was uphill. Joking aside, for more historically attuned eastern Montanans, the winter this past one most brought to mind was the "Winter of Blue Snow." That was the fabled winter of 1886–1887, immortalized in several famous drawings and paintings by Charlie Russell and, later, Frederick Remington. That was the winter that, with far more finality than any range war, brought to a close the reign of the cattle barons. As David Laskin puts it in his riveting history *The Children's Blizzard*:

> The relentless blizzards and freezes of the Winter of Blue Snow proved that the "open range" system—running cattle on the western prairie without the supplemental food or winter shelter— was just another foolish American dream, like the fantasy that rain follows the plow. Scores of the big ranches went under. Blue-blooded investors pulled out or declared bankruptcy, and lots of ordinary ranchers with a few dozen head were clamoring to sell, cut, and run.

Laskin uses his account of the Winter of 1886–1887 to pave the way for his own subject: the freak blizzard of January 13, 1888, that bore down on the High Plains with such sudden and intense ferocity that it left hundreds dead, many of them children who failed to make it home that day from school. Hence it came to be known as the Children's Blizzard. That storm barreled through eastern Montana too but, mercifully, it arrived early enough in the day that schools cancelled classes and businesses were shuttered. Communities in the Dakotas and Nebraska were not so fortunate. The day had dawned unseasonably warm for January, and sunny. Many of the children who subsequently succumbed to the storm had been cheerily sent off to school hatless and gloveless in this midwinter spring weather, in lightweight jackets and thin shoes. It was, I suppose, not unlike our own warm preblizzard weekend. Weather prognostication has improved considerably in the last hundred and twenty years, but in this part of the country the more some things change, the more others—like the weather—remain the same. Laskin assesses the impact of the storm on homesteaders' psyches as follows:

> The truth was beginning to sink in: The sudden storms, the violent swings from one meteorological extreme to another, the droughts and torrents and killer blizzards were not freak occurrences but facts of life on the prairie. This was not a garden. Rain did not follow the plow. Laying a perfect grid of mile-sided squares on

the grassland did not suppress the chaos of the elements. The settlers had to face the facts. Living here and making a living off this land was never going to be easy.

And yet, as happened fifty years later in the Dust Bowl, many of them stayed. The question is, why?

This was essentially the same question Frank and Deborah Popper were pressing a hundred years after the history-making High Plains blizzards of 1886–1888. And interestingly enough, it generated approximately the same set of responses earlier as later. As Laskin recounts the history, in the aftermath of the Children's Blizzard a major controversy emerged between the local and national news media over the issue of just how many fatalities could be attributed to the storm. The national press picked up on the idea that there had been nearly a thousand dead; regional papers put the figure far lower. Laskin's insight is astute here:

> What was at issue here was not just the accuracy of the death toll figures, but the truth about the climate of the prairie. A region that could slay a thousand innocent American citizens in the course of an afternoon did not look like a fit place for human habitation—quite the contrary—whereas if the figure stood at a mere couple of hundred, that could be written off as an unfortunate sacrifice on the path to progress. In essence it was an argument over image and reputation: prairie public relations.

That essential argument continues, unabated, today.

On April 24, 2009, the *Billings Gazette* ran a story about the storms' aftermath in southeastern Montana: "Ranchers count up losses to weather: Snow in Montana's southeast hit during calving, lambing." It provoked a vigorous exchange of reader comments in the newspaper's online edition, most of which in one way or another replayed a litany by now well over a century old. On the one side, there were comments like these:

- "Livestock is the same as kids. 'If you can't feed 'em, don't breed 'em.' The usual whining from the rural welfare crowd."
- "Poor Poor Ranchers. NOT! If it's that bad, sell, subdivide, move on. I don't feel bad one bit. If you think they don't have insurance or some sort of Govt. check waiting, your wrong. Like I said, if its that bad, cash out and move on. Only a fool does the same thing over and over

and expects a different result. Like a kid touching a stove, first time I feel sorry, after that its you own fault. Nuff said."

• "There are risks in every business. Mother nature is indeed a risk for farmer/ranchers. These ranchers will be looking to garner sympathy as justification for the government to give them disaster money. They should get no more than what their insurance covers. Unfortunately, disaster will be declared and they will get ridiculous amounts of money and the taxpayer will bear this burden as well."

Countering remarks like those above were classic justifications of the pioneer spirit that will see southeastern Montanans through. For example:

• "The good thing is these people come from a heritage that knows how to roll up their sleeves and do what has to be done now. Yes times will be hard but the ranchers will band together and lend a hand to each other. Obama sure won't offer to bail them out and they don't need it."
• "Regardless of what you think of ranching . . . it is a hard life and the men and women who make their living off the land should be thanked every day for supplying food to people. A general population who are generally thankless and have no clue where the food even comes from."
• "If you ask any rancher/farmer they know they will never be rich, that's not why they do this. It is a passion and a life style that few people understand. If you really knew these people and their situation you might understand too."

And there was one response, written by an Ekalaka native, that is worth quoting at length:

I used to live in Ekalaka . . . and my parents raised cattle there. It's no secret that in Eastern MT you can expect awfully intense, cold, snowy winters followed by major flooding in the spring. This winter has just not quit for them. Ranching/farming is hard work but it's a choice these ranchers and farmers make—they're tougher than most people—they can handle it. It's been a way of life for them for generations and something to be proud of. To any of you out there who think that any of these eastern Montana folk are looking for a handout, you're seriously mistaken. If they were offered one, they probably wouldn't even take it. Eastern MT folk are some of the toughest, most hardworking people to live and they will pick themselves up by their bootstraps as they have for generations. Anyone who thinks they will attempt to "garner sympathy" just isn't strong enough to understand this simple, honest, hardworking way of life. Excuses and handouts aren't in Eastern MT folks vocabulary.

As I read, and reread, this comment, it struck me how utterly true to the ethos of eastern Montanans it is—and how it simultaneously gives voice to the frontier mythology that has served to create the most powerful fictions of the West. I noticed, as well, that the woman (for so her screen name identified her) who wrote this impassioned apologia is among the generation of children who have moved away from here.

My friend Verna likes to say we live in "next year country." You can call that country wisdom. You can also call it a country cliché; I doubt that it's original with her. Nevertheless, like other clichés—especially those to which we resort when other words fail us—it rings true. Farming and ranching are all about planning, and then hoping against hope that one's plans will pan out in the face of myriad forces that are beyond one's control, the most capricious among them being the weather. It becomes an almost natural reflex to think in terms of next year. Next year, things will be different. And next year, they generally are. But remember, in these parts, "different" is not necessarily better.

By mid-May, around the time of year I would typically be arriving home at the end of the school year, spring had finally, definitively, "sprung." The grass was growing by inches every day and was a luscious moisture-rich and nutrient-laden green. Wild plum thickets turned several draws into festivals of tiny white blossoms, and the several varieties of introduced cherries Doug had planted were a panoply of deep pinks. Our apple trees were in delicate flower, the yellow currants bounding our yard an explosion of buttercup blossoms, and the "Indian magic" crabapple a profusion of ruby blooms.

Love was in the air: Turkeys were gobbling in the early morning hours, and the toms took every opportunity to strut their stuff. Sharptail grouse were drumming, and nesting pairs of mallards and teal had settled in on several of our reservoirs. Goldfinches, having exchanged their winter olive-drab for brilliant yellow, hopped about in the grass, giving the illusion, as Doug remarked, of dandelions suddenly airborne. Deer and pronghorn were dropping their fawns. And we were seeing a bison baby boom: the most calves we'd had in years, and by all indications, the most robust as well.

Winter's memory remained, close to the surface and reinforced by a short-lived shot of late-season snow on May 14. But in the main, it was possible to believe that the future held better things than the past few months had witnessed. It was as if the very landscape itself was heaving a massive sigh of relief.

There was for us one thread of poignancy in all this. Among the birdsongs to which we would drift into wakefulness each morning in the predawn half-light, we could for the past several years count on hearing the crowing of pheasants, roosters calling back and forth to one another in the creek. They were conspicuously silent now. We hadn't seen any of our familiar roosters since spring set in, in earnest. Nor had Henrietta, that plucky little hen, made any more appearances. We could only assume that a predator—possibly a fox, maybe a raccoon, or perhaps more likely a large raptor—had gotten them all. Having survived that brutal winter, the birds must one by one have been seized and forever quieted, their resilient energy and iridescent vigor too roughly stilled.

There is an object lesson here, of the sort this "next year country" always offers. We humans are, like Chinese ring-necked pheasants, an introduced species in these parts. We forget that fact at our own peril. Ranching has never been a comfortable way of life. But if mere comfort were what we were after, we never would have settled here in the first place.

It presents a perennial conundrum. Even as we stay on here, as our roots here paradoxically grow deeper and more tenuous, Doug and I ask, "Where do we go from here?" That is the "next year" question, and we are hardly alone in asking it. It is a question the rapidly changing West is, with increasing urgency, asking about itself.

Little Joe's Place today. Photo by Mary Stange.

CHAPTER 12
New West, True West?

🐎 It seemed so out of place. Nestled at the base of the Chalk Buttes, a little house painted a bright robin's egg blue: so jarringly distinct from everything around it that it might as well have been airlifted in from some cozy suburb somewhere. Doug and I had noticed it—one couldn't *help* but notice it—immediately after we moved here, and had often wondered about it. The house looked fairly new, yet appeared to be windowless and uninhabited. Clearly visible from the Chalk Buttes Road, it was on private land (we weren't sure whose), and far enough removed from the road that we didn't feel right about venturing closer to it.

We finally got around to asking one of our neighbors about it. "Oh, that place," he chuckled. "It's an old homesteader's cabin, been there probably since the 'twenties, 'teens maybe. A few years back, folks that own that land figured they could fix it up. So they slapped that blue vinyl siding on it. But they couldn't restore it. The cabin was too far gone to be livable anymore. About the only thing standing now is the siding. Everything inside has pretty much rotted away."

There has got to be a parable in there somewhere, about the encounter between past and present, and between image and reality in what has come to be called the "New West."

HOMESTEADING, TWENTY-FIRST–CENTURY STYLE?

There are, on our ranch, three surviving homesteads, all dating to the Woodrow Wilson administration, their ruins in varying stages of deterioration. The best preserved—and also the only one with electrical power available—has a house, a granary, and a shed, the remnants of a garden and corrals, an old McCormick reaper, and the rusted out hulk of a Ford Model T. It is called the "Radey Place," the Radeys having apparently been a family that tried, and subsequently failed, to turn it into a pig farm. They had taken it over from the more colorfully named original homesteader, one Porkypine Johnson—who, so they say, operated a still there during Prohibition and produced some excellent moonshine, although this may be pure fiction. There is also the "Smith-Davis Place," today a caving-in shell of a dwelling, with a now roofless barn and a collapsed root cellar. It was, nonetheless, the most recently inhabited. We have actually met a woman who grew up there, in the 1950s, and a spartan childhood it must have been. Finally, there's the "Little Joe Place," which I've already mentioned. All that remains of Little Joe's homestead are a few logs that once defined the walls of a very modest cabin.

Were we of a mind to subdivide our place, which of course we most definitely are not, all three homesteads would probably appeal as potential building sites. The Model T would be displaced by a Ford F-150, and the reaper by a DR Trimmer and a Toro rider mower. The houses would be somewhat larger and have indoor plumbing, and satellite TV and Internet connections. But little else would have changed, especially when it comes to the myths and fictions driving the impulse to stake a claim on a few frontier acres.

The idea of homesteading and the myth of self-sufficiency that goes along with it are trendy again, as even the most casual Google search bears out. Variously construed as an exercise in personal independence, as spiritual practice, and/or as crisis preparedness, this deeply American assertion of back-to-the-land self-reliance exerts as powerful an influence on the American imagination now as it did a hundred and more years ago. There are urban homesteaders "living small" in big cities, latter-day hippies questing after as much of "the good life" as can be carved out in a cabin on an acre or so, upscale hobby farmers on subdivided ranchettes, and separatist evangelical Christian homesteaders plotting the gardens of their new Eden. There are high-tech experimenters in permaculture and off the grid organic farmers, ruggedly individualist property-rights activists, and advocates of "homesteading on the electronic frontier," whatever on earth that means. Except, perhaps, for this latter group, they are all in the market for some variation on the American Dream, Western-style. And over the past generation or so, Montana realtors have seen them as a major growth market, as eager for western adventure and surely as gullible as their homesteading forebears who, a century ago, were lured westward by railroad pamphlets promising a piece of paradise.

The *Montana Land Magazine* is a bimonthly clearinghouse of real estate offerings throughout Big Sky Country. When Doug and I were looking at ranch properties back in 1987, it amounted to a few black-and-white tabloid pages. Today its six annual issues are thicker than the Mid-Rivers telephone book that covers roughly the southeastern quadrant of the state. Many ads are in lavish color, and most of them guarantee, in one way or another, that Eden awaits the savvy buyer.

The Radey Place. Photo by Doug Stange.

The Smith-Davis Place. Photo by Mary Stange.

Eden, of course, does not come cheap. "Share the Montana lifestyle," one ad trumpets. "Live the dream . . . in a fabulous, tastefully furnished 3BR log home on 20 acres with breathtaking views." $190,000 will buy you eight weeks' occupancy a year in this gem of a time-share. If the views don't take your breath away, the price of admission to the twenty-first century version of the Montana Dream certainly might.

Flipping through the pages of the *Montana Land Magazine*, one drifts from cliché to myth and back again, born along on wave upon wave of the kind of hype that only realtors seem capable of producing with such uncritical self-parody. "A river runs through" an awful lot of these properties—although in more than a few cases the waterway in question is actually either an irrigation ditch or a seasonally flowing spring creek. Virtually every spread offers "panoramic views"—not infrequently of mountain ranges fifty or more miles in the distance, "viewsheds" that amount to little more than dark ripples on the horizon.

Then there's the ubiquitous phrase "Montana Country Living." This might mean anything from a massive trophy home to a cozy cabin. It may also mean a dilapidated old clapboard-sided farmhouse—sure to be the case if it features a "quaint ranch kitchen," or is described as being in any way "historic." Or the phrase may connote a trailer house dating to the post–World War II era and reeking of mold. Or a drafty shack with an outhouse in back. Or, just possibly, no dwelling at all.

If you've got money to burn—that is, if you are in the lingo a "qualified buyer"—your imagination may run wild indeed, say toward a 2,700-acre ranch with "majestic views" (in this particular case, the Absarokee Mountains, barely visible in the distance), "an ideal Family Getaway, Hunter's Paradise, or 'off the grid' lifestyle." All this for a mere $5.2 million dollars. No house, of course. And in this parcel's neighborhood, nestled as it is between a National Forest, a Wilderness Area, and Yellowstone Park, "off the grid" is not necessarily a lifestyle choice. More than likely, you can't get power to it.

Some of the properties offered are, like the one mentioned above, rangeland that has never been suitable for human settlement. But most are ranches, some still intact as big parcels of land, others as subdivisions or potential subdivisions (otherwise known, until recently, as "investment opportunities"). Their owners are mostly now departed, that is, either fled to condos in Missoula or Great Falls, or else deceased. They called these spreads by other names. "Lazy Bar L" or "Rockin' R" or "Circle T." Or, more familiarly still, "The Place" or "The Money Pit," which is what just about every working ranch is. But names like these won't sell the Montana Dream. And that is what realtors in Big Sky Country are selling.

The fact of the matter is that fewer and fewer ranches are making it today. South Dakota bison rancher Dan O'Brien captures the essence of the contemporary farm and ranch economy in the introduction to his *Buffalo for the Broken Heart*, when he quotes a neighbor with whom he was embarking on a cost-share project: "I sure hope we break even on this deal," the man remarked, "I need the money." With the kids moving away to greener (that is, urban) pastures, federal subsidies becoming harder to come by, and conservation easements that actually pay increasingly tough to find, selling off and investing in a motor home for one's sunset years doesn't look like a bad alternative.

In most parts of the state, the result has been subdivision. *Montana Land Magazine* suggests a Montana Dreamscape full of five- to twenty-acre parcels with names like Lonesome Dove Ranch, Pronghorn Meadows, Chico Peak Estates, Gallatin River Ranch (where "Life's a Vacation"), Deep Creek Estates, Shining Mountains, Trail Creek Ranches, Mustang Ranch, Yellowstone Trails Ranch (where "Your Piece of Paradise is Waiting for You"), Paradise Meadows, Willow Creek,

Grand View at Remington Ranch, Stallion Ridge Ranch ("A Lifestyle Worth Living"), Silver Bow Estates, Elk Park at Duck Creek. Some of these minispreads used to be called the Last Best Place, but that phrase became the subject of trademark litigation a few years ago. One realtor cunningly uses the phrase "Best Last Place"—although that might strike some potential buyers as sounding just a tad funereal.

For wannabe Montana Dreamers who cannot afford cash on the barrelhead, payment plans are available: Ponderosa Pines ranch offers ten-acre plots with "seasonal access" for a mere ninety-six dollars per month for the next fifteen years. If your pockets are somewhat deeper, Yellowstone River Ranch—"perfect for horses," with "power close"—is yours for seven grand down and fifteen years worth of three-hundred-dollar monthly payments. Whether you want a "Gentleman's Ranchette" or a "Woman's Pocket Ranch," you can "Own your own piece of Heaven."

If money is really not an issue—as, during the 1990s and the early part of this present decade it was not for a growing number of buyers of seasonal recreational properties—there are a growing number of gated communities, like investment guru Charles Schwab's Stock Farm outside of Hamilton, Montana. There, for a membership fee of $125,000, one can pay some really serious money (a million dollars and up) for a home designed by an approved architect, and conforming to neighborhood aesthetic standards—there are "ranch" homes (with wraparound porches and requisite outbuildings), "mountain" homes (reminiscent of National Park lodges and made of hand-hewn logs), and a "homestead village" of 2,000 to 4,500 square foot "cabins" with up to six bedrooms with accompanying baths.

Strictly speaking, of course, these little subdivided properties are merely fictions of homesteads, although a fair proportion of their proprietors probably like to fancy they are the real McCoy. As, perhaps, do buyers who respond to an ad promising that one can "Own a piece of Montana like it used to be! Wide open spaces and breathtaking views," on 160-acre parcels for $352,000 a crack. Long gone are the days when all it took to secure title to a quarter-section was five years' worth of one's time, savings, sweat, and tears.

And yet the motivations of these contemporary landowners are in many respects akin to those that drew the original homesteaders to this part of the country. They have, in part, to do with—to use the jargon that became fashionable during the second Bush Administration—an "ownership society," in which one can, along with those dazzling views, buy freedom, and rugged individualism, and roots, and if one has the requisite spirit (or the ready cash), some degree of self-sufficiency. These latest would-be homesteaders as a group are, like their forebears, mostly urbanites who believe these things are best achieved someplace away from it all—"it all" being city life. A century and more ago, that life most likely meant tenement living, factory work, and the limited opportunities most first-generation immigrants and their offspring confronted. Today, it's more likely to be pollution, and crime, and the high cost and higher stress of urban living that instill a longing for open country.

Those with deeper roots in this part of the world have not been entirely welcoming of these latest settlers. A few years ago, one began seeing pickups with bumper stickers saying "Don't Californicate Montana!" Whereas the original Euro-American pioneers had to reckon with the hostility of the Native Americans whom they were displacing, today's transplants more often than not find themselves at odds with their next door neighbors. But now, as then, a large part of the problem owes to their downright ignorance as to what they were getting themselves into in the first place. Urbanites tend to believe the simple life is so simple they needn't bother to read up on it in advance. As farmer and writer Gene Logsdon remarks in his *Living at Nature's Pace*, "My mother read *The New Yorker* faithfully on her farm in Ohio. I wonder how many people in New York read *The Ohio Farmer?*"

THE CODE OF THE NEW WEST

Latter-day settlers who have harkened to the "Westward Ho!" of enterprising developers face a rude awakening, when they discover that their twenty-acre "ranchette" in Big Sky Country is a very different proposition than the same size parcel in, say, pastoral Massachusetts would be. Even Robert Frost, in his celebrated poem debunking the idea that "Good fences make good neighbors," made an exception for cows. Here, under the open-range law, if you object to a rancher's cattle moseying onto your property, it's up to you to fence them out. If you don't like the way those cattle smell, well, you'll have to learn to live with it. You'll also have to learn to live with the facts that although your hilltop trophy home has a commanding view, you can't even coax a petunia in the rocky soil and your thousand-foot-deep well produces a dribble of mineral-laden water. The wind never seems to stop rattling the windows. Electrical storms feel terrifyingly life-threatening. The premium for fire insurance gives you a nosebleed. A pack of coyotes did in your Pomeranian. Your cell signal keeps breaking up. A power outage crashed your hard drive. And your neighbors are all annoyed with you because your house destroyed *their* view.

According to the University of Colorado's Center of the American West, the population in the Rocky Mountain/High Plains states has been steadily growing, thanks primarily to retirees and urban refugees, and the trend is expected to continue through 2050. With longtime ranchers, generally resistant to change, increasingly coming into contact with naïve newcomers, disgruntled about what unexpected lifestyle changes awaited them in the rural West, social tensions in some areas arguably haven't been as high in the region since its original settlers in the nineteenth century were trying to decide whether the farmer and the cowboy could be friends. And with a farm-and-ranch economy threatened by everything from NAFTA to mad cow disease, the last thing your average rancher wants to contend with is the clueless city slicker who bought the miniranch down the road.

This has led many counties in Montana to promote something called the "Code of the New West," a pamphlet intended to acquaint newcomers with the realities of ranch-country life: that residents in these parts can expect far fewer services for their tax dollars than city-folk, and that they need to exhibit considerable self-sufficiency, the desire for which is supposedly what brought them there in the first place. In the words of the Gallatin County code, "Often newcomers are much more romantic about the West than the old-timers and have false hopes about bringing their urban lifestyles into the great outdoors. They come with false expectations. They believe they can fax and e-mail from the mountaintop. In the New West, the information superhighway is often a dirt road." And as to cows: "Animal manure can, and often does, cause 'objectionable' odors. What else can we say? No whining!"

But every wave of settlers in the West came with "false expectations" of one sort or another, mostly having to do with striking it rich or living off the fat of the land. Those ranchers who have hung on, many by a thread, are living with an increasingly dim set of expectations, and harboring their own nostalgia for a West that, for the most part, no longer exists.

Its promoters say the Code of the New West was inspired by Zane Grey's idea of an older, unwritten Western code, founded on values like integrity, self-reliance, accountability, and cooperation: all, one might observe, good "homestead" virtues. But the contemporary call for a shared spirit of community and stewardship of the land often rings hollow, to the extent that neither side in this newest range war has exhibited much interest in changing their ways.

The environmental stakes are especially high. Those same ranches that newcomers resent for being dirty, smelly, and inconvenient represent the only sizable tracts of largely unfenced land in private hands, and as such are of massive ecological importance. Yet ranchers have mostly been behind the curve when it comes to adopting more environmentally friendly practices. Meanwhile, their ranchette neighbors are accelerating the drain on limited water resources, disrupting wildlife migration corridors, and increasing the costs and inefficiency of range fire control.

This collision of "New West" with "True West" is occurring on a terrain at once literal and metaphorical. The heft of the *Montana Land Magazine* attests to two things that unite present with past: On the one hand, the attractive pull of the Montana Dream is arguably as strong today as it was when the Homestead Act first opened the way for western settlement. At the same time—judging by the sheer number of ranchette properties on the market—that dream is probably failing at a rate not unlike that of the original homesteaders, whose relics still dot the landscape.

The *Montana Land Magazine* also, of course, attests to the fact that to date nearly all of this neohomesteading, with all its attendant problems, has been happening far west of Carter County, in the Rocky Mountain end of the state. Indeed, in the popular imagination "Montana" so literally equates with "Mountains" that the eastern two-thirds of the state—the High Plains fly-over region—might as well not exist. This point is made eloquently, if quite unintentionally, by Jared Diamond in *Collapse: How Societies Choose to Fail or Succeed*, his 2005 follow-up to *Guns, Germs, and Steel*. It is a wide-ranging work that addresses, among other things, the environmental factors at play in failed societies and lost civilizations from Easter Island to the Mayan Empire. In it, Diamond uses Montana as his introductory case study of a possible collapse-in-the-making, to illustrate how the human transformation of the landscape can set in motion potentially disastrous, and generally unforeseen, ecological consequences. These consequences have to do with problems like water depletion, deforestation, soil erosion, the noxious by-products of mineral extraction, air pollution, toxic waste, disease, and the relative safety of the food supply.

Why Montana? In part, because all of the above factors figure in the state's environmental history. In part, because Diamond annually summers in southwestern Montana with his family, and so has some deep familiarity with the state. And also, because it is a "land of paradoxes": the U.S. state with the fourth largest land area and the sixth smallest population, increasingly populated by "immigrants" from other parts of the country even as a high percentage of its native high school graduates move elsewhere, and in which the newcomers tend to be far more affluent than those born and raised here. These paradoxical factors, he suggests, lead to a good deal of polarization, "along many axes: rich versus poor, old-timers versus newcomers, those clinging to a traditional lifestyle versus others welcoming change, pro-growth versus anti-growth voices, those for and against governmental planning, and those with and without school-age children."

True—all true—of Montana at large. But Diamond's Montana is limited to the Rocky Mountain west. Aside from a couple of pages treating the problem of saline content in groundwater, eastern Montana receives no mention in his analysis. It is as if we might as well not be here. The map of "Contemporary Montana" that he provides (on page thirty-one of the paperback edition of the book) shows nothing—and I mean *nothing*—east of Billings, aside from the Yellowstone River. In this rendering, Carter and Powder River counties are simply a convenient place to locate the compass icon indicating which way is north. It isn't the Big Open, it's the Big Empty.

From a Carter County point of view this is ironic, to say the least. Up until the collapse of the housing market nationally—which was reflected in yet more ranchettes in the pages of the most recent issues of the *Montana Land Magazine*—the eastward march of developmental "progress" across Big Sky Country seemed inevitable. Most folks around here figured it was just a matter of time before ranchettes began to dot our landscape, too. It was already happening down by Broadus (the Powder River County seat), thanks in part to the influx of workers, and their substantial paychecks, from the mineral development taking place just south of there, on Wyoming's side of the Powder River Basin. One or two Carter County landowners were flirting with subdivision, with the details of zoning, power, and suchlike presumably to be worked out in due time.

When the ranch immediately east of ours was on the market—a strip of land about a mile wide, between our place and the National Forest boundary of the Chalk Buttes, and advertised by the broker as "Ideal for Subdivision!"—Doug remarked, "I can see it now: ranch lights twinkling all along the base of the Buttes." He was not joking.

Fortunately, the person who bought that place, an absentee owner from the Midwest, was not of a mind to subdivide. He built a cabin and spends a few weeks here every fall during hunting season. In the summer, the land is leased for grazing to local cattlemen, as it had been for years by the previous owner as well. The good news, on the face of things, is that the property remains intact. The not so good news is that there is a persistent noxious weed problem, in the form of leafy spurge. The successive leasers have had no personal stake in the land, apart from its providing grass for protein conversion into beef. With no apparent rest-rotational grazing program in place, the grass over there is taking a real beating. From our side of the fence one can see the effects of its annually being chewed down to nothing, never allowed to head out and reproduce. In a phenomenon called "pedestaling," isolated clumps of tufted grass remain, the topsoil surrounding them having eroded away. Aside from that, there is some sagebrush, and a shrub called greasewood that, when consumed without additional good forage, can be toxic to some animals.

Last fall, when we were hunting the protected riparian area on our side of the fence, the contrast was stark: Doug and I were making our way through several inches of snow, while on the other side of the fence there was mostly bare dirt, there being scarcely any vegetation over there to trap and hold the snow. One cannot help but wonder whether absentee ownership of intact ranches, which is a growing trend in Montana, is ultimately all that preferable to their subdivision. Either way, the result is likely to be environmental depredation. And these eastern Montana lands are, for a variety of reasons, arguably more vulnerable today than they have ever been.

NEW RANCH, TRUE RANCH?

One strong argument in favor of preserving the ranching tradition in the West has to do with the advantages—both cultural and ecological—of large tracts of land remaining in private hands. But it obviously all comes down to how those lands are managed, and the value system to which their managers adhere. At this historical juncture, and no doubt at least partly in response to the past generation's passion for subdivision, the question of sustainable ranching has begun to gain considerable traction throughout the West—even here, in granola-averse Carter County. When we moved here in the late 1980s, I never would have dreamed farmer/ranchers in these parts would be experimenting with canola or safflowers as a crop, or experimenting with no-till planting, or foregoing summer-fallowing their fields, or employing insects rather than herbicide to control some noxious weeds—not to mention taking seriously the Parelli method of "natural horsemanship," and other forms of gently training (rather than "breaking") horses. Call these baby steps if you wish, but at least they are in the right direction. Can real sustainability be far behind?

Wes Jackson, one of the primary voices in the sustainable agriculture movement, has said it is vital to keep rural/agrarian folk on their land because they amount to "cultural seed stock" that needs to be kept in place, just like those native grasses upon which they rely. Gene Logsdon, thinking along similar if somewhat more florid lines, declares: "Sustainable farms are to today's headlong rush toward global destruction what the monasteries were to the Dark Ages: places to preserve human skills and crafts until some semblance of common sense and common purpose returns to the public mind."

As a scholar of religion, I'm not sure I buy his notion of Lindisfarne on the Prairie, but a sense of near-prophetic zeal approaching the religious does tend to run through much of the literature relating to the ways a new kind of environmentally friendly ranching might save the rural West. And the sense of getting back to basic skills and crafts, rooted in the more intimate experience of nature, is not restricted to Euro-Americans. One not infrequently hears traditionalist Native Americans assert that, when Anglo society and economy have run their self-destructive course, only they will have the skills and accompanying lore to survive, in harmony once again with the land, their Mother.

Of course, to live—as Logsdon phrases it—"at nature's pace" assumes one has a handle on what "nature" is, and how it works. In a fascinating study of "modern homesteading and spiritual practice in America," religion scholar Rebecca Kneale Gould observes that many contemporary transplants from town to country display "a kind of cultivated ignorance toward nature." For them, "Nature" wields undisputed authority:

"Nature" suggests that new structures of time, work, and play are "more appropriate." "Nature" requires vegetarianism (and, for some, Nature requires meat eating). "Nature" dictates that technology is "bad" (or "good") or that certain foods, herbs, and physical regimes are "healthy" (because they are "natural"). Not surprisingly, while Nature is presumed to be authoritative, what Nature wants (as, in other settings, what God wants) differs depending on the interpreter of Nature's "truths."

The necessary antidote to such simplified, and romanticized, readings of "Nature" is, it seems to me, the perspective that longtime farmers and ranchers bring to bear on the complexity of what it means to live up close and personal with "Nature"—as rancher/environmentalist Barney Nelson would put it, cowshit and all.

This is where the sustainability movement suggests a provocative new model for ranchers. Or, to invoke the movement's terminology, "New Ranchers." Put most simply and starkly, the future of the West depends upon the survival of its mixed-grass prairie. "New Ranch" proponent Courtney White quotes, in this regard, U.S. senator from Kansas James Ingalls (the father of *Little House on the Prairie* author Laura Ingalls Wilder): "Grass is the forgiveness of nature—her constant benediction. Fields trampled with battle, saturated with blood, torn with the ruts of cannon, grow green again with grass, and carnage is forgotten. Streets abandoned by traffic become grass grown like rural lanes, and are obliterated: forests decay, harvests perish, flowers vanish, but grass is immortal." White continues:

> Few understand these words better than ranchers, who depend on the forgiveness of nature for a livelihood while simultaneously nurturing its benediction. And like grass, ranching's adaptive response to adversity over the years has been patience: to outlast its troubles. The key to survival for both has been endurance, the ability to hold things together until the next rainstorm.

Nonetheless, one cannot fail to see the negative mark of ranching on the western landscape, and perhaps more particularly on those public lands that ranchers lease from the BLM. The prairie can be abused to the point where its "forgiveness" is in perilously short supply. When we moved to Carter County, Doug and I immediately noticed when driving rural roads that one didn't need the BLM markers to distinguish public rangeland: it was almost invariably the most ravaged. Private lands faired somewhat better, unless or until—as with this ranch we took over in 1988—an unfortunate combination of bad weather and worse finances laid the groundwork for persistent and punishing overgrazing. This has been the unfortunate pattern throughout the High Plains West.

For New Ranchers, the obvious problems have to do with conventional patterns of cattle grazing and the ways in which ranchers manage, and imagine, their interactions with nature. And their equally obvious solutions entail changing those patterns. White's definition of the New Ranch is as follows:

> The New Ranch describes an emerging progressive ranching movement that operates on the principle that the natural processes that sustain wildlife habitat, biological diversity and functioning watersheds are the same processes that make land productive for livestock. New Ranches are ranches where grasslands are productive and diverse, where erosion has diminished, where streams and springs, once dry, now flow, where wildlife is more abundant, and where landowners are more profitable as a result.

Our Crazy Woman Bison Ranch would exemplify White's New Ranch—but for one curious divergence from his model.

The progressive ranching movement has something of a patron saint: Allan Savory, a native of Zimbabwe who pioneered something called holistic ecosystem management, and who has toured the world introducing livestock managers to its advantages. The Savory system involves radically altering the patterns of livestock grazing. In conventional grazing, cattle are released into a large pasture and allowed to graze it down until the grass is essentially depleted; then they are moved to another large pasture. This is the case even in typical rest-rotation programs. In Savory's system, cattle are released into much smaller and more concentrated paddocks—mere slices of the larger pasture—which they graze intensively before being moved to another paddock. The effect of grazing a big pasture area sliver by sliver is that, overall, the pasture gets plenty of time to replenish itself because of vastly decreased overall grazing pressure. Hence, healthier grassland results.

The idea is brilliant in its simplicity, and—in the spirit of progressive ranching—it is derived from close observation of the way nature works. Savory obtained his insight about how most efficiently to manage grassland not by observing domestic cattle, but by observing wild animals' patterns of movement. Domestic cows, left to their own devices, are selective grazers. They will focus on their favorite grasses first, eating them down to the roots and hammering certain pasture areas while leaving other areas largely untouched. They also tend to be relatively sedentary. Wild grazers, by contrast, are more wide-ranging both in their tastes and in their behavior. They cover a considerable amount of ground every day, grazing a greater variety of grasses more lightly than do cattle. Savory's paddock system is an artificial way of duplicating the effects of wild grazers, and in North America, the aim is to achieve a pattern of cattle grazing that duplicates the effects of a bison herd.

In his *Revolution on the Range*, White profiles dozens of progressive ranching operations throughout the High Plains and Rocky Mountain West and Southwest. Time and again, he explains how different ranchers have created systems to manage their livestock in such a way as to mimic the more environmentally friendly grazing impact of bison. The odd thing—and this is where we seem to diverge from the New Ranch model—is that, apart from an obligatory mention of Ted Turner as a progressive ranching visionary, none of the ranches White profiles raise bison.

Now, isn't this strange? If the goal is to bring grasslands back to peak, self-renewing condition by achieving the effects of bison grazing the land, why not just replace the beef cattle with buffalo? From a producer's point of view, economics no doubt have something to do with it. So, too, does the lingering prejudice in favor of the role cattle played in the winning of the West, and against anything that sounds too, shall we say, Popperesque.

Meanwhile, with a more explicit nod to the Poppers' idea of the Buffalo Commons, the World Wildlife Fund in cooperation with the American Prairie Foundation is attempting to bring bison back to the eastern Montana prairie as part of a larger restoration project called the American Prairie Reserve. Located northwest of where we live, between the town of Malta and the Charles M. Russell Wildlife Refuge, the reserve is projected, according to its Web site, to "one day become larger than Yellowstone National Park and rival in splendor the Serengeti of Africa and the Arctic National Wildlife Refuge." It is an ambitious conservation project, promoted as the potential salvation of the faltering local farm and ranch economy. It will replace ranching with tourism and public education. As it is almost entirely funded by wealthy investors outside of the state of Montana, I'd say the jury is still out regarding the degree of needed local support it stands to receive over the long term.

But efforts like the American Prairie Reserve, and variations on New Ranching, are at the very least preferable potential uses for public and private range land than what has, in recent years, threatened to become its dominant use in eastern Montana: mineral extraction. Our friend Bobby, who works as a wildlife biologist for the BLM, has told us that in recent years he has spent almost all his time working on mineral leases. While there are some natural gas wells, by far the most lucrative potential market has been for coalbed methane (CBM), the production of which involves pumping massive amounts of ground water out of underground coal seams to free and capture trapped methane gas.

CBM development is doubly hazardous to our fragile eastern Montana ecology: it depletes the aquifer on the one hand, and releases to the surface nonpotable mineral-laden waste water on the other. CBM development is hazardous for ranchers as well: not only might they discover that the government has decided to lease away their BLM grazing allotments to the modern day equivalent of wildcatters, they also may well discover that someone has acquired the right to exploit federal mineral resources on their private land. And there is not a thing they can do about it: most ranchers, Doug and I included, own "surface rights" to land for which the undersurface mineral rights are far more complicated to sort out, and of which the federal government is almost invariably a partial owner. To date, the most egregious mineral development has been south of our border, in Wyoming, which has less stringent environmental regulations than Montana. But, on both sides of the state border, for ranchers in the Powder River Basin who have been facing the choice between foreclosure and subdivision, the mineral extraction industry has provided a profitable, if ecologically unsound, way to stay in business.

For a part of the state that even many Montanans regard as nothing but sage and gumbo, the threat of massive environmental depredation posed by mineral extraction has in recent years been real, and growing. Yet there are signs that the situation may be changing, thanks in part to public pressure to protect wild lands held in the public trust. Some of this pressure has come from environmentalists, and some of it from hunters, and it has primarily centered around concern for the western sage grouse. Bird numbers have been declining sharply in the Powder

River Basin, and the decline is clearly linked to the standing wastewater generated by CBM extraction. That water, pumped into surface pools, attracts mosquitoes, a significant percentage of which are liable to be carrying West Nile virus. Sage grouse are among the bird species that are highly susceptible to the virus. Throughout the Bush Administration, environmental groups sought "threatened" status for sage grouse, under the Endangered Species Act, to no avail. The birds may or may not fair better under the Obama Administration. But the vigorous public debate engendered by the plight of the sage grouse, and allied concerns for antelope, deer, and elk populations whose patterns of mating and migration are sharply curtailed by intensive mineral development, has apparently impacted BLM decision-making regarding mineral leases. Bobby is now getting back to being able to focus on wildlife habitat preservation and restoration.

Public environmental concern aside, another more practical force has been at work in putting the breaks on CBM and other mineral exploitation in this region. With the economic downturn and attendant decreased demand for fuel, many of the mineral companies have either gone bankrupt or are cutting back on development in the face of falling prices. It's not the first time that the High Plains region's "boom and bust" economic pattern has been the decisive factor in environmental change. Nor, surely, will it be the last.

Of course, as I write in the early summer of 2009, there is still so-called clean coal on the horizon, and along with it the tantalizing prospect of Montana becoming a major exporter of energy to other parts of the nation. Taking into consideration that we are "The Treasure State," and that the state motto is "Oro y Plata" ("Gold and Silver"), eastern Montanans might well worry about another unwelcome influx from the western part of the state—the home of toxic mine tailings and several Superfund sites—in comparison with which a few subdivisions might not seem half bad.

Nothing is ever easy, or predictable, out here. But, against all the odds, any environmentally concerned person can only trust that done right, which means done better in some ways than it has been, ranching is this country's last best hope. This is the hope that keeps us going, at any rate. On good days, it is enough. On not so good days, it is all we have.

The one thing we know for sure is that once we humans have made our mark on a landscape like this one, we cannot just walk away from it. This is a matter of moral responsibility. But more: it is a matter of not breaking trust with the powerful spirits that drew us here in the first place, and that keep us here until our time on this land one way or another draws to a close. Neither Doug nor I can imagine, right now, living here forever. Nor can we, right now, imagine leaving here forever. On days, both good and bad, this knowledge too, right now, is enough.

Starvation Butte. Photo by Mary Stange.

EPILOGUE
Rockfall

It was a midsummer morning, several years ago. We had gotten up quite early, to take advantage of the cool dawn hours and do ranch chores before the heat of the day set in. I was straightening up after our morning tea when Doug went outside, and walked down our road to water the horses. Moments later, he was back in the front yard, calling me, the tone of his voice one of urgency, though not alarm: "Mary, come out here! You've got to see something."

"What is it?" I called back, just a bit trepidatious. Ever since Garth Brooks's snakebite, I am always a little edgy about early morning ranch surprises.

"You have just got to see this. Come on out!"

I tossed my dish towel onto the counter, and went to the screen door. "See *what*?" I asked.

"I am not going to tell you, you've got to see it for yourself," he replied.

I ventured onto the porch.

"The Buttes," Doug said. "Look at the Buttes."

"They're . . . lovely," I said. We often call to each other, to draw attention to especially striking sunrises, or sunsets, or cloud formations hugging the Chalk Buttes. They are constantly changing, remaking themselves, in the shifting light. But, to be candid, this morning's rosy sunrise was nothing out of the ordinary.

"Go down the road, and *look at the Buttes*," he said. And so, somewhat bemused, I did.

And then I immediately saw it. Starvation Butte—only visible when one gets some hundred or so yards from the house—had changed dramatically. Its entire northern end, hundreds of thousands of tons of sandstone, had sheared completely free. The rockslide had obliterated the pine forest on the upslope below, creating a field of scree made up of boulders, some of which must have been the size of small houses. It had happened overnight. That such a violent alteration of the landscape could occur without awakening us, its explosive force muted by the singing of crickets, speaks to the vastness of this place.

We stood together in the road, arms entwining each other's waists, wordlessly gazing at the slightly altered skyline. Between the earliness of the hour and the sparse human population around here, we were certainly the first people to see this change. "We'll have to call the *Eagle*," Doug said. "They'll want to come out to take a picture of this for Friday's paper." I nodded agreement.

But for now, it was enough to savor this moment, and this gift of the Chalk Buttes, their lesson in impermanence. Nothing lasts forever; the things of this earth are constantly refashioning themselves. "We are just moving through; don't tarry long."

Doug went back to his horse chores, and I headed for the vegetable garden.

It was another ordinary day. The ancient Earth had rearranged itself.

Now-golden rays of sunshine burst, in a sunrise benediction, over Starvation Butte.

Resources

CHAPTER I

The Lay of the Land

For information about the history of Ekalaka I relied primarily on information available from the Carter County Museum, including *Shifting Scenes: A History of Carter County Montana*, a three-volume compilation of local lore, and Jessie Sundstrom's "Montana Town of Colorful Past Was Named for Relative of Red Cloud and Hiram Kelly," *Hills and Plains History* (Vol. 3, Issue 1: March 1997). Roberta Carkeek Cheney's *Names on the Face of Montana: The Story of Montana's Place Names* (Missoula, MT: Mountain Press Publishing Company, 1983) proved a surprisingly useful resource as well. Walter Nugent's *Into the West: The Story of Its People* (New York: Alfred A. Knopf, 1999) and Robert V. Hine and John Mack Faragher's *Frontiers: A Short History of the American West* (New Haven and London: Yale University Press, 2007) are good general histories of homesteading in the region. As to the explicit use of homesteading to displace Native Americans from their tribal lands, see Douglas W. Allen, "Homesteading and Property Rights: Or, 'How the West Was Really Won,'" *Journal of Law and Economics* (Vol. 34, No. 1 April 1991, 1–23). On the Dust Bowl years, the definitive work is Donald Worster's *Dust Bowl: The Southern Plains in the 1930s* (Oxford and New

York: Oxford University Press, 1979, 2004); Timothy Egan's more recent *The Worst Hard Time: The Untold Story of Those Who Survived the Great American Dust Bowl* (Boston: Mariner Books, 2006) presents an equally compelling history of the "dirty thirties." While both books are geographically focused farther south, much of what they say translates to eastern Montana and the Dakotas; and Egan's work, particularly, gets into the mind-set of those who stuck it out in those worst of times. Other sources cited relative to local history include: Jonathan Raban, *Bad Land: An American Romance* (New York: Pantheon Books, 1996); Percy Wollaston, *Homesteading: A Montana Family Album* (New York: Lyons Press, 1997); Jennie Carlson, *Thru the Dust* (Boston: The Christopher Publishing House, 1952); and Russell Rowland, *In Open Spaces* (New York: Harper Perennial, 2002). Since the publication of this last book, Rowland has relocated to Billings, Montana. He has since published its sequel, *The Watershed Years* (Helena, MT: Riverbend Publishing, 2007), and as of the summer of 2009 was at work on a "prequel" set in Carter County's homesteading days.

The quotation from Granville Stuart is taken from P. J. Hill, "The Non-Tragedy of the Buffalo Commons," published online at www.isnie.org/ISNIE05/Papers05/hill.pdf (accessed June 12, 2007). Wayne Yost, of the Ekalaka office of the U.S. Natural Resources and Conservation Service, is the source of the NRCS estimate of four to five acres of grazing land per AUM (animal unit month), based on seven months of grazing and five of feeding hay. For information on population fluctuations in Carter County, I am indebted to Pamela Castleberry, the Carter County clerk and recorder.

CHAPTER 2
Being "Differnt"
Works cited in this chapter include Natalie Merchant's "Gold Rush Brides," which is on 10,000 Maniacs' *Our Time in Eden* (1992), and my *Woman the Hunter* (Boston: Beacon Press, 1997).

CHAPTER 3
Intrepid Hippies, Homesteaders, and Other Survivors
Relative to women's homesteading experience, my major resources in this chapter include H. Elaine Lindgren, *Land in Her Own Name: Women as Homesteaders in North Dakota* (Norman and London: University of Oklahoma Press, 1996); Susan Armitage and Elizabeth Jameson, *The Women's West* (Norman and London: University of Oklahoma Press, 1987); Sandra L. Myres, *Westering Women* (Albuquerque: University of New

Mexico Press, 1982); and Barbara Handy-Marchello, *Women of the Northern Plains: Gender and Settlement on the Homestead Frontier 1870–1930* (St. Paul: Minnesota Historical Society Press, 2005). The May Wing quotation is from Jameson's essay "Women as Workers, Women as Civilizers: True Womanhood in the American West," in *The Women's West*. Melody Graulich's "Violence Against Women: Power Dynamics in Literature of the Western Family" appears in that same volume. I accumulated an additional treasure trove of information about the homesteading period at "Homesteading Reconsidered," a research symposium sponsored by the Center for Great Plains Studies, University of Nebraska–Lincoln, May 17–19, 2007. John Mack Faragher's remarks about women homesteaders and "proving up," are from his keynote address at that conference, "Home, Home on the Range: The Homestead Act in American Myth and American History." The Gerard Baker anecdote—which I have taken the liberty of somewhat embellishing—is from his keynote at the same conference, "The Dawes Act—A Loss of Land."

Judy Blunt's *Breaking Clean* was published by Alfred A. Knopf (New York) in 2002. *The New York Times* article cited here is "Writers in Place; Suffering and Creativity" by Blaine Harden (May 28, 2002).

CHAPTER 4

The Law of the Frontier

Works cited in this chapter include Jane Tompkins, *West of Everything: The Inner Life of Westerns* (New York and Oxford: Oxford University Press, 1992); Sharman Apt Russell, *Kill the Cowboy: A Battle of Mythology in the New West* (Reading, MA: Addison-Wesley Publishing Company, 1993); and Darrell Arnold, *The Cowboy Kind* (Missoula, MT: Mountain Press Publishing Company, 2001).

CHAPTER 5

Animal Affinities

Works cited in this chapter include Peter Decker, *Old Fences, New Neighbors* (Golden, CO: Fulcrum Publishing Company, 1998, 2006); Barney Nelson, *The Wild and the Domestic: Animal Representation, Ecocriticism, and Western American Literature* (Reno and Las Vegas: University of Nevada Press, 2000); Jeremy Rifkin, *Beyond Beef: The Rise and Fall of Cattle Culture* (New York: E. P. Dutton, 1992); Susan Kent, ed., *Farmers as Hunters: the Implications of Sedentism* (Cambridge: Cambridge University Press, 1989); Michael Pollan, *The Botany of Desire: A Plant's-Eye View of the World* (New York: Random House, 2001); Stephen Budiansky, *The Covenant of the Wild:*

Why Animals Chose Domestication (Leesburg, VA: The Terrapin Press, 1992); Jared Diamond, *Guns, Germs, and Steel: The Fates of Human Societies* (New York: W. W. Norton, 2005); and Gary Snyder, "Survival and Sacrament," in *The Practice of the Wild* (New York: North Point Press/Farrar, Straus and Giroux, 1990).

The Helen Spurway remark about "goofies" comes from a discussion of domestication in Paul Shepard, *Coming Home to the Pleistocene* (Washington, DC: Island Press/Shearwater, 1998), Chapter VI, "Romancing the Potato."

As to the evolution of horses, recent evidence unearthed in Kazakhstan appears to establish their domestication as much as a millennium earlier than previously believed; see "Equine Alternative," *The New York Times* (March 18, 2009), A26, for a fascinating "thought experiment" on the implications not only of this discovery, but of its alternative: What would be the implications for human cultures, had horses never been domesticated?

CHAPTER 6
Hard Grass

Among works cited early on in this chapter are Richard Manning, *Grassland: The History, Biology, Politics, and Promise of the American Prairie* (New York: Penguin Books, 1995), and John A. Byers, *American Pronghorn: Social Adaptations & the Ghosts of Predators Past* (Chicago and London: University of Chicago Press, 1997). For information on deer evolution, I relied primarily on Richard Nelson, *Heart and Blood: Living with Deer in America* (New York: Alfred A. Knopf, 1998). Information about the prehistory of this area derives primarily from sources available through the Carter County Museum.

Sources for the section on Native Americans include Robert M. Utley, *The Lance and the Shield: The Life and Times of Sitting Bull* (New York: Henry Holt and Company, 1993), from which the quotation from Sitting Bull is taken along with most of the details of the Lakota history of this area; James Donovan, *A Terrible Glory: Custer and the Little Bighorn—the Last Great Battle of the American West* (New York: Little, Brown and Company, 2008); and Alston Chase, *Playing God in Yellowstone: The Destruction of America's First National Park* (New York: Harcourt, Brace and Company, 1987), on national park literature relating to Native "visitors." On the Northern Cheyenne background, I relied primarily on *The Northern Cheyenne Tribe and Its Reservation: 2002 A Report to the U.S. Bureau of Land Management and the State of Montana Department of Natural Resources and Conservation,*

prepared by the Northern Cheyenne Tribe and accessible online at: http://
www.blm.gov/mt/st/en/fo/miles_city_field_office/og_eis/cheyenne.
print.html.

Particularly relevant is Chapter 7 of this report, "Northern Cheyenne
Cultural Resources," which was coauthored by Sherri Deaver and
Cheyenne elder Joe Little Coyote. Also, Bill Tallbull, Sherri Deaver, and
Halcyon LaPoint, "A New Way to Study Cultural Landscapes: The Blue
Earth Hills Assessment," *Landscape and Urban Planning* 36 (1996), 125–
33. The quotation from N. Scott Momaday is from "The Native Way of
Seeing," in Walter H. Capps, ed., *Seeing With A Native Eye: Essays in Native
American Religion* (San Francisco: Harper and Row, 1976). As of winter
2010, the Chalk Buttes and environs had yet to be accorded any special
cultural status, or protection.

On Native American place-names, my resources included Linea
Sundstrom, "The Crazy Mule Maps: A Northern Cheyenne's View of
Montana and Western Dakota in 1878," *Montana: The Magazine of Western
History* (Spring 1999); Carrie Moran McCleary, "Giving voice to Crow
Country—the Crow place name project," *Tribal College Journal* (Vol. XII,
Issue 2, Winter 2000); and Becky Bohrer, "Cheyenne president: Town
names unfit," *The Billings Gazette* (September 8, 2005). And I am majorly
indebted to Richard Nelson's *The Island Within* (New York: Random House,
1989).

CHAPTER 7

Hunting Nature, Hunting Culture

Works cited in the first few pages of this chapter include David Quammen,
*Monster of God: The Man-Eating Predator in the Jungles of History and the
Mind* (New York: W. W. Norton, 2003); David Baron, *The Beast in the Garden:
A Modern Parable of Man and Nature* (New York: W. W. Norton, 2004);
Annette Kolodny, *The Lay of the Land: Metaphor as Experience and History in
American Life and Letters* (Chapel Hill: University of North Carolina Press,
1975); Val Plumwood, "Wilderness Skepticism and Wilderness Dualism,"
in F. Baird Callicott and Michael P. Nelson, eds., *The Great New Wilderness
Debate* (Athens and London: University of Georgia Press, 1998); and Ted
Kerasote, *Bloodties: Nature, Culture and the Hunt* (New York: Random
House, 1993).

Regarding ecoregionalism and locavorism: Eric Schlosser, *Fast Food
Nation* (New York: Harper Perennial, 2005); Michael Pollan, *The Omnivore's
Dilemma: A Natural History of Four Meals* (New York: Penguin Press, 2006);
Barbara Kingsolver, *Animal, Vegetable, Miracle: A Year of Food Life* (New

York: Harper Collins, 2007); Michael Pollan, *In Defense of Food: An Eater's Manifesto* (New York: Penguin, 2008); Bill McKibben, *Deep Economy: The Wealth of Communities and the Durable Future* (New York: Henry Hold and Company, 2007); Alice Waters, *The Art of Simple Food: Notes, Lessons and Recipes from a Delicious Revolution* (New York: Crown Publishing Group/ Clarkson Potter, 2007) and *Slow Food Nation's Come to the Table: The Slow Food Way of Living* (Emmaus, PA: Rodale Press 2008). Jan Zita Grover's review of *Animal, Vegetable, Miracle* appeared in *The Women's Review of Books* (November/December 2007).

The interchange between Gerard Baker and the woman in the audience took place at the Center for Great Plains Studies Symposium cited above (Chapter 3). The women's remarks, as they appear here, are not an exact quotation, but represent my best approximation of what she said.

My sources for the discussion of Paleolithic cave art, bison hunting, and hunting history and culture include: Jared Diamond, "Drowning Dogs and the Dawn of Art," *Natural History* (102:3, March 1993); Stephen Jay Gould, "Up Against a Wall," *Natural History* (105:7, July 1996); John Halverson, "Paleolithic Cave Art and Cognition," *Journal of Psychology Interdisciplinary and Applied* (126:3, May 1992); Jesper Christensen, "Heaven and Earth in Ice Age Art: Topography and Iconography at Lascaux," *Mankind Quarterly* (36:3–4, Spring/Summer 1996); Paul Shepard, "A Theory of the Value of Hunting," (*Transactions of the Twenty-Fourth North American Wildlife Conference*. Washington, DC; American Wildlife Institute, 1959); Stephen Kellert, "Attitudes and Characteristics of Hunters and Anti-Hunters and Related Policy Suggestions," a working paper presented to the Fish and Wildlife Service, U.S. Department of the Interior (November 4, 1976); Stephen Kellert, *The Value of Life: Biological Diversity and Human Society* (Washington, DC: Island Press/Shearwater Books, 1996); Paul Shepard, "A Post-Historic Primitivism," in Max Oelschlaeger, ed., *The Wilderness Condition* (San Francisco: Sierra Club Books, 1992) and Paul Shepard, *Coming Home to the Pleistocene*, edited by Florence Shepard (Washington, DC: Island Press/Shearwater Books, 1998). Luther Standing Bear is quoted in Linda Hasselstrom, *Bison: Monarch of the Plains* (Portland, OR: Graphic Arts Center Publishing Company, 1998).

CHAPTER 8

The Business of Buffalo

On the controversy over bison subsidies, see Lisa Anderson, "How Buffalo Ted Hunts Bison Bucks," *Insight on the News* (July 28, 1999); Theo Stein, "Crash in market prices tramples bison ranchers," *Denver Post* (January 25,

2002); and Bill Hogan, "Star-Spangled Lobbyists," *Mother Jones* (March/ April 2002).

Our Web site is www.crazywomanbison.com.

Aldo Leopold's remarks on the "split-rail value" of hunting appear in his essay "Wildlife in American Culture," in *A Sand County Almanac* (New York: Ballantine Books, 1966).

CHAPTER 9
The First, and Last, Annual Buffalo Gals Hunt

My *Bugle* article was called "Hunting With a Difference: Do women make better hunters than men?" (January/February 2000). As to the article about disagreement among feminists: see Jane Gallop, Marianne Hirsch, and Nancy K. Miller, "Criticizing Feminist Criticism," in Hirsch and Evelyn Fox Keller, eds., *Conflicts in Feminism* (New York: Routledge, 1990).

CHAPTER 10
A Nice Place to Visit

Tompkins's book is cited above (Chapter 4). *Annie Oakley* ran in syndication on TV from 1954–1957, and in reruns in the late 1950s and early 1960s, when I watched it. Gail Davis was the first woman to star in a TV western.

A good source of background and information on the Johnson County War is David Dary's classic history, *Cowboy Culture: A Saga of Five Centuries* (Lawrence: University Press of Kansas, 1981, 1989), Chapter 14, "End of the Open-Range Culture."

As to the Poppers and the Buffalo Commons: see Anne Matthews's *Where the Buffalo Roam* (New York: Grover Weidenfeld, 1992). The photograph of the Poppers that I discuss in this section is the frontispiece to Chapter 1 of that book. Articles by Frank and Deborah Popper that I cite in this chapter include "The Great Plains: From Dust to Dust," *Planning* (December 1987); "The Buffalo Commons, Then and Now," *FOCUS* (43:4, Winter 1993); "The Onset of the Buffalo Commons," *Journal of the West* (45:2, Spring 2006); and "The Buffalo Commons: Its Antecedents and Their Implications," *Online Journal of Rural Research and Policy* (Issue 6: December 31, 2006). Also, Florence Williams, "Plains Sense: Frank and Deborah Popper's 'Buffalo Commons' is creeping toward reality," *High Country News* (January 15, 2001); Lorna Thackeray, "Unsettling Times: Buffalo Commons idea lingers," *Billings Gazette* (June 18, 2005); and Lauren Donovan, "20 years later, Buffalo Commons theory still being debated," *Bismarck Tribune* (September 2, 2007).

CHAPTER 11
Next Year Country

Works referred to in this chapter include Kathleen Norris, *Dakota: A Spiritual Biography* (New York: Ticknor and Fields, 1993); Linda Hasselstrom, *Windbreak: A Woman Rancher on the Northern Plains* (Berkeley: Barn Owl Books, 1987); Henry David Thoreau, *Walden, Or Life in the Woods* (Victoria, BC: Castle Books Reprint, 2007); Annie Dillard, *Pilgrim at Tinker Creek* (New York: Harper Perennial, 2007); and David Laskin, *The Children's Blizzard* (New York: Harper Collins, 2004).

The author of the *Billings Gazette* piece on the storm's aftermath was Lorna Thackeray. The online comments are quoted verbatim, spelling and grammatical errors and all.

CHAPTER 12
New West, True West?

Books cited in this chapter include Dan O'Brien, *Buffalo for the Broken Heart: Restoring Life to a Black Hills Ranch* (New York: Random House, 2001, 2002); Gene Logsdon, *Living at Nature's Pace: Farming & The American Dream* (White River Junction, VT: Chelsea Green Publishing Company, 1994, 2000); Jared Diamond, *Collapse: How Societies Choose to Fail or Succeed* (New York: Penguin Books, 2005); Rebecca Kneale Gould, *At Home in Nature: Modern Homesteading and Spiritual Practice in America* (Berkeley: University of California Press, 2005); Laura Pritchett, Richard L. Knight, and Jeff Lee, eds., *Home Land: Ranching and a West That Works* (Boulder, CO: Johnson Books, 2007); Courtney White, *Revolution on the Range: The Rise of a New Ranch in the American West* (Washington, DC: Island Press/Shearwater Books, 2008).

On the Stock Farm, see Florence Williams, "Behind the Gate," *High Country News* (November 11, 2002). Diamond also focuses on this gated development, to epitomize basically everything that is wrong with the changes occurring in Big Sky Country today.